General editor: Graham H

Brodie's Notes on Chaucer

The Knight's Tale

F. W. Robinson MA

MACMILLAN

First published by James Brodie Ltd
New edition published 1976 by Pan Books Ltd
This revised edition first published 1978
by Pan Books Ltd

Reprinted 1992 by
THE MACMILLAN PRESS LTD
Houndmills, Basingstoke, Hampshire RG21 2XS
and London
Companies and representatives
throughout the world

ISBN 0–333–58063–X

Printed in Great Britain by
Clays Ltd, St Ives plc, Bungay, Suffolk

Contents

To the student

A close reading of the *Tale* is the student's primary task. These Notes will help to increase your understanding and appreciation of the *Tale*, and to stimulate *your own* thinking about it: *they are in no way intended as a substitute* for a thorough knowledge of the work.

Editor's note and bibliography

Chaucer is our greatest comic poet, and *The Canterbury Tales* is his masterpiece. Yet Chaucer's poetry is not a subject for general reading, but of specialist study. The reason for this is that his language is not easy for the general reader to read and understand. The English language of the fourteenth century was different from the language we speak today, and some trouble must be taken in learning these differences before a proper understanding of the meaning can be gained. And further, when one has learned to read Chaucer and to understand the meaning, some knowledge is necessary of the age in which he lived, and his place in it, before the work of this colourful and humorous poet can be fully appreciated and enjoyed.

These notes are aimed primarily at students coming fresh to Chaucer in their studies of English literature. An attempt has been made to set out, as briefly and simply as possible, the areas of knowledge which are necessary for the proper understanding and appreciation of a selected text in the context of examination requirements.

It is hoped, however, that the notes have been prepared in such a way that the student will enjoy the task of understanding and appreciating this wonderful poetry with its melodic style, gentle satire and rollicking humour, and even to acquire a taste for Chaucer which will lead to wider reading and a deeper appreciation of his work.

The Editor wishes to acknowledge his indebtedness to the various works he has studied, and particularly to the editions of Chaucer's works by Professors W. W. Skeat and F. N. Robinson (it is on the latter's work that the text of this edition is based – *The Complete Works of Geoffrey Chaucer*, 2nd ed., 1957, with revised punctuation and spelling by James Winny. CUP,

1971); and the editions of several of Chaucer's *Tales* edited by F. W. Robinson.

Bibliography

For those who wish to carry their study of Chaucer beyond what is possible to include in a small volume of notes, a selection of books that may be helpful is listed below:

The Poet Chaucer, Nevill Coghill, OUP Paperbacks

An Introduction to Chaucer, Hussey, Spearing and Winny, CUP

English Social History, Trevelyan (Chaps 1 and 2) Longmans, also Penguin

Chaucer's World, ed. M. Hussey, CUP

Pelican Guide to English Literature, Vol. 1, The Age of Chaucer, Penguin

It is recommended that students should read a selection of the tales from the translation into modern verse by Nevill Coghill – *The Canterbury Tales*, translated by Nevill Coghill, Penguin Classics.

It is also recommended that students should listen to a recording of Chaucer read with the original pronunciation – *The Prologue to The Canterbury Tales*, read in Middle English by Nevill Coghill, Norman Davis and John Burrow, Argo Record Company, London, No. PLP 1001 (LP).

A brief description of
Chaucer's life and works

Geoffrey Chaucer was born about 1340 near the Tower of London. He was born into the age of Edward III, and of the Black Prince, into the Age of Chivalry and the magnificent court of Edward III with knights and ladies, heraldry and tournaments, minstrels and poetry, music and story-telling.

Chaucer entered into this rich and colourful courtly world at an early age, when he became a page in the household of the Countess of Ulster, wife to Lionel, later Duke of Clarence, and one of the sons of Edward III. This was clearly arranged by his parents, who had some contacts at Court. His mother's first husband had been Keeper of the King's Wardrobe, and there can be little doubt that she had something to do with the appointment of Chaucer's father as deputy to the King's Butler. The first record of Geoffrey Chaucer appears in an account book, dating from 1357, which records a payment by the royal household to a London tailor for a cloak, multi-coloured breeches and a pair of shoes for the young page Chaucer. It was in the Duke's great houses in London and Yorkshire that the young page would have learned the elegant and aristocratic code of manners, and made the acquaintance of the high and the noble. He would have learned French and Latin, the language of the Court, the Church and the educated classes. It was also one of the duties of a page to play and sing, and to recite poetry.

The next record we have is that Chaucer was taken prisoner by the French in 1359, during one of the campaigns in The Hundred Years' War, and ransomed in the following year – the King himself contributing £16 (a very large sum in those days) of the money. So Chaucer must have seen active service in the French wars, probably as a squire attending on one of the nobles, like the squire in the *Canterbury Tales* who attended on the Knight, his father. For the upper classes, the experience of being a prisoner of war in the Age of Chivalry was not too uncomfortable. It was normal for the 'prisoner' to be entertained as a 'house guest' until the ransom was paid, and it is probable that during this enforced stay in France Chaucer became thoroughly versed in French literature, particularly the *Roman de la Rose* (the procedure manual, as it were, for 'courtly love'), which was to have such an important influence on his literary work.

After his ransom was paid, Chaucer returned to his Court duties, and soon in a more elevated position. He became one of the valets in attendance on the King. In 1366 his father died and his mother married again. It is probable that in the same year he married Philippa, daughter of Sir Payne Roet and sister of Katherine Swynford, the mistress and later third wife to John of Gaunt. Philippa was a lady-in-waiting to the Queen. As a valet to the King, Chaucer would carry candles 'before the King', tidy up his bedroom and attend to a variety of duties which were to become more and more concerned with affairs of state. In 1386 he was sent abroad on the official business of the Crown. About this time he was promoted from valet to palace official. It appears that Chaucer went soldiering again in 1369, probably on one of John of Gaunt's campaigns in Picardy. In 1370 he was abroad again on the King's service, and we can now see him becoming a trusted civil servant as he was frequently sent on missions to France, Flanders and Italy. During his visits to Italy on official business Chaucer took the opportunity to become familiar with Italian literature, most especially the works of Petrarch, Boccaccio and Dante, which were to influence much of his subsequent poetry.

In 1374 he was promoted to a senior position as Comptroller of Customs and Subsidy (for wool, skins and hides) at the Port of London, and the City of London bestowed on him the lease of a house in Aldgate.

From about 1380 Chaucer settled down to his life as senior customs official, as there is only one record of further journeys abroad. He must have been respected as a man of affairs, as he became a Justice of the Peace in 1385, and a Member of Parliament, or Knight of the Shire for Kent, soon afterwards.

It was during these years that Chaucer found time to write seriously. His early literary attempts were influenced considerably by French literature. Then, when John of Gaunt left the country in 1386 on an adventure to claim the crown of Castile, the King's uncle, the Duke of Gloucester, took charge of the country's affairs (Richard being not yet of age), and Chaucer suffered from the new influences in royal patronage. He lost his Comptrollership of Customs, he was not re-elected to Parliament and he had to give up his house in Aldgate. We even learn that he felt himself in danger of being sued for debt. Chaucer had now plenty of time to ponder and at this time he must have been preparing *The Canterbury Tales*.

In 1389 a rumour was abroad that the great Duke of Lancaster (Chaucer's patron John of Gaunt) was returning home. This helped the young King Richard II in taking over the reins of power from his uncle Gloucester. It has been stated that the young King Richard knew Chaucer and liked his poetry. There must be some substance in this, as shortly afterwards Chaucer was appointed Clerk of the King's Works. John of Gaunt returned to England in November 1389, and for the rest of his life Chaucer was to enjoy royal patronage and a comfortable living. It was in these years of semi-retirement that *The Canterbury Tales* were written. Alas, Chaucer died without having finished his masterpiece. His tomb in Westminster Abbey gives the date of his death – October 1400.

It seems probable that 1387 was the approximate date of commencement for *The Canterbury Tales*. Chaucer's renown rests mainly on this work, but in terms of volume the *Tales* form less than half of his writing which has come down to us. Besides a number of shorter poems, there are five other major works in verse and two or three in prose. Chaucer's most important production during his first tentative years as a writer was his translation he probably made of the *Roman de la Rose*, the style and content of which was to have such a great influence on his writing. His first major poem was *The Book of the Duchess*, a poem steeped in the French tradition, written about 1370 to commemorate the death of Blanche, Duchess of Lancaster, and wife of his patron, John of Gaunt. This was the first of four love-vision poems, the others being *The House of Fame*, *The Parliament of Fowls* and *The Legend of Good Women* (whose date is doubtful). Chaucer's works can be conveniently grouped into three parts, the French period, the Italian period and the English period; and, generally speaking, the periods follow one another in chronological sequence. The French period showed influence of the *Roman de la Rose*, and included the love-vision poems. The Italian period (1380–5) is marked by the narrative poem *Troilus and Criseyde*, which rehandles a theme of the Italian poet Boccaccio. *Troilus and Criseyde* is a masterpiece, and is still considered to be the finest narrative poem in English, full of beauty and lyrical quality, and delightful humour in the character of Pandarus. The English period (1389–1400) is the last, and is the period when Chaucer reached his full maturity as a dramatic poet. This is the period of *The Canterbury Tales*, a collection of tales and tellers which is unique in English literature. Chaucer died before he could complete this great masterpiece.

It must be emphasized that these terms, 'French', 'Italian', 'English' for Chaucer's literary life only indicate predominant influences: the stories in *The Canterbury Tales* are drawn from far and wide; *The Knight's Tale*, for instance, again owes its theme to a story by Boccaccio.

The setting of the *Tales*

The Knight's Tale is but one of a collection of stories which make up *The Canterbury Tales*, his most ambitious and comprehensive work, and his last. Some of the tales may have been composed during earlier periods of Chaucer's literary career and brought together, with others specially written for the purpose, as a collection of stories told within the framework of a pilgrimage to Canterbury. There are many examples in the literature of the Middle Ages of collections of stories, and there is no doubt that Chaucer was familiar with some of them. Most of Chaucer's stories did not originate with him, any more than Shakespeare originated his own plots; nevertheless, *The Canterbury Tales* are unique. By choosing a pilgrimage as the frame-story within which to tell his tales, Chaucer, in a brilliant stroke of genius, was able to bring together as pilgrims a representative group of many of the various classes of English society of his time, and to allocate to each pilgrim a tale suited to character and status.

Chaucer's ambitious plan for *The Canterbury Tales* was never completed. In the *Prologue* we are told that each pilgrim will tell four tales, two on the outward and another two on the homeward journey. But the company never reaches Canterbury and there are manuscripts of tales for only twenty-three of the thirty pilgrims, and these incompletely arranged, and in some cases unfinished. Nevertheless, this partly completed work is the masterpiece of comic poetry in English literature.

The dramatic coherence of *The Canterbury Tales* is fashioned by the *Prologue*, which sets the scene of the pilgrimage to Canterbury, and introduces the pilgrims by a striking series of word portraits. The portraits of the pilgrims leap out of the pages with all the vividness of description and character of great portrait-painting, and with astounding originality and realism. As Nevill Coghill comments, 'The result was a new sort of poetical truth, the creation of a poetry of fact by a wise, sure-eyed and sensitive selection of daily detail, mellowed and harmonized by a humane and often an amused approval, qualified wherever approval was withdrawn by an ironical wit. It was a new way of looking at people.' So diverse are the characters, and so vivid the portraiture, that the *Prologue* has been described as the National Portrait Gallery of medieval England; the portraits of a nation, of 'high and low, old and young, male and female, lay and clerical, learned and ignorant, rogue and righteous, land and sea, town and country.' In the *Prologue* to *The Canterbury Tales* we learn that Chaucer had already taken up his quarters at the Tabard Inn, Southwark in preparation for his pilgrimage the next day to Canterbury, when some twenty-nine other people arrive at the inn for the same purpose. The landlord of the Tabard Inn, the host, Harry Bailly, learning the purpose of the assembled company, proposed that the pilgrims should entertain themselves during the journey by telling one another stories. The company accepted this suggestion, and when the Host announced his intention to join the party on the pilgrimage, decided to appoint him as organizer and judge of the tales. There would be a prize for the best tale told, which would be a good supper at the Tabard Inn at the expense of the other companions. Certain matters of discipline were also discussed, and all the company agreed to abide by the rules laid down by the Host, any breach of which would involve a fine amounting to the travelling expenses of the whole company. The company started off on the journey to Canterbury early the next morning. It was decided by lot that the Knight, the most distinguished member of the pary, should tell the first tale.

The Knight, very properly and entirely according to character, tells a tale of chivalric romance, abounding in the artificial manners of courtly love, of descriptions of temples and gardens, of battle and of nobility and philosophy. The

Knight's tale is greatly applauded by the company, and the Host is very pleased by the successful start to his arrangements.

The end of the *Knight's Tale* is followed by the *Prologue* to the *Miller's Tale*. This *Prologue* is the link joining the two tales, and serves as comment on the tale just told, and as an introduction to the next. The *Prologues*, or links, also act as dramatic interludes between the tales, adding drama and giving movement and reality to the frame-story.

The origin and plot of the *Tale*

Chaucer acknowledges his indebtedness for the tale to writers of 'olde stories', though he does not name them. The brief quotation from Statius which is found in some manuscripts suggests an indebtedness to this author of the *Thebiad*; but it was a very small one. Statius lived in the first century AD and wrote in twelve books of verse an account of the wars against Thebes, the chief town of Boeotia, in central Greece – not to be confused with the Egyptian city of the same name. Chaucer's principal source however was the *Teseide*, a long poem by the Italian poet, Giovanni Boccaccio, who died in 1375. He was a native of Florence, and it is just possible that Chaucer actually met him during a visit there in 1372–3.

Boccaccio's poem about Theseus is 9,896 lines long: Chaucer's *Knight's Tale* totals 2,250. It will be obvious that Chaucer treated the *Teseide* rather as a source book than as one to be translated into English, and the *Knight's Tale* does contain matter of Chaucer's own. One notable feature of Chaucer's version is that he has taken a classical story and transformed it into a medieval romance, for highly-placed young knights fall in love with the same princess, and a tournament is arranged in which their rivalry can be settled by combat. Continually the Knight, who is telling the story to interest the pilgrims on their way to Becket's shrine at Canterbury, remarks on his need to get on with the story quickly, and he omits very much of what Boccaccio included. Nevertheless, Chaucer's *Knight's Tale* remains the longest of the Canterbury tales, and well deserves the opinion of its original hearers that it is 'a noble storie'.

Boccaccio divided his *Teseide* into twelve books: Chaucer's version is in four 'parts'. He introduces first the Duke Theseus of Athens, returning from a successful war against the Amazons and bringing with him his newly married queen,

Hippolyta, and her younger sister, Emelye. Just about to enter his capital he is addressed by the eldest of a company of ladies, all in mourning, who ask him to intervene on their behalf with Creon, Lord of Thebes, who had slain their husbands and had had their bodies piled up in a heap, refusing them burial or cremation. Theseus immediately delayed his entry into Athens and marched against Creon, whom he killed. He was about to return to his own country when he was told of two royal princes who had been found alive, though badly wounded, amongst the slain. These two he ordered to be taken to Athens and to be imprisoned for life. They were Palamon and Arcite.

From their prison tower they espied Emelye on a May morning walking below. Palamon is smitten with her beauty, supposing her to be Venus, and Arcite in his turn falls in love with her but considers her to be a mortal. Both realize, however, that they are prisoners, and that they must be content with gazing on her, as there was no chance of their being freed. It happened, however, that Duke Perotheus, a bosom friend of Theseus, came to Athens and, seeing there his friend Arcite, begged Theseus to release him. This he agreed to do, on the condition that Arcite was not to set foot on any territory belonging to Theseus, on pain of losing his life. Arcite accepted these conditions, though bewailing inwardly that his fate separated him from any chance of seeing Emelye: it was indeed Palamon who would have the joy of beholding her. On the other hand, it was Palamon who wept bitter tears, for Arcite was now freed from prison, while he himself must remain there, though he still had the privilege of seeing Emelye.

At this point the Knight pauses at the end of the first part, leaving it to the company to consider which of the two was really the better off.

Part 2 shows us Arcite in Thebes, tormented by the cruelty of his position. After a year or two, however, he dreamed that the god Mercury told him to return to Athens where his troubles would come to an end. He arose from his sleep determined to obey the vision, and a glance at a mirror convinced him that so changed was he in appearance by his grief he would not be recognized there. In the disguise of a poor workman and with one servant as his comrade, he reached Athens where he was fortunate enough to obtain a position at court as an attendant in the service of Emelye herself. Before long he was appointed squire of the Duke and his confidential servant, under the name of Philostrate.

Meanwhile, Palamon was still confined to the dark, horrible, strong prison, where for seven years he had suffered so greatly that he had almost lost his reason. By the help of a friend, however, he was able to drug his gaoler and escape as far into a forest as he could in the short night of the late spring, intending to make his way to Thebes, where he might muster his friends and with their help endeavour to win Emelye as his wife.

It happened, however, that Arcite entered that same forest early the next morning, intent on paying his homage to the month of May. Palamon saw him, but so changed was Arcite that Palamon did not recognize him. Soon, however, he was heard lamenting his fate: he had to serve a man who was his mortal enemy: 'cruel Mars has killed all my kindred excepting Palamon, and him Theseus tortures in prison, while Emelye slays me with her eyes'. At these words Palamon sprang up from his hiding place and revealed himself to Arcite who now drew his sword, but, seeing Palamon had no weapon, sheathed it and proposed that he should bring armour for Palamon, and that they should fight to the death for Emelye. Palamon consented and the next day, as soon as they were armed, the two began to fight 'as if they were lion and tiger, or a couple of wild boars'.

It happened that Theseus himself had decided to hunt in this same wood that day, and with Hippolyta and Emelye went to rouse a hart which was known to be there. He soon saw the other two fighting desperately, stopped them, and demanded an explanation of their quarrel. Palamon replied that they both deserved death, for he was Palamon and the other Arcite, whom the Duke now called Philostrate. The Duke commanded that they should both be put to death, but relented when the ladies begged for their lives, for he realized it was love and not hate which had brought them into conflict. But as only one of them could marry the princess, he decreed that the two should go free, but should return in 'fifty weeks', each with a hundred knights, while he himself would have a lists prepared in which the question of who should have Emelye should be decided by tournament. The rivals were overjoyed at the suggestion, thanked the Duke, and rode homeward to Thebes 'with his olde walles wyde'.

Part 3 describes the making of the lists and gives details of its notable features. It relates also the preparations made by the rivals and their prayers to the immortals to grant them success. Palamon prayed to Venus and received a sign which he interpreted as assuring him the victory, while Arcite received an assurance from Mars of his own success. To solve the difficulty arising from the two contradictory promises, Saturn intervened on behalf of Venus, promising that Palamon should indeed marry Emelye, though there would seem to be some uncertainty at first. Emelye had appealed to Diana, the protectress of unmarried women, but had been told that one of the cousins would certainly have her as his bride.

Part 4 describes the tournament in great detail, but Theseus announced an innovation. None of the combatants was to lose his life. And, furthermore, if the leader of one side was captured the tourney was to cease immediately, and the other side was to be awarded the victory. During the combat Palamon was wounded and taken off the field, and Arcite was declared the victor. At this point Saturn interfered, for as Arcite looked towards Emelye a spirit from Hades frightened Arcite's horse, which reared and threw his rider, so that he fell head first to the ground and lay as if dead. He was taken to the palace; but realizing that his life could not be saved, he sent for Emelye and begged her, if ever she married, not to forget Palamon. He died almost as he spoke, his last words being 'Mercy, Emelye'.

Theseus was overcome with grief, but his aged father, Egeus, comforted him with the thought that death is inevitable for us all. The last rites were observed and the body of Arcite was consumed on the funeral pyre.

As the years passed, however, and the mourning for Arcite was over, Theseus sent for Palamon and Emelye, and, having spoken at some length about the inevitability of death, suggested first to Emelye and then to Palamon that they should marry. The marriage was celebrated, and the two lived happily together.

It is interesting to note that Palamon and Arcite figure as the chief characters in a play entitled *The Two Noble Kinsmen*, written by John Fletcher (1579–1625) with possibly some help from Shakespeare. The play introduces a feature not found in Chaucer's poem, in that Palamon is released from prison by the jailer's daughter who has fallen in love with him. She kills herself when she realizes that he is still true to Emelye.

A better-known reference to some of the other characters is found in Shakespeare's *A Midsummer Night's Dream*. The first stage direction reads: 'Athens, the Palace of Theseus. Enter Theseus, Hippolyta, Philostrate, and attendants'. The time of this opening scene is four days before the Duke's wedding. Philostrate is sent to stir up the youth of Athens to merriment in honour of the occasion. One of the items suggested in the last act is rejected by Theseus as having been played 'when I from Thebes came last a conqueror'. One of the characters in the Duke's entourage bears the name of Egeus, but he is no longer his old father who tried to console him on the death of Arcite.

The characters

Theseus

And in his tyme switch a conquerour,
That gretter was ther noon under the soone.

Theseus was one of the legendary heroes of ancient Greece. He appears with Hippolyta in Shakespeare's *Midsummer Night's Dream*. It is to celebrate their marriage that Bottom and his fellow workmen perform their play. In *The Knight's Tale*, as in Shakespeare's play, Theseus is a figure in the background. He is a spectator of rather than a participant in the main action of the tale.

Chaucer is clearly fascinated by the character of Theseus. His impact is immeasurably greater than his role in the story can justify. His part in the plot is that of a god, for he controls the destinies of the other characters. It is he who takes Arcite and Palamon prisoner and refuses to release them; it is he who decides first that Arcite and then later Palamon shall marry Emily. He has the power of life and death over the knights who take part in the tournament. He is a man of power and magnificence.

He is a great conqueror and a great soldier, although his valour is matched by his wisdom. There is a repetitive emphasis on his nobility, his conquests and his glory. He is a true knight, and in his chivalry is not corrupted by love.

Throughout the *Tale* he displays a humane attitude towards the plight of others. He feels his heart will break at the sight of the women mourning for the fate of their husbands and he tries to comfort them. His humanity is shown in his decision to forbid the taking of life at the jousting – a decision universally approved for its mercy.

He is diplomatic in his clemency; he assures both sides that they were equal in valour. After the jousting, he displays his concern for the injured. He is so overwhelmed with sorrow by the death of Arcite that only the sage advice of his father Aegeus can save him from despair.

His heroic stature is constantly emphasized. When he states that Greece will resound with the account of his revenge upon Creon, this is not vainglory but a true appraisal of his own valour and strength in war. In everything he does there is both glory and magnificence. His banners are 'white and large':

And by his baner born is his penoun of gold ful riche.

His earlier heroic exploits with the Minotaur are emblazoned on it. He is surrounded by knights:

And in his host of chivalrye the flour.

True to the codes of medieval knighthood, he slays Creon in open battle. He shows no hesitation in parting Arcite and Palamon when they are fighting to the death; his courage and his authority are unquestionable.

Everything he does matches the magnificence of his own person. Be it a funeral or a tournament, Theseus will organize it with a glorious extravagance that needs several pages to describe. On such occasions he looks like a god and the populace crowd to see him and pay their respects.

He combines philosophy with a great deal of practical common sense. He indicates that both men cannot have Emily, although in a sense, this indication is ironically wrong; common sense is not always a sound guide in this world of romance. His common sense borders on humour when he observes that Emily knows nothing of the furore she has caused, no more than a cuckoo or a hare.

He has the benevolence and the experience to recognize the extremes to which love can drive men; he even suggests that he has experienced its power. Youth, he observes, can be foolish, but so, he adds, can old age. Certainly his own marriage to Hippolyta betrays no signs of real emotion. Perhaps, however, we should applaud his knightly sense of duty in turning aside to take vengeance on Creon, rather than comment on his seeming lack of haste to arrive home with his bride Hippolyta. When Chaucer describes his greatest joy, the reference is to hunting and not to Hippolyta.

His vengeance can be terrible. He destroys the city of Thebes; he threatens Arcite with death if he is found within his jurisdiction; he decides without hesitation to execute Arcite and Palamon. His anger however soon gives way to mercy and the ready forgiveness and acceptance of the offender. Perhaps his comments on his change of heart are priggish in their conscious justification – or so they would be in a lesser man.

If he is an enemy to be feared, he is also a good friend. His gift of friendship with Perotheus is such that each is prepared to seek the other in hell.

Theseus's wisdom and philosophy – largely inspired by Boethius's *The Consolations of Philosophy*, which Chaucer had himself translated from the Latin – provide the necessary balance to a Tale that would otherwise swing between the violent extremes of the two lovers. Thus Chaucer emphasizes the importance of the whole. Everything changes; nothing can last for ever. We must accept the passing of time; to rebel is foolish. We must 'maken vertu of necessitee'. Happiness must prevail: 'After wo, I rede us to be merye.'

It is Theseus who comes to terms with the facts of life, accepting its sorrows and the inevitability of death. But it is also Theseus who asserts the need for happiness and brings the love of Emily and Palamon to fulfilment in marriage.

Arcite

'Thou hast wysdom and manhede.'

Arcite is a prince of the royal house of Thebes; like Palamon he is imprisoned by Theseus who has refused a ransom. He is more philosophical in his acceptance of fate than Palamon. In his belief that their misfortune is the result of a fate determined by the malevolence of the planets, he is something of a fatalist: 'We moste endure it: this is the short and playn.'

Ironically, after Palamon has been overwhelmed by Emily's beauty, Arcite is also struck by her loveliness. In love, he is wholly selfish. In Palamon's eyes, he is false and a traitor to his knightly duty to help a brother-in-love. He is a clever, and argues that his love is justified, as Palamon's is a bodiless spiritual love whereas his is human and physical. This suggests from the start that Palamon's love is purer and, therefore, more akin to that of Emily's. Perhaps Arcite, with his devotion to Mars the god of war, is inevitably destined to lose the battle for Emily to Palamon, a follower of Venus.

He is almost cynical in his attempt at justification. He says:

'Who shall yeve a lover any lawe?
Love is gretter lawe, by my pan,
Than may be yeve to any erthly man.'

His conception is earthy. He compares two lovers to two dogs fighting over a bone. He concludes on a note of cynical realism:

Heere in this prisoun moote we endure
And everich of us take his aventure.

However, there can be no doubt about the strength of his love. He is constant and suffers agonies:

And, shortly, turned was al up so doun
Bathe habit and eek disposicioun.

Arcite, who once counselled Palamon to accept fate, now meditates at length on the futility of human desires and ambitions. He closely mirrors the Russian melancholy of a despairing Tolstoy, asserting that we seek happiness without knowing in what our happiness consists. There is no philosophy he can summon to his aid when he is dying for love. No 'Consolation of Philosophy' is for him. He will sacrifice all for love: position, safety, even his life. The young, powerful, large-boned warrior has become the weak slave of love.

His mental state is mirrored in his social condition; in order to be near Emily, he sacrifices the position to which his princely birth entitles him. Even in his lowly position, Arcite becomes famous throughout the court. His good deeds and polite address lead to advancement under Theseus. He rises through his own merit, helped by the secret transference of his personal wealth to Athens. His patience is exemplified by the fact he is content to bide his time in his pursuit of Emily. Indeed, he seems somewhat slow to use his newly established position in the court of Theseus. Palamon would have acted with more urgency and decision. There is almost an element of the playboy in the way he disports himself, wearing a garland of hawthorn and honeysuckle leaves and singing to welcome May. His love is seen only in his sudden depressions. Then the shame of his position strikes home: a slave to his enemy, a denier of his own name and a humble squire.

He does, however, retain his honour – illustrated in his refusal to kill the defenceless Palamon. In the best tradition of the medieval knight, he challenges him to combat. In the ensuing battle, he fights like a tiger to Palamon's lion. He is a worthy follower of Mars; yet he is not without a measure of humility: to Mars he acknowledges that he is both young and ignorant. He is more objective than Palamon; he realizes that Emily cannot care for him and is humbler in his hopes that she may.

Arcite has his reward in Theseus's decision to give Emily to him after the jousting. He has achieved his aim even if his desires are not satisfied. His death mirrors his philosophy. Life is uncertain; it can shift from the warmth and delights of life to the cold harsh reality of the grave. He is perhaps ungrateful in blaming Emily for his death. Yet his love lasts until the end; his final word is 'Emily'.

In death, Arcite displays nobility and magnanimity. His death brings out those knightly qualities that have been woefully lacking under the influence of love. His end is moving as he speakes to Emily:

As in this world right now ne knowe I non
So worthy to ben loved as Palamon,
That serveth yow, and wol don al his lyf.
And if that ever ye shul been a wyf,
foryet nat Palamon, the gentil man.

His is the death of a tragic hero, which brings peace and reconciliation, the awareness of truth and a realization of the nobility of life to all those around him. He is valued more in death than he was in life.

There is more individuality of characterization in Arcite than in Palamon. Both, however, are flat characters. Some contemporary philosophy finds its expression in Arcite; he has the capacity to look objectively at his position and at himself. He represents a tentative study in the limitations as well as the virtues, of the medieval knight and the concept of courtesy. The study is tentative because Arcite is a creation of a narrator, the Knight, who himself is a representative of that tradition. Chaucer's satire is only fitfully directed at Arcite.

Palamon

'That gentil Palamon, thyn owene knyght,
That serveth yow with wille, herte, and myght.'

Palamon is the perfect man to Emily's perfect woman. The
only faults he shows are those brought on by the intensity of
his love. In the world of chivalry and romance such madness
is acceptable. Even Theseus acknowledges the power of love.
Palamon prays to Venus, and it is fitting that his life should
be governed by love.

He is a royal prince of the House of Thebes. It is in defeat
that we first meet him. He and Arcite have been conquered
by Theseus, and have become his prisoners. Palamon is less
philosophical about his fate than is Arcite. He wishes he had
not been born; this is, however, understandable, since he has
nothing to look forward to in life except imprisonment in a
dungeon in the heart of the grim tower.

From the very beginning, Palamon's is the pattern of perfect
love. In this tale, Chaucer changes Boccaccio's story, where
it is Arcite who first sees Emily, and where there is no rivalry
between the two cousins. Chaucer's approach is much more
direct and dramatic:

He cast his eyen upon Emelye,
And therewithal he bleynte, and cride 'A'!
As though he stongen were unto the herte

Palamon is highly emotional, as befits a lover. From this point
forward his whole mind and being are completely given over
to his love for Emily.

His standards of chivalry are higher than those of Arcite,
though there is a degree of self-interest in his complaints
about Arcite. He considers that, since he saw Emily first, it is
false and traitorous of Arcite to aspire also to her love, and a
sad falling-away from his knightly oath. It is interesting to
speculate how Palamon would have behaved and spoken had
Arcite seen Emily first.

Palamon's extravagantly emotional temperament is seen when Arcite achieves his freedom: in his despair he weeps and howls. He is more direct than Arcite who, when he is free, tries to achieve his aims secretly and patiently. Palamon thinks in terms of conquering Theseus and winning Emily for his wife. For Palamon the direct way is the only way: he regards Arcite's subtlety as dishonourable cheating. When finally he escapes, and sees Arcite, it is the obvious and direct solution of killing him that occurs to Palamon.

Yet both knights are heroes. They help each other to put on their armour before they begin their fight to the death. When Theseus finds them it is Palamon who, immediately and openly, admits who they are. There is no attempt to deceive, no grovelling for mercy; only the courage to accept punishment and death. He asks only that Arcite shall suffer the same fate.

Just as Palamon can wish that he had never been born, so he can complain against the gods – but not in a spirit of rebellious defiance, rather in a mood of dejection, self-pity and sadness at the miserable lot of mankind. There is no feeling of the glory of man. Palamon considers that beasts are happy in the satisfaction of their lust, and in not having a future life. His true nobility and generosity are revealed only at the death of Arcite: at this moment sorrow transcends love and rivalry.

Palamon is not a fully rounded human character: Chaucer does not intend him to be. He has a part to play as the lover of Emily, and he plays it fully and obsessively. Emily is the love of his life, and his salvation lies in winning her in marriage:

For now is Palamon in alle wele,
Lyvynge in blisse, in richesse, and in heele;
And Emelye hym loveth so tendrely,
And he hire serveth al-so gentilly.

Emily (Emelye)

That Emelye, that fairer was to sene
Than is the lylie upon his stalke grene,
And fresher than the May with flowers newe.

In Boccaccio's *Teseide*, which Chaucer used as his source for
The Knight's Tale, the character of Emily is differently drawn.
There she plays a more active part, enjoys being gazed at,
and reveals the vanity that – according to Boccaccio – is
innate in women.

Chaucer portrays Emily as the pattern of all loveliness: he
spares no pains to present her as beautiful, fresh and virgin-
ally pure. The purity of her beauty is likened to that of
the lily; the freshness of her colouring is like the roses of May:
the beauty of the flowers complements the exquisite loveliness
of her person. The sun's radiance matches her own: Emily
and the sun rise together; light surrounds them both. Inevit-
ably, her long hair is golden.

While she gathers flowers Emily sings like an angel. When
first he sees her, Arcite is so overwhelmed that he wonders
whether she is woman or goddess. With her radiance, fresh-
ness and beauty, the reader is willing to accept that she can
arouse the sudden, violent love of both Arcite and Palamon.

Emily has all the virtues: she is demure, calm and serene.
Passion she may arouse in others: she herself is pure and
virginal. Diana is the goddess to whom she prays: she begs
the goddess to allow her to remain a virgin; hopes that Arcite
and Palamon will become friends, and wishes them both to
forget her. Yet she can, in her virgin innocence, show a touch
of reality; she is careful to ask Diana to ensure that, if she
cannot be a virgin, she can have the one that will love her
most.

Emily has a pitying heart: she is easily and profoundly
moved by suffering. The slightness of her connection with
Arcite in no way moderates her grief at his death: for many

years she remains in a continued state of virginity and grief.

Obedience is fundamental to Emily. It never occurs to her to question the will of Diana when, to her terror, she appears to her, saying that Emily will marry. At the command of Theseus, she is prepared to marry first Arcite and then Palamon. She looks softly and sweetly on Arcite when it seems he is to be her husband, for – as Chaucer comments – Emily is a woman, and women favour those who are successful.

When at last she marries Palamon, Emily becomes the perfect wife: tender, faithful, constant in love, trusting and patient. The marriage of these loving and high-born partners brings happiness to both – and a resolution to the story.

Chaucer gives to Emily a faint suggestion of genuine womanliness, which saves her from seeming merely an exercise in cold perfection – of appearance and character. Yet it is *only* a faint suggestion: fundamentally she belongs to the Knights' idealized world of romance and chivalry – where the young ladies are beautiful, pure and virginal; graced with all the accomplishments; and perfect in their sympathy and tenderness.

Theseus may comment on the remarkable depth and strength of the love of Arcite and Palamon for a girl they have seen but not known: there is the realist speaking. In the world of chivalry, distance and unattainability are no bar to passion. And the psychology of this is not completely absurd: it remains a commonplace of observation that passion feeds on its own lack of satisfaction. (It is essential, in order to understand a 'Wife of Bath' to know a lot about her. The vision of beauty that is Emily would be partly destroyed by a closer knowledge of her character.)

Hippolyta (Ypolita)

The faire, hardy quene of Scithia.

Hippolyta plays little part in *The Knight's Tale*. Theseus had, among his many conquests, defeated the Amazons, a race of warrior women, whose queen was Hippolyta. She is a worthy wife for Theseus, who marries her after he has conquered her in battle. Like Emily, who is her younger sister, Hippolyta is easily moved to pity; and it is her tears that move Theseus to show mercy to Arcite and Palamon.

The Character of the Knight

A Knight ther was, and that a worthy man,
That fro the tyme that he first bigan
To ryden out, he loved chivalrye,   45
Trouthe and honour, fredom and curteisye.
Ful worthy was he in his lordes werre,
And therto hadde he riden (no man ferre)
As well in Cristendom as hethenesse,
And ever honoured for his worthinesse.   50
  At Alisaundre he was, whan it was wonne;
Ful ofte tyme he hadde the bord bigonne
Aboven alle naciouns in Pruce.
In Lettow hadde he reysed and in Ruce,
No Cristen man so ofte of his degree.   55
In Gernade at the sege eek hadde he be
Of Algezir, and riden in Belmarye.
At Lyeys was he, and at Satalye,
Whan they were wonne; and in the Grete See
At many a noble armee hadde he be.   60

  At mortal batailles hadde he been fiftene,
And foughten for our feith at Tramissene
In listes thryes, and ay slayn his fo.
This ilke worthy knight had been also
Somtyme with the lord Palatye,   65
Ageyn another hethen in Turkye:
And evermore he hadde a sovereyn prys.
And though that he were worthy, he was wys,
And of his port as meke as is a mayde.
He never yet no vileinye ne sayde   70
In al his lyf, un-to no manner wight.
He was a verray parfit gentil knight.
But for to tellen yow of his array,
His hors were gode, but he was nat gay.
Of fustian he wered a gipoun   75
Al bismotered with his habergeoun;
For he was late y-come from his viage,
And wente for to doon his pilgrimage.

There was a Knight, an honourable man, who, from the time that he first became a soldier, loved knightly conduct, truth, honour, freedom and courteous manners. He had been brave and capable in his Lord's war and, moreover, no man had served farther afield, not only in Christendom but also in heathen countries, and he had always been held in the highest respect for his moral excellence. He was at Alexandria when it was captured and very often in Prussia he had occupied the most honoured place at table above all ranks. He had served as a soldier in Lithuania and Russia. Indeed, no Christian man of equal rank had served as often as he. He had also been in Granada at the time of the siege of Algeciras and had served in Ben-Marin. He was at Ayas and Attalia when they were captured and had accompanied many magnificent expeditions to the Mediterranean Sea.

He had been present at fifteen fierce battles, had fought in three tournaments for our faith at Tlemsen and had killed his adversary every time. This renowned Knight had also been once with the lord of Palatia, still another heathen ruler of Turkey. He always gained very great renown *but*, although he was brave, he was prudent and as meek as a girl in his behaviour. He had never uttered foul language in his whole life to any person whatsoever. He was a true, perfect and refined Knight. But, to tell you about his clothes, although he had a good horse, he himself was not finely dressed. He wore a fustian tunic, soiled all over by his coat of mail, for he had only lately returned from his travels and had decided to fulfil his pilgrimage straightaway.

'Who shal telle the firste tale?'

A-morwe, whan that day bigan to springe,
Up roos our host, and was our aller cok,
And gadrede us togidre, alle in a flok,
And forth we riden, a litel more than pas,   825
Un-to the watering of seint Thomas.
And there our host bigan his hors areste,
And seyde; 'Lordinges, herkneth, if yow leste.
Ye woot your forward, and I it yow recorde.
If even-song and morwe-song acorde,   830
Lat see now who shal telle the firste tale.
As ever mote I drinke wyn or ale,
Who-so be rebel to my jugement
Shal paye for al that by the weye is spent.
Now draweth cut, er that we ferrer twinne;   835
He which that hath the shortest shal biginne.
Sire knight,' quod he, 'my maister and my lord,
Now draweth cut, for that is myn acord.
Cometh neer,' quod he, 'my lady prioresse;
And ye, sir clerk, lat be your shamfastnesse,   840
Ne studieth noght; ley hond to, every man.'

Anon to drawen every wight bigan,
And shortly for to tellen, as it was,
Were it by aventure, or sort, or cas,
The sothe is this, the cut fil to the knight,   845
Of which ful blythe and glad was every wight;
And telle he moste his tale, as was resoun,
By forward and by composicioun,
As ye han herd; what nedeth wordes mo?
And whan this gode man saugh it was so,   850
As he that wys was and obedient
To kepe his forward by his free assent,
He seyde: 'Sin I shal beginne the game,
What, welcome be the cut, a Goddes name!
Now lat us ryde, and herkneth what I seye.'   855
And with that word we riden forth our weye;
And he bigan with right a mery chere
His tale anon, and seyde in this manere.

'Who shall tell the first tale?'

When dawn came the next morning, our Host arose before us all and, collecting us together in a company, we rode forth at hardly more than walking pace to St Thomas's Well. Here our Host stopped his horse and said, 'Gentlemen, listen to me please. Although you probably remember your agreement, I shall remind you of it. If you agree this morning with what you said last evening, let us decide who will tell the first story. By my intention never to drink anything except wine or ale, the one who will not obey my decision will pay for everything that we spend during the journey. Now, let us draw lots before we go any farther. The person who draws the shortest straw will begin. Sir Knight, my lord and master,' he continued, 'take your draw as I say. Come nearer, my Lady Prioress, and you, Sir Clerk, don't be shy. Don't stand there day-dreaming. Let us all begin.'

Straightaway every one came forward for the draw and, to be brief, whether it was by luck, chance or fortune, the fact is that the lot fell upon the Knight. This pleased every one immensely, and he had to tell his story, as was right, according to our agreed decision, as you have heard. Need I say more? When the gentleman saw that it was so, like one who is wise and obedient in keeping to his agreement, he said, 'Since I must begin the entertainment, in God's name, let the draw be welcome! Now let us ride forward and listen to what I shall say.'

With these words we rode forth on our journey and the Knight began to tell his story in a right happy manner at once and related it thus.

The Knight's Tale

Iamque domos patrias, Scithice post aspera gentis
Prelia, laurigero, &c. (Statius, *Theb*, 12, 519)

Part 1

Whylom, as olde stories tellen us,
Ther was a duk that highte Theseus;   860
Of Athenes he was lord and governour,
And in his tyme swich a conquerour,
That gretter was ther noon under the sonne.
Ful many a riche contree hadde he wonne;
What with his wisdom and his chivalrye,   865
He conquered al the regne of Femenye,
That whylom was y-cleped Scithia;
And weddede the quene Ipolita,
And broghte hir hoom with him in his contree
With muchel glorie and greet solempnitee,   870
And eek hir yonge suster Emelye.
And thus with victorie and with melodye
Lete I this noble duk to Athenes ryde,
And al his hoost, in armes, him bisyde.

  And certes, if it nere to long to here,   875
I wolde han told yow fully the manere,
How wonnen was the regne of Femenye
By Theseus, and by his chivalrye;
And of the grete bataille for the nones
Bitwixen Athenës and Amazones;   880
And how asseged was Ipolita,
The faire hardy quene of Scithia;
And of the feste that was at hir weddinge,
And of the tempest at hir hoom-cominge;
But al that thing I moot as now forebere.   885
I have, God woot, a large feeld to ere,
And wayke been the oxen in my plough.
The remenant of the tale is long y-nough.
I wol nat letten eek noon of this route;
Lat every felawe telle his tale aboute,   890
And lat see now who shal the soper winne;
And ther I lefte, I wol ageyn biginne.

The Knight's Tale

Part 1

Once upon a time there was, so the old stories tell us, a Duke called Theseus. He was the lord and governor of Athens and in his day he conducted himself so well that there was no greater conqueror under the heavens. Many a wealthy country had he subdued and, through his foresight and personal exploits, he had overrun the whole Kingdom of the Amazons, formerly called Scythia. After he had wedded Queen Hippolyta, he brought her and her young sister, Emily, with great pomp and glory home with him to his own country. And so, amid victory and music-making, I shall leave this noble Duke and all his host in arms beside him to ride to Athens.

Indeed, if it were not too long for you to hear, I should describe to you in detail the way in which the Kingdom of the Amazons was conquered by Theseus and his excellent knights, the great battle that was fought between the Athenians and the Amazons on that occasion, how Hippolyta, the beautiful, brave Queen of Scythia, was besieged, the feast that was held at their wedding and the storm that occurred on their home-coming: but I must pass over all that for the time being. God knows, I have a large field to plough and the oxen in my plough are weak (i.e. I have much ground to cover and my facilities are scanty). The rest of my story is long enough and, as I do not wish to stand in the way of anyone in this company, I prefer that everyone should tell his story in turn and then we shall see who will win the supper. Now, then, I shall continue my story where I left it.

This duk, of whom I make mencioun,
When he was come almost unto the toun,
In al his wele and in his moste pryde,   895
He was war, as he caste his eye asyde,
Wher that ther kneled in the hye weye
A companye of ladies, tweye and tweye,
Ech after other, clad in clothes blake;
But swich a cry and swich a wo they make,   900
That in this world nis creature livinge,
That herde swich another weymentinge;
And of this cry they nolde never stenten,
Til they the reynes of his brydel henten.

'What folk ben ye, that at myn hoom-cominge   905
Perturben so my feste with crynge?'
Quod Theseus, 'have ye so greet envye
Of myn honour, that thus compleyne and crye?
Or hath yow misboden, or offended?
And telleth me if it may been amended;   910
And why that ye ben clothed thus in blak?'

The eldest lady of hem alle spak,
When she hadde swowned with a deedly chere,
That it was routhe for to seen and here,
And seyde: 'Lord, to whom Fortune hath yiven   915
Victorie, and as a conquerour to liven,
Noght greveth us your glorie and your honour;
But we biseken mercy and socour.
Have mercy on our wo and our distresse.
Som drope of pitee, thurgh thy gentilesse,   920
Up-on us wrecched wommen lat thou falle.
For certes, lord, there nis noon of us alle,
That she nath been a duchesse or a quene;
Now be we caitifs, as it is wel sene:
Thanked be Fortune, and hir false wheel,   925
That noon estat assureth to be weel.
And certes, lord, t'abyden your presence,
Here in the temple of the goddesse Clemence
We han ben waytinge al this fourtenight;
Now help us, lord, sith it is in thy might.   930

When this Duke, about whom I am telling you, in all his good fortune and great pride, had almost reached the town, he noticed, on looking around him, a company of ladies, all dressed in black clothes, kneeling in pairs, one behind the other, on the highway. They were weeping and wailing so bitterly that no one living anywhere could have heard such grief; and, what is more, they would not stop their mourning till they had taken hold of the reins of Theseus's bridle.

'Who are you who dare with this weeping to disturb this feast to celebrate my home-coming?' Theseus asked. 'Are you so envious of my renown that you should wail and weep like this? If not, who has harmed or done you wrong? Tell me if I can do anything to help you. And why are you dressed in black in this manner?'

After the eldest of them all had swooned in such a death-like manner most pitiful to see and hear, she answered, 'My lord, to whom Fortune has granted victory and the right to live as a conqueror, we do not begrudge your glory and renown. We beg only for mercy and assistance. Take pity on our troubles and our distress. Show some measure of pity from your own gentle heart to us wretched women, for indeed, lord, there is not one among us who has not been a duchess or a queen. Thanks to Fortune and her fickle wheel, as you can clearly see, we are in misery and no one will assure us that our lives are secure. For a fortnight, Sire, we have been watching in this Temple of the goddess, Clemency, to wait your coming. Please, help us Sire, for it lies in your power.

I wrecche, which that wepe and waille thus,
Was whylom wyf to king Capaneus,
That starf at Thebes, cursed be that day;
And alle we, that been in this array,
And maken al this lamentacioun,   935
We losten alle our housbondes at that toun,
Whyl that the sege ther-aboute lay.
And yet now th'olde Creon, weylaway!
The lord is now of Thebes the citee,
Fulfild of ire and of iniquitee,   940
He, for despyt, and for his tirannye,
To do the dede bodyes vileinye,
Of alle our lordes, whiche that ben slawe,
Hath alle the bodyes on an heep y-drawe,
And wol nat suffren hem, by noon assent,   945
Neither to been y-buried nor y-brent,
But maketh houndes ete hem in despyt.'
And with that word, with-outen more respyt,
They fillen gruf, and cryden pitously,
'Have on us wrecched wommen som mercy,   950
And lat our sorwe sinken in thyn herte.'

This gentil duk doun from his courser sterte
With herte pitous, whan he herde hem speke.
Him thoughte that his herte wolde breke,
Whan he saugh hem so pitous and so mat,   955
That whylom weren of so greet estat.
And in his armes he hem alle up hente,
And hem conforteth in ful good entente;
And swoor his ooth, as he was trewe knight,
He wolde doon so ferforthly his might   960
Up-on the tyraunt Creon hem to wreke,
That al the peple of Grece sholde speke
How Creon was of Theseus y-served,
As he that hadde his deeth ful wel deserved.

And right anoon, with-outen more abood,   965
His baner he desplayeth, and forth rood
To Thebes-ward, and al his host bisyde;
No neer Athenës wolde he go ne ryde,
Ne take his ese fully half a day,
But onward on his wey that night he lay;   970

I, who am weeping and wailing in my misery like this, was once the wife of King Capaneus who met his death at Thebes – Cursed be that day! – and all of us who are thus dressed in black and are wailing in this fashion lost our husbands while the siege was being conducted round that town. Now, to our sorrow, aged Creon who is the lord of the city of Thebes is filled with anger and wickedness and, from mere spite and for the sake of tyranny, has purposed to ill-treat the corpses of all our slain lords by piling them all in a heap and will not allow them, under any circumstances, to be buried or burnt. Instead, from sheer spite, he is letting the dogs eat them.' With these words they straightaway fell prostrate on the ground and cried piteously, 'Take some pity on us unfortunate women and let our sorrow sink into your heart.'

When the noble Duke heard them speak these words, he leapt from his horse with such a compassionate heart that he thought it would break at the sight of these ladies, who had once held such high rank in society, so pitiful and dejected. He raised them all up in his arms and comforted them with a kind heart, swearing an oath that, as he was a true knight, he would use his utmost power to wreak vengeance upon that tyrant, Creon. He promised that everyone in Greece would remember how Creon was punished by Theseus and would say that Creon had right well merited his death.

Delaying no longer, he unfurled his banner and rode with all his army towards Thebes, even refusing to ride any nearer Athens or to rest for more than half a day but continued on his way into the night.

And sente anoon Ipolita the quene,
And Emelye hir yonge suster shene,
Un-to the toun of Athenës to dwelle;
And forth he rit; ther nis namore to telle.

The rede statue of Mars, with spere and targe,   975
So shyneth in his whyte baner large,
That alle the feeldes gliteren up and doun;
And by his baner born is his penoun
Of gold ful riche, in which ther was y-bete
The Minotaur, which that he slough in Crete.   980
Thus rit this duk, thus rit this conquerour,
And in his host of chivalrye the flour,
Til that he cam to Thebes, and alighte
Faire in a feeld, ther as he thoghte fighte.
But shortly for to speken of this thing,   985
With Creon, which that was of Thebes king,
He faught, and slough him manly as a knight
In pleyn bataille, and putte the folk to flight;
And by assaut he wan the citee after,
And rente adoun bothe wal, and sparre, and rafter;   990
And to the ladyes he restored agayn
The bones of hir housbondes that were slayn,
To doon obséquies, as was tho the gyse.

But it were al to long for to devyse
The grete clamour and the waymentinge   995
That the ladyes made at the brenninge
Of the bodyes, and the grete honour
That Theseus, the noble conquerour,
Doth to the ladyes, whan they from him wente;
But shortly for to telle is myn entente.   1000
Whan that this worthy duk, this Theseus,
Hath Creon slayn, and wonne Thebes thus,
Stille in that feeld he took al night his reste,
And dide with al the contree as him leste.

To ransake in the tas of bodyes dede,   1005
Hem for to strepe of harneys and of wede,
The pilours diden bisinesse and cure,
After the bataille and disconfiture.

He at once sent Hippolyta and her fair, young sister, Emily, to remain in the town of Athens. I think all I need say is that he proceeded on his way.

The red figure of Mars, holding a spear and shield, shone so brightly on his large, white banner that all the fields around glittered; next to his banner was carried a pennon, richly embroidered in gold and on which were worked the Minotaurs which he had slain in Crete. The Duke, the conqueror, the very flower of the knights of his army, rode in this fashion till he came to Thebes. Here he dismounted in a field where he intended the fight should take place. To be brief, he fought with Creon, the King of Thebes, and just like a true knight he slew him in manly fashion in open fight and put his followers to flight. Later, he captured the city by assault, tore down its walls, beams and rafters and restored the bones of their slain husbands once again to the wives so that they could carry out the funeral rites in the fashion then prevailing.

It would, however, take me too long to describe the great outcry and lamentation the ladies made at the burning of the bodies, and also the deep respect the renowned conqueror, Theseus, paid to the ladies when they left him. It is, indeed, my intention to be brief. When the noble Duke Theseus had killed Creon and had taken Thebes in this way, he rested quietly the whole night in that field of battle and used the country just as he thought fit.

After the battle rout, of course, the pillagers performed their due work in ransacking the piles of dead bodies and stripping them of armour and clothing.

And so bifel, that in the tas they founde,
Thurgh-girt with many a grevous blody wounde,   1010
Two yonge knightes ligging by and by,
Bothe in oon armes, wroght ful richely,
Of whiche two, Arcite hight that oon,
And that other knight hight Palamon.
Nat fully quike, ne fully dede they were,   1015
But by hir cote-armures, and by hir gere,
The heraudes knewe hem best in special,
As they that weren of the blood royal
Of Thebes, and of sustren two y-born.
Out of the tas the pilours han hem torn,   1020
And han hem caried softe un-to the tente
Of Theseus, and he ful sone hem sente
To Athenës, to dwellen in prisoun
Perpetuelly, he nolde no ransoun.

And whan this worthy duk hath thus y-don,   1025
He took his host, and hoom he rood anon
With laurer crowned as a conquerour;
And there he liveth, in joye and in honour,
Terme of his lyf; what nedeth wordes mo?
And in a tour, in angwish and in wo,   1030
Dwellen this Palamoun and eek Arcite,
For evermore, ther may no gold hem quyte.

 This passeth yeer by yeer, and day by day,
Til it fil ones, in a morwe of May,
That Emelye, that fairer was to sene   1035
Than is the lilie upon his stalke grene,
And fressher than the May with floures newe –
For with the rose colour stroof hir hewe,
I noot which was the fairer of hem two –
Er it were day, as was hir wone to do,   1040
She was arisen, and al redy dight;
For May wol have no slogardye a-night.
The sesoun priketh every gentil herte,
And maketh him out of his sleep to sterte,
And seith, 'Arys, and do thyn observaunce.'   1045
This maked Emelye have remembraunce
To doon honour to May, and for to ryse.

It so happened that they found in the heap two young knights lying side by side, both pierced through with many grievous bloody wounds, and both clad in identically-fashioned armour, very elaborately wrought. One was called Arcite and the other Palamon. They were not quite dead but the heralds particularly recognized from their coat of arms and their accoutrements that they were members of the blood-royal of Thebes and the sons of two sisters. The pillagers rescued them from the heap of dead and gently carried them to the tent of Theseus who, as he did not desire any ransom, despatched them to Athens to be confined to prison for ever.

When he had done this, the noble Duke collected his army and, crowned with laurel in the fashion of a conqueror, at once rode towards his home where he passed his whole life in joy and honour. There is no point in saying any more about it, except that Palamon and Arcite, his comrade, were left in bitter sorrow for ever in a tower from where no money could ransom them.

Thus, day after day, year after year, went by until the occasion came one May morning that Emily had arisen early in her usual way and was already dressed before daylight. She was fairer to look at than a lily on its green stalk and fresher than the month of May with its lovely flowers; her complexion rivalled the colour of the rose and I cannot say which was the fairer of the two. The month of May will not tolerate slothfulness at night because that is the period when every decent heart is urged to arise from sleep and say, 'Get up to perform your rites.' This made Emily remember that she too had to pay her respects to May and get up early.

Y-clothed was she fresh, for to devyse;
Hir yelow heer was broyded in a tresse,
Bihinde hir bak, a yerde long, I gesse   1050
And in the gardin, at the sonne up-riste,
She walketh up and doun, and as hir liste
She gadereth floures, party whyte and rede,
To make a sotil gerland for hir hede,
And as an aungel hevenly she song.   1055
The grete tour, that was so thikke and strong,
Which of the castel was the chief dongeoun,
(Ther-as the knightes weren in prisoun,
Of whiche I tolde yow, and tellen shal)
Was evene joynant to the gardin-wal,   1060
Ther as this Emelye hadde hir pleyinge.

Bright was the sonne, and cleer that morweninge,
And Palamon, this woful prisoner,
As was his wone, by leve of his gayler,
Was risen, and romed in a chambre on heigh,   1065
In which he al the noble citee seigh,
And eek the gardin, ful of braunches grene,
Ther-as this fresshe Emelye the shene
Was in hir walk, and romed up and doun.
This sorweful prisoner, this Palamoun,   1070
Goth in the chambre, roming to and fro,
And to him-self compleyning of his wo;
That he was born, ful ofte he seyde, 'alas!'
And so bifel, by aventure or cas,
That thurgh a window, thikke of many a barre   1075
Of yren greet, and square as any sparre,
He caste his eye upon Emelya,
And ther-with-al he bleynte, and cryde 'a!'
As though he stongen were un-to the herte.

And with that cry Arcite anon up-sterte,   1080
And seyde, 'Cosin myn, what eyleth thee,
That art so pale and deedly on to see?
Why crydestow? who hath thee doon offence?
For Goddes love, tak al in pacience
Our prisoun, for it may non other be;   1085
Fortune hath yeven us this adversitee.

If I were to describe her, I should say that she was most attractively dressed, with her golden hair, which was a yard long, I suppose, plaited in a tress down her back. At sun-rise she was already walking in the garden, picking to her heart's content some white and red flowers to make an exquisite garland for her head, and while she did so, she sang as divinely as an angel. The great tower which was the chief dungeon of the castle, so broad and strongly-constructed, was joined close to the garden wall where Emily was taking her recreation; and it was here that the knights, around whom the story is centred, were imprisoned.

The sun was shining beautifully that clear morning and the unhappy prisoner, Palamon, had secured leave from the gaoler to get up and roam around, in his usual way, in his upper room from where he could see the beautiful city and also the garden, full of green foliage, where the fair Emily too was strolling to and fro. This miserable prisoner, Palamon, began wandering about in his room, bewailing his troubles to himself, wondering why he had ever been born and sighing all the time. Luck or chance had it that, through a window strengthened by iron bars, huge and squared like pieces of timber, his glance alighted upon Emily. At once he started back and said, 'Ah!' as if he was stricken to the heart.

Arcite immediately arose when he heard the cry. 'My cousin,' he asked, 'What is hurting you that you look so ghastly pale? Why do you cry out? Who has wronged you? For heaven's sake, endure this prison patiently for we can't do anything about. Fortune has given us this adversity.

Som wikke aspect or disposicioun
Of Saturne, by sum constellacioun,
Hath yeven us this, al-though we hadde it sworn;
So stood the heven whan that we were born; 1090
We moste endure it: this is the short and pleyn.'

 This Palamon answerde, and seyde ageyn
'Cosyn, for sothe, of this opinioun
Thou hast a veyn imaginacioun.
This prison caused me nat for to crye. 1095
But I was hurt right now thurgh-out myn yë
In-to myn herte, that wol my bane be.
The fairnesse of that lady that I see
Yond in the gardin romen to and fro,
Is cause of al my crying and my wo. 1100
I noot wher she be womman or goddesse;
But Venus is it, soothly, as I gesse.'
And ther-with-al on kneës doun he fil,
And seyde: 'Venus, if it be thy wil
Yow in this gardin thus to transfigure 1105
Bifore me, sorweful wrecche creature,
Out of this prisoun help that we may scapen.
And if so be my destinee be shapen
By eterne word to dyen in prisoun,
Of our linage have som compassioun, 1110
That is so lowe y-broght by tirannye.'

And with that word Arcite gan espye
Wher-as this lady romed to and fro.
And with that sighte hir beautee hurte him so,
That, if that Palamon was wounded sore, 1115
Arcite is hurt as muche as he, or more.
And with a sigh he seyde pitously:
'The fresshe beautee sleeth me sodeynly
Of hir that rometh in the yonder place;
And, but I have hir mercy and hir grace, 1120
That I may seen hir atte leeste weye,
I nam but deed; ther nis namore to seye.'
 This Palamon, whan he tho wordes herde.
Dispitously he loked, and answerde:
'Whether seistow this in ernest or in pley?' 1125
 'Nay,' quod Arcite, 'in ernest, by my fey!
God help me so, me list ful yvele pleye.'

Some contrary planetary relation or adjustment of Saturn with reference to some constellation has caused this ill turn of circumstance. I believe the long and short of it is that the heavens were in this position when we were born, so we must endure it.'

'Indeed, cousin,' replied Palamon, 'you obviously misunderstand things when you make a remark like that. This prison did not cause me to cry out. Rather, I was hurt because what my eye saw pierced my heart and it will be the death of me. The beauty of that lady whom I see strolling in the garden down there is the cause of my crying aloud and my trouble. I do not know whether she is a woman or a goddess but I believe, indeed, that she is Venus herself.' Falling immediately on his knees, he continued, 'If it is your wish, Venus, to transform yourself in this manner in this garden before the eyes of one who is a sad, wretched person, please grant us help that we may escape from this prison. If my fate is so ordained, by eternal word, for me to die in prison, do have some mercy on our birth that has been brought so low through this tyranny.'

On hearing these words Arcite looked at the place where this lady was walking to and fro. He too was so smitten by the sight of her beauty that, even if Palamon had been sorely wounded, Arcite was as equally, if not more, struck than he. He sighed pitifully and said, 'The exquisite beauty of the maiden walking down there almost takes my breath away. Unless I gain her pity and have her favour to see her for a short time, to say the least, I shall die. I can say no more.'

When he heard these words, Palamon gave him a disdainful look and said, 'Are you speaking in earnest or in jest?'

'No,' said Arcite, 'in earnest, on my honour. So help me God, I'm not jesting.'

This Palamon gan knitte his browes tweye:
'It nere,' quod he, 'to thee no greet honour
For to be fals, ne for to be traytour   1130
To me, that am thy cosin and thy brother
Y-sworn ful depe, and ech of us til other,
That never, for to dyen in the peyne,
Til that the deeth departe shal us tweyne,
Neither of us in love to hindren other,   1135
Ne in non other cas, my leve brother;
But that thou sholdest trewely forthren me
In every cas, and I shal forthren thee.
This was thyn ooth, and myn also, certeyn;
I wot right wel, thou darst it nat withseyn.   1140
Thus artow of my counseil, out of doute.
And now thou woldest falsly been aboute
To love my lady, whom I love and serve,
And ever shal, til that myn herte sterve.
Now certes, fals Arcite, thou shalt nat so.   1145
I loved hir first, and tolde thee my wo
As to my counseil, and my brother sworn
To forthre me, as I have told biforn.
For which thou art y-bounden as a knight
To helpen me, if it lay in thy might,   1150
Or elles artow fals, I dar wel seyn.'

  This Arcite ful proudly spak ageyn,
'Thou shalt,' quod he, 'be rather fals than I;
But thou art fals, I telle thee utterly;
For *par amour* I loved hir first er thow.   1155
What wiltow seyn? thou wistest nat yet now
Whether she be a womman or goddesse!
Thyn is affeccioun of holinesse,
And myn is love, as to a creature;
For which I tolde thee myn aventure   1160
As to my cosin, and my brother sworn.
I pose, that thou lovedest hir biforn;
Wostow nat wel the olde clerkes sawe,
That "who shal yeve a lover any lawe?"
Love is gretter lawe, by my pan,   1165
Than may be yeve to any erthly man.
And therefore positif lawe and swich decree
Is broke al-day for love, in ech degree.

Palamon knit his brows. 'It would not be very honourable,' he said, 'for you to be false or traitorous to me, your cousin and sworn brother. We are both bound to each other solemnly by oaths that, even if we should die in torture, we shall never part till Death shall separate us nor hinder each other in love or in any other circumstances. My dear brother, we swore that you would truly help me in every eventuality and I should help you. That was certainly our oath and I know very well that you dare not deny it. Although it is true that you are my counsellor and my sworn brother, yet you would now falsely purpose to love my lady whom I love and serve and shall ever do so till my heart breaks. I tell you, false Arcite, you shall not have her. I loved her first and told you my trouble just as I should to my counsellor, my sworn brother, so that you could help me, as I have already reminded you. I consider you are bound by knightly honour to help me, if it lies in your power. If not, I dare maintain you are false.'

Arcite replied very proudly to this. 'You are more likely to prove false than I. I declare that you are utterly false, for I loved her first, with true love, before you. What can you say to that? You did not know just now if she was a woman or a goddess. Yours is mere aspiration after holiness while mine is genuine love for a human being. And that is why I told you my experience just as I should to my cousin and sworn brother. Even if you loved her first, don't you remember the old saying of the old scholar that no one can make laws for a lover? I can assure you Love is a greater law than any that can be given to any mortal man. As a result of this, fixed laws and such enactments are broken every day for the sake of Love in every rank of life.

A man moot nedes love, maugree his heed.
He may nat fleen it, thogh he sholde be deed, 1170
Al be she mayde, or widwe, or elles wyf.
And eek it is nat lykly, al thy lyf,
To stonden in hir grace; namore shal I;
For wel thou woost thy-selven, verraily,
That thou and I be dampned to prisoun 1175
Perpetuelly; us gayneth no raunsoun.
We stryve as dide the houndes for the boon,
They foughte al day, and yet hir part was noon;
Ther cam a kyte, whyl that they were wrothe,
And bar awey the boon bitwixe hem bothe. 1180
And therfore, at the kinges court, my brother,
Ech man for him-self, ther is non other.
Love if thee list; for I love and ay shal;
And soothly, leve brother, this is al.
Here in this prisoun mote we endure, 1185
And everich of us take his aventure.'

Greet was the stryf and long bitwise hem tweye,
If that I hadde leyser for to seye;
But to th'effect. It happed on a day,
(To telle it yow as shortly as I may) 1190
A worthy duk that highte Perotheus,
That felawe was un-to duk Theseus
Sin thilke day that they were children lyte,
Was come to Athenes, his felawe to visyte,
And for to pleye, as he was wont to do, 1195
For in this world he loved no man so:
And he loved him as tendrely ageyn.

So wel they loved, as olde bokes seyn,
That whan that oon was deed, sothly to telle,
His felawe wente and soghte him doun in helle; 1200
But of that story list me nat to wryte.
Duk Perotheus loved wel Arcite,
And hadde him knowe at Thebes yeer by yere;
And fynally, at requeste and preyere
Of Perotheus, with-oute any raunsoun, 1205
Duk Theseus him leet out of prisoun,
Freely to goon, wher that him liste over-al,
In swich a gyse, as I you tellen shal.

A man must needs love in spite of every thing. Whether the object of his affection is a maiden, a widow or a wife, he cannot avoid it even if he should die. I also tell you that you are not likely in your whole life to win her affection. But neither shall I, if it comes to that, for you yourself know that you and I are unhappily condemned for ever to prison. Ransom is no use to us. We are quarrelling just like the dogs who fought all day for a bone and gained nothing from it because a kite came on the scene during the fight and stole the bone from between the two of them. I can assure you, my brother, it is the same at the king's court, where every man takes care of himself. Nothing else can be done about it. Love her if you wish but I too shall love her and shall always love her. Even so, my dear brother, the fact of the matter is that we must endure here in prison and each of us must watch for his own opportunity.'

I haven't time enough to describe the sustained struggle between these two and I shall tell you only what directly happened. To put it as briefly as I can, one day a noble Duke, named Perotheus, who had been the companion of Duke Theseus since their childhood days happened to make his customary visit to Athens to have some sport with his friend. Perotheus loved no man in this world as much as Theseus and Theseus loved him dearly in return.

They loved each other so dearly, as the old books say, that when one of them died, to tell the truth, his friend went and sought him in Hell but I do not wish to tell you about that story. Duke Perotheus also liked Arcite very much and had known him for years in Thebes; and, finally, at the request and petition of Perotheus, Duke Theseus released him from prison without any ransom to go around freely wherever he wished in the manner I shall explain.

This was the forward, pleynly for t'endyte,
Betwixen Theseus and him Arcite: 1210
That if so were, that Arcite were y-founde
Ever in his lyf, by day or night or stounde
In any contree of this Theseus,
And he were caught, it was acorded thus.
That with a swerd he sholde lese his heed;   1215
Ther nas non other remedye ne reed,
But taketh his leve, and homward he him spedde;
Let him be war, his nekke lyth to wedde!

How greet a sorwe suffreth now Arcite!
The deeth he feleth thurgh his herte smyte;   1220
He wepeth, wayleth, cryeth pitously;
To sleen him-self he wayteth prively.
He seyde, 'Allas that day that I was born!
Now is my prison worse than biforn;
Now is me shape eternally to dwelle   1225
Noght in purgatorie, but in helle.
Allas! that ever knew I Perotheus!
For elles hadde I dwelled with Theseus
Y-fetered in his prisoun ever-mo.
Than hadde I been in blisse, and nat in wo.   1230
Only the sighte of hir, whom that I serve,
Though that I never hir grace may deserve,
Wolde han suffised right y-nough for me.

O dere cosin Palamon,' quod he,
'Thyn is the victorie of this aventure,   1235
Ful blisfully in prison maistow dure;
In prison? certes nay, but in paradys!
Wel hath fortune y-turned thee the dys,
That hast the sighte of hir, and I th'absence.
For possible is, sin thou hast hir presence,   1240
And art a knight, a worthy and an able,
That by som cas, sin fortune is chaungeable,
Thou mayst to thy desyr som-tyme atteyne.
But I, that am exyled, and bareyne
Of alle grace, and in so greet despeir,   1245
That ther nis erthe, water, fyr, ne eir,
Ne creature, that of hem maked is,
That may me helpe or doon confort in this:
Wel oughte I sterve in wanhope and distresse;
Farwel my lyf, my lust, and my gladnesse!   1250

To put it clearly, the agreement between Theseus and Arcite was to the effect that, if Arcite should at any time in his life be found for one moment, by day or night, in any territory belonging to Theseus and if he should be caught in the act, it was agreed that he should forfeit his head by the sword. He had no other means or course but to take his leave and hasten homewards with the warning that his neck was pledged as a guarantee.

Arcite suffered very deep sorrow at that time. He felt Death smiting him through his heart. While he wept, wailed and cried pitifully, he secretly watched for a chance to kill himself. 'Alas, the day I was born!' he cried. 'My prison is now stronger than before. I am now destined not to stay in purgatory but even in hell. Alas, that I ever knew Perotheus! If I had not known him, I should have remained fettered in Theseus's prison for ever; and, if that had been the case, I should have been very happy and not sorrowful. The mere sight of my lady whom I serve would have been sufficient for me though I may never deserve her favour.

O dear cousin Palamon,' he went on, 'you have gained the victory in this affair! You can remain very happy in prison. In prison? Nay, indeed, in Paradise! Fortune has thrown the dice so well that you can see her but I am to be far from her. As you are near her and you too are a capable and eminent knight and Fortune is so fickle, it is even possible that you may, in some way, attain your desire some time. On the other hand, I who am exiled and have lost all favour am in such despair that there is no earth, water, fire, air or any person created from them who can heal me or afford me comfort in this matter. It is best for me to die in the midst of my despair and distress. Farewell my life, my desire and my happiness.

  Allas, why pleynen folk so in commune
Of purveyaunce of God, or of fortune,
That yeveth hem ful ofte in many a gyse
Wel bettre than they can hem-self devyse?
Som man desyreth for to han richesse,   1255
That cause is of his mordre or greet siknesse.
And som man wolde out of his prison fayn,
That in his hous is of his meynee slayn,
Infinite harmes been in this matere;
We witen nat what thing we preyen here.   1260
We faren as he that dronke is as a mous;
A dronke man wot wel he hath an hous,
But he noot which the righte wey is thider;
And to a dronke man the wey is slider.
And certes, in this world so faren we;   1265
We seken faste after felicitee,
But we goon wrong ful often, trewely.

Thus may we seyen alle, and namely I,
That wende and hadde a greet opinioun,
That, if I mighte escapen from prisoun,   1270
Than hadde I been in joye and perfit hele,
Ther now I am exyled fro my wele.
Sin that I may nat seen yow, Emelye,
I nam but deed; ther nis no remedye.'
  Up-on that other syde Palamon,   1275
Whan that he wiste Arcite was agon,
Swich sorwe he maketh, that the grete tour
Resouneth of his youling and clamour.
The pure fettres on his shines grete
Weren of his bittre salte teres wete.   1280

'Allas!' quod he, 'Arcita, cosin myn,
Of al our stryf, God woot, the fruyt is thyn.
Thow walkest now in Thebes at thy large,
And of my wo thou yevest litel charge.
Thou mayst, sin thou hast wisdom and manhede,   1285
Assemblen alle the folk of our kinrede,
And make a werre so sharp on this citee,
That by som aventure, or som tretee,
Thou mayst have hir to lady and to wyf,
For whom that I mot nedes lese my lyf.   1290

Why do people generally complain about the providence of God or of Fortune who gives them gifts so abundantly in many different ways far better than they themselves can devise? Some men desire to acquire wealth and this is the cause of murder or great sickness; another would be glad to escape from his prison and as a result he is slain by his retinue in his own house. There are such huge difficulties in this life that we do not know what we want. We behave like a person as drunk as a mouse. A drunken man is well aware he has a home but he does not know the right way to it and even that road is slippery for any one who is drunk. I suppose that is the way we must take things in this world. We are constantly seeking for happiness but, indeed, most usually we go astray.

We can all say this, and especially I who fantastically thought that, if I could escape from prison, I should then be very happy and enjoy perfect health, whereas I am now exiled from my good fortune. As I cannot see you, Emily, I am as good as dead and there is no remedy for it.'

Meanwhile, when Palamon who was still in prison knew that Arcite had gone, he wept so bitterly that the great tower resounded with his cries and shouts. The very fetters round his powerful shins were wet with his bitter salt tears.

'Alas!' he said, 'Arcite, my cousin, God knows that the fruits of our entire struggle rest with you. At this moment you are walking around, a free man, in Thebes and giving little thought to my misery. With the wisdom and manliness you possess you could collect all the members of our family and wage such a deadly war against the city that, in some way or by some agreement, you could have the woman for whom I must needs lose my life as your wife.

For, as by wey of possibilitee,
Sith thou art at thy large, of prison free,
And art a lord, greet is thyn avauntage,
More than is myn, that sterve here in a cage.
For I mot wepe and wayle, whyl I live,   1295
With al the wo that prison may me yive,
And eek with peyne that love me yiveth also,
That doubleth al my torment and my wo.'
Ther-with the fyr of jelousye up-sterte
With-inne his brest, and hente him by the herte 1300
So woodly, that he lyk was to biholde
The box-tree, or the asshen dede and colde.

Tho seyde he; 'O cruel goddes, that governe
This world with binding of your word eterne,
And wryten in the table of athamaunt   1305
Your parlement, and your eterne graunt,
What is mankinde more un-to yow holde
Than is the sheep, that rouketh in the folde?
For slayn is man right as another beste,
And dwelleth eek in prison and areste,   1310
And hath siknesse, and greet adversitee,
And ofte tymes giltelees, pardee!

 What governaunce is in this prescience,
That giltelees tormenteth innocence?
And yet encreseth this al my penaunce,   1315
That man is bounden to his observaunce,
For Goddes sake, to letten of his wille,
Ther as a beest may al his lust fulfille.
And whan a beest is deed, he hath no peyne;
But man after his deeth moot wepe and pleyne, 1320
Though in this world he have care and wo:
With-outen doute it may stonden so.

Th'answere of this I lete to divynis,
But wel I woot, that in this world gret pyne is.
Allas! I see a serpent or a theef,   1325
That many a trewe man hath doon mescheef,
Goon at his large, and wher him list may turne.
But I mot been in prison thurgh Saturne,
And eek thurgh Juno, jalous and eek wood,
That hath destroyed wel ny al the blood   1330
Of Thebes, with his waste walles wyde.

This course is well within the bounds of possibility for, as you are now at large, free of the prison, and are a lord, you have an unlimited advantage, far greater than that which is at the disposal of myself who is dying here in prison. I must weep and wail during my lifetime and suffer all the trouble this prison can inflict upon me and the pain that Love too is causing me, Love which doubles all my torment and trouble.' On that the fire of jealousy welled up within his breast and sized him so madly in his heart that his face took on the colour of a box-tree or dead, cold ashes.

'O cruel goddess,' he went on, 'who governs this world with the bonds of your everlasting words and whose decree and eternal permission are written on a tablet of adamant, how does mankind concern you more than the sheep which lie huddled together in the fold? Man, too, is killed just like another beast and also dwells in prison and custody, suffering sickness and great tribulation, even though he is oftentimes guiltless.

What studied plan is there in this foreknowledge which results in guiltless, innocent men being tormented? Yet, this knowledge that Man is bound to his duty, for God's sake, to restrain the scope of his desire, whereas an animal may follow his own inclination, greatly increases my penance. When an animal dies, it suffers no pain but Man, even though he may have had no care or trouble in this world, must weep and suffer after his death: I do not doubt this is the true conclusion.

I leave its solution to the divines. I know only too well, however, that there is great suffering in this world. Alas! I see a serpent or a thief who has done evil to many an honest man wandering around the place and going wherever he may please; but I must remain in prison on account of Saturn and jealous, mad Juno who has well-nigh destroyed all the people of Thebes, now desolate in its massive walls.

And Venus sleeth me on that other syde
For jelousye, and fere of him Arcite.'
  Now wol I stinte of Palamon a lyte,
And lete him in his prison stille dwelle,   1335
And of Arcita forth I wol yow telle.
  The somer passeth, and the nightes longe
Encresen double wyse the peynes stronge
Bothe of the lovere and the prisoner.
I noot which hath the wofullere mester.   1340
For shortly for to seyn, this Palamoun
Perpetuelly is dampned to prisoun,
In cheynes and in fettres to ben deed;
And Arcite is exyled upon his heed
For ever-mo as out of that contree,   1345
Ne never-mo he shal his lady see.

  Yow loveres axe I now this questioun,
Who hath the worse, Arcite or Palamoun?
That oon may seen his lady day by day,
But in prison he moot dwelle alway.   1350
That other wher him list may ryde or go,
But seen his lady shal he never-mo.
Now demeth as yow liste, ye that can,
For I wol telle forth as I bigan.

Part 2

Whan that Arcite to Thebes comen was,   1355
Ful ofte a day he swelte and seyde 'allas,'
For seen his lady shal he never-mo.
And shortly to concluden al his wo,
So muche sorwe had never creature
That is, or shal, whyl that the world may dure.   1360
His sleep, his mete, his drink is him biraft,
That lene he wex, and drye as is a shaft.
His eyen holwe, and grisly to biholde;
His hewe falwe, and pale as asshen colde,
And solitarie he was, and ever allone,   1365
And wailling al the night, making his mone.
And if he herde song or instrument,
Then wolde he wepe, he mighte nat be stent;

At the same time I am being killed by Venus for jealousy and fear of Arcite.'

Now I shall tell you no more about Palamon for a while and let him stay quietly in his prison. Instead, I shall tell you more about Arcite.

As the summer went on, the long nights doubly increased the great tortures of both the lover and the prisoner. I do not know which of them had the more miserable existence. To put it in a few words, Palamon was condemned to prison for life, to die in chains and fetters, while Arcite was exiled on pain of death for ever from that country nor would he ever again see his lady.

Now, you lovers, I put this question to you – Who had the worse lot, Arcite or Palamon? One could see his lady daily but he must remain in prison always; while the other could ride or go wherever he pleased but he would never see his lady again. Now, you who have knowledge of the question, decide about it yourselves, for I shall continue with my story as I intended.

Part 2

After Arcite had arrived at Thebes, he fainted and sighed many times a day because he would never see his lady love again. To sum up about his trouble, no person living or who shall ever live as long as this world lasts suffered so much sorrow as he. He could no longer sleep, eat or drink; and he grew thin and withered like a piece of wood, his eyes sunken and frightful to look at and his complexion yellow and pale as cold ashes. Not only was he always on his own, wailing and moaning all night, but if he heard a song or a musical instrument he would weep so much that he could not be prevailed upon to cease.

So feble eek were his spirits, and so lowe,
And chaunged so, that no man coude knowe   1370
His speche nor his vois, though men it herde.
And in his gere, for al the world he ferde
Nat oonly lyk the loveres maladye
Of Hereos, but rather lyk manye
Engendred of humour malencolyk,   1375
Biforen, in his celle fantastyk.
And shortly, turned was al up-so-doun
Bothe habit and eek disposicioun
Of him, this woful lovere daun Arcite.

  What sholde I al-day of his wo endyte?   1380
Whan he endured hadde a yeer or two
This cruel torment, and this peyne and wo,
At Thebes, in his contree, as I seyde,
Up-on a night, in sleep as he him leyde,
Him thoughte how that the wingéd god Mercurie   1385
Biforn him stood, and bad him to be murye.
His slepy yerde in hond he bar uprighte;
An hat he werede up-on his heres brighte.
Arrayed was this god (as he took keep)
As he was whan that Argus took his sleep;   1390
And seyde him thus: 'T'Athénës shaltou wende;
Ther is thee shapen of thy wo an ende.'
And with that word Arcite wook and sterte.
'Now trewely, how sore that me smerte,'
Quod he, 't'Athénës right now wol I fare;   1395
Ne for the drede of deeth shal I nat spare
To see my lady, that I love and serve;
In hir presence I recche nat to sterve.'

  And with that word he caughte a greet mirour,
And saugh that chaunged was al his colour,   1400
And saugh his visage al in another kinde.
And right anoon it ran him in his minde,
That, sith his face was so disfigured
Of maladye, the which he hadde endured,
He might well, if that he bar him lowe,   1405
Live in Athénes ever-more unknowe,
And seen his lady wel ny day by day.

His spirits grew so feeble and dejected and his appearance so altered that people, even when they heard him, could not recognize his speech or his voice. In his manner he behaved for all the world not only as if he was suffering from the love-sickness of Eros but also as if he was possessed of a madness provoked by a sullen humour from the front of his brain. Indeed, both the behaviour and the character of this sorrowful lover, Master Arcite, were completely reversed.

Why should I talk all day about his trouble? When he had endured this cruel torment and painful sorrow for a year or two, one night as he laid himself down to sleep in his country of Thebes, as I told you, he dreamt how the winged god, Mercury, wearing a hat upon his glistening hair and carrying his sleep-bringing wand upright in his hand, stood before him and bade him be cheerful. He noticed that he was dressed the same as when he put Argus to sleep. 'You shall go to Athens,' he said, 'where an end to your troubles is determined for you.' When he heard this, Arcite awoke and leapt up. 'Now, indeed, I shall go to Athens however sorely that torments me,' he said. 'Nor shall I spare myself through fear of death to see the woman I love and serve. As long as I am near her, I care nothing about Death.'

After he had said this he looked into a large mirror and saw that his complexion was transformed and his face was completely changed. Immediately it flashed through his mind that as his face was so disfigured by the sickness he had suffered he could easily, if he behaved himself unostentatiously, live unrecognized in Athens for ever and also see his lady almost every day.

And right anon he chaunged his array.
And cladde him as a povre laborer,
And al allone, save oonly a squyer, 1410
That knew his privetee and al his cas,
Which was disgysed povrely, as he was,
T'Athénës is he goon the nexte way.
And to the court he wente up-on a day,
And at the gate he profreth his servyse, 1415
To drugge and drawe, what so men wol devyse.
And shortly of this matere for to seyn,
He fil in office with a chamberleyn,
The which that dwelling was with Emelye;
For he was wys, and coude soon aspye 1420
Of every servaunt, which that serveth here.

Wel coude he hewen wode, and water bere,
For he was yong and mighty for the nones,
And ther-to he was strong and big of bones
To doon that any wight can him devyse. 1425
A yeer or two he was in this servyse,
Page of the chambre of Emelye the brighte;
And 'Philostrate' he seide that he highte.
But half so wel biloved a man as he
Ne was ther never in court, of his degree; 1430
He was so gentil of condicioun,
That thurghout al the court was his renoun.
They seyden, that it were a charitee
That Theseus wolde enhauncen his degree,
And putten him in worshipful servyse, 1435
Ther as he mighte his vertu excercyse.

And thus, with-inne a whyle, his name is spronge
Both of his dedes, and his good tonge,
That Theseus hath taken him so neer
That of his chambre he made him a squyer, 1440
And yaf him gold to mayntene his degree;
And eek men broghte him out of his contree
From yeer to yeer, ful prively, his rente;
But honestly and slyly he it spente,
That no man wondred how that he it hadde. 1445
And three yeer in this wyse his lyf he ladde,
And bar him so in pees and eek in werre,
Ther nas no man that Theseus hath derre.

Changing his clothes at once and dressing himself as a poor labourer, he went out alone save for a poor squire who knew his secrets and his whole condition, also disguised as a poor man like himself. He went to Athens by the nearest route and, one day coming to the Court, he offered his services at the gate to drudge and draw water just as he should be commanded. To put this matter in a few words, he came to be employed by the chamberlain who dwelt with Emily; and, as he was prudent, he soon found out about every servant who was employed there.

He could cut wood and carry water efficiently, for he was young and strong for that purpose. In addition, as he was tall and of a sturdy body, he was able to do whatever anyone ordered him to do. He served a year or two in this employment as a page-in-waiting in the apartment of the illustrious Emily, giving his name out as Philostrate. There was no man of his rank so beloved as he. He was so kind in his disposition that his good name spread throughout the whole court. They even said it would be a good thing if Theseus elevated his rank and placed him in an honourable post where he could give full scope to his virtues.

Indeed, his reputation so spread abroad both as the result of his good deeds and polished speech that Theseus took him closely into his service and made him a squire in his own apartment and gave him gold to maintain his rank. Although friends secretly brought him his income from his own country year after year, he spent it so honourably and prudently that no man suspected how he acquired it. In this way he passed three years of his life and conducted himself so well in peace and war that no one was dearer to Theseus than he.

And in this blisse lete I now Arcite,
And speke I wol of Palamon a lyte.   1450
  In derknesse and horrible and strong prisoun
This seven yeer hath seten Palamoun,
Forpyned, what for wo and for distresse;
Who feleth double soor and hevinesse
But Palamon? that love destreyneth so,   1455
That wood out of his wit he gooth for wo;
And eek therto he is a prisoner
Perpetuelly, noght oonly for a yeer.
Who coude ryme in English proprely
His martirdom? for sothe, it am nat I;   1460
Therefore I passe as lightly as I may.

  It fel that in the seventhe yeer, in May,
The thridde night, (as olde bokes seyn,
That al this storie tellen more pleyn,)
Were it by aventure or destinee,   1465
(As, whan a thing is shapen, it shal be,)
That, sone after the midnight, Palamoun,
By helping of a freend, brak his prisoun,
And fleeth the citee, faste as he may go;
For he had yive his gayler drink so   1470
Of a clarree, maad of a certeyn wyn,
With nercotikes and opie of Thebes fyn,
That al that night, thogh that men wolde him shake,
The gayler sleep, he might nat awake;
And thus he fleeth as faste as ever he may.   1475

The night was short, and faste by the day,
That nedes-cost he moste him-selven hyde,
And til a grove, faste ther besyde,
With dredful foot than stalketh Palamoun.
For shortly, this was his opinioun,   1480
That in that grove he wolde him hyde al day,
And in the night than wolde he take his way
To Thebes-ward, his freendes for to preye
On Theseus to helpe him to werreye;
And shortly, outher he wolde lese his lyf,   1485
Or winnen Emelye un-to his wyf;
This is th'effect and his entente pleyn.

I now leave Arcite in this happy state and shall say a little about Palamon.

Palamon had sat for seven years in darkness in this horrible, strong prison. Wasted by the pain of his trouble and distress, no one could feel this double sorrow and despair more than Palamon. Love so afflicted him that he nearly went out of his wits with his misery. Besides that, he was a prisoner not merely for one year but for life. Who could put his martyrdom in correct English rhymes? Indeed, I am not capable of doing it so I shall pass him over as gently as I can.

On the third night of May in the seventh year (so the old books, which treat this story in clearer fashion, tell us) it so happened, whether by accident or fate – for when an event is ordained it must happen – that Palamon broke prison soon after midnight with the help of a friend and fled from the city as fast as he could. To bring this about, he had given his gaoler a spiced drink made from a certain wine, with narcotics and fine opium of Thebes, in such a way that, though people shook him, the gaoler slept all that night and could not be awakened. Then he fled as fast as he could.

As, however, the night was short and day was approaching, he was compelled to hide himself and so he made his way apprehensively to a grove nearby. Briefly, it was his idea to hide himself all day in the grove, making his way by night to Thebes where he would beg his friends to help him make war on Theseus. The principal idea behind his whole plan was that he would either lose his life or win Emily as his wife.

Now wol I torne un-to Arcite ageyn,
That litel wiste how ny that was his care,
Til that fortune had broght him in the snare.   1490
  The bisy larke, messager of day,
Saluëth in hir song the morwe gray;
And fyry Phebus ryseth up so brighte,
That al the orient laugheth of the lighte,
And with his stremes dryeth in the greves   1495
The silver dropes, hanging on the leves.
And Arcite, that is in the court royal
With Theseus, his squyer principal,
Is risen, and loketh on the myrie day.
And, for to doon his observaunce to May,   1500
Remembring on the poynt of his desyr,
He on a courser, sterting as the fyr,
Is riden in-to the feeldes, him to pleye,
Out of the court, were it a myle or tweye;

And to the grove, of which that I yow tolde,   1505
By aventure, his wey he gan to holde,
To maken him a gerland of the greves,
Were it of wodebinde or hawethorn-leves,
And loude he song ageyn the sonne shene;
'May, with alle thy floures and thy grene,   1510
Wel-come be thou, faire fresshe May,
I hope that I som grene gete may.'
And from his courser, with a lusty herte,
In-to the grove ful hastily he sterte,
And in a path he rometh up and doun,   1515
Ther-as, by aventure, this Palamoun
Was in a bush, that no man mighte him see,
For sore afered of his deeth was he.

No-thing ne knew he that it was Arcite:
God wot he wolde have trowed it ful lyte.   1520
But sooth is seyd, gon sithen many yeres,
That 'feeld hath eyen, and the wode hath eres.'
It is ful fair a man to bere him evene,
For al-day meteth men at unset stevene.
Ful litel woot Arcite of his felawe,   1525
That was so ny to herknen al his sawe,
For in the bush he sitteth now ful stille.

Now I shall return to Arcite who little realized how near was the person for him to fear till Fortune had caught him in her snare.

The busy lark, the messenger of the day, saluted the grey morning in her song, and fiery Phoebus arose so brilliantly that all the East laughed with the sunshine, whose sunbeams dried the silver drops hanging on the leaves in the grove. And now Arcite, member of the royal court and personal squire to Theseus, arose and looked on this delightful day. He remembered the object of his desire and, deciding to pay homage to May, rode on a charger of fiery spirit into the fields, a mile or two from the Court, to amuse himself.

By mere chance he made his way to the grove, about which I have told you, to make himself a garland of twigs, woodbine or hawthorn leaves. He sang aloud to the shining sun, 'Welcome, May, beautiful fresh May with all your flowers and foliage! I do hope I can get myself a green garland.' In a light-hearted manner he leapt very quickly from his horse into the grove and began strolling up and down a path near where Palamon happened to be hiding in a bush lest any one should see him, as he was sore afraid of death.

He did not realize in the slightest that it was Arcite. God knows he would have hardly believed it! Still, it was said truly many years ago that 'the field has eyes and the wood ears.' It was only right for him to behave cautiously for every day people meet when they least expect it. Arcite was completely unaware of his comrade who was so near that he could hear all his conversation, as he was sitting very quietly in the bush.

Whan that Arcite had romed al his fille,
And songen al the roundel lustily,
In-to a studie he fil sodeynly,   1530
As doon thise loveres in hir queynte geres,
Now in the croppe, now doun in the breres,
Now up, now doun, as boket in a welle.
Right as the Friday, soothly for to telle.
Now it shyneth, now it reyneth faste,   1535
Right so can gery Venus overcaste
The hertes of hir folk; right as hir day
Is gerful, right so chaungeth she array.
Selde is the Friday al the wyke y-lyke.

Whan that Arcite had songe, he gan to syke,   1540
And sette him doun with-outen any more:
'Alas!' quod he, 'that day that I was bore!
How longe, Juno, thurgh thy crueltee,
Woltow werreyen Thebes the citee?
Allas! y-broght is to confusioun   1545
The blood royal of Cadme and Amphioun;
Of Cadmus, which that was the firste man
That Thebes bulte, or first the toun bigan,
And of the citee first was crouned king,
Of his linage am I, and his of-spring   1550
By verray ligne, as of the stok royal:
And now I am so caitif and so thral,
That he, that is my mortal enemy,
I serve him as his squyer povrely.

And yet doth Juno me wel more shame,   1555
For I dar noght biknowe myn owne name;
But ther-as I was wont to highte Arcite,
Now highte I Philostrate, noght worth a myte.
Allas! thou felle Mars, allas! Juno,
Thus hath your ire our kindrede al fordo,   1560
Save only me, and wrecched Palamoun,
That Theseus martyreth in prisoun.
And over al this, to sleen me utterly,
Love hath his fyry dart so brenningly
Y-stiked thurgh my trewe careful herte,   1565
That shapen was my deeth erst than my sherte.
Ye sleen me with your eyen, Emelye;
Ye been the cause wherfor that I dye.

When he had strolled about to his satisfaction and had sung a roundelay lustily, Arcite, just as lovers in their strange moods do, suddenly fell into a reverie. One moment these lovers are on top of the world, the next they are down in the depths, now up, then down, like a bucket in the well. Just as on a Friday, to tell the truth, the sun is shining at one moment while the next it is raining hard, so does fickle Venus overcast the hearts of her servants; just as her day is changeable, so she changes her dress. Seldom is a Friday like the rest of the week.

When Arcite had finished his song, he sighed and then sat down. 'Alas, the day I was born!' he said. 'How long, Juno, will you wage cruel war against the city of Thebes? Alas, the blood royal of Cadmus and Amphion has been brought to confusion. By lineage I am directly descended in royal line from Cadmus who was the first man to build Thebes or who laid the foundations of the city and was the first crowned King of the city. I am now so wretched and enslaved that I serve as a squire in lowly fashion to the man who is my deadly enemy.

Juno, too, is giving me even greater shame, for I dare not confess my own name and, whereas I used to be called Arcite, I am now called Philostrate and am not worth a farthing. Alas, you cruel Mars! Alas, Juno! Save for me and wretched Palamon whom Theseus holds as a martyr in his prison, your anger in this affair has quite destroyed our lineage. Love, intending to compass my complete destruction as well, has pierced his fiery dart so fiercely through my faithful, troubled heart that death was ordained for me before my shirt was spun. Emily, your mere looks are killing me. You are the cause of my dying.

Of al the remenant of myn other care
Ne sette I nat the mountaunce of a tare,   1570
So that I coude don aught to your plesaunce!'
And with that word he fil doun in a traunce
A long tyme; and after he up-sterte.
   This Palamoun, that thoughte that thurgh his herte
He felte a cold swerd sodeynliche glyde,   1575
For ire he quook, no lenger wolde he byde.
And whan that he had herd Arcites tale,
As he were wood, with face deed and pale,
He sterte him up out of the buskes thikke,
And seyde: 'Arcite, false traitour wikke,   1580
Now artow hent, that lovest my lady so,
For whom that I have al this peyne and wo,
And art my blood, and to my counseil sworn,
As I ful ofte have told thee heer-biforn,
And hast by-japed here duke Theseus,   1585
And falsly chaunged hast thy name thus;
I wol be deed, or elles thou shalt dye.

Thou shalt nat love my lady Emelye,
But I wol love hir only, and namo;
For I am Palamoun, thy mortal fo.   1590
And though that I no wepne have in this place,
But out of prison am astert by grace,
I drede noght that outher thou shalt dye,
Or thou ne shalt nat loven Emelye.
Chees which thou wilt, for thou shalt nat asterte.'   1595

   This Arcite, with ful despitous herte,
Whan he him knew, and hadde his tale herd,
As fiers as leoun, pulled out a swerd,
And seyde thus: 'by God that sit above,
Nere it that thou art sik, and wood for love,   1600
And eek that thou no wepne hast in this place,
Thou sholdest never out of this grove pace,
That thou ne sholdest dyen of myn hond.
For I defye the seurtee and the bond
Which that thou seyst that I have maad to thee.   1605
What, verray fool, think wel that love is free,
And I wol love hir, maugre al thy might!

I do not care the value of one tare for the rest of my troubles as long as I can do any thing to please you.' No sooner had he uttered these words than he fell down in a trance lasting some time. Later, he arose once more.

Palamon, who thought that he felt a cold sword suddenly glide through his heart, shook with anger and could wait no longer. When he heard Arcite's remarks, he leapt out of the dense bushes with a deathly-pale face, as if he was mad. 'Arcite, you false, wicked traitor,' he cried. 'Now, you who loves so passionately my lady Emily, for whom I suffer all this pain and misery, are caught, you who are of my own blood and are my sworn counsellor, as I have often told you before. By falsely changing your name you have deceived this Duke Theseus. Either you or I will have to die.

You shall not love my lady Emily for I alone, and no one else, shall love her. I am Palamon, your deadly enemy. As I have only just escaped from prison with some assistance, I have no weapons with me but I don't doubt but either you will die or you will give up your love for Emily. Choose whichever course you prefer, for you shall not escape.'

When Arcite had heard what he had to say, he recognized him and scornfully clutched his sword like a fierce lion. 'By the God who rules above us.' he declared, 'were it not for the fact that you were sick and insane with love and have no weapon with you, you would never leave this grove for you should die by my hand. I care nothing for the sanctity of the promise you say I made with you. You fool, don't you realize that Love is free and I shall continue to love her however powerful you are!

But, for as muche thou art a worthy knight,
And wilnest to darreyne hir by batayle,
Have heer my trouthe, to-morwe I wol nat fayle, 1610
With-outen witing of any other wight,
That here I wol be founden as a knight,
And bringen harneys right y-nough for thee;
And chees the beste, and leve the worste for me.
And mete and drinke this night wol I bringe 1615
Y-nough for thee, and clothes for thy beddinge.
And, if so be that thou my lady winne,
And slee me in this wode ther I am inne,
Thou mayst wel have thy lady, as for me.'
This Palamon answerde: 'I graunte it thee.' 1620
And thus they been departed til a-morwe,
When ech of hem had leyd his feith to borwe.

 O Cupide, out of alle charitee!
O regne, that wolt no felawe have with thee!
Ful sooth is seyd, that love ne lordshipe 1625
Wol noght, his thankes, have no felaweshipe;
Wel finden that Arcite and Palamoun.
Arcite is riden anon un-to the toun,
And on the morwe, er it were dayes light,
Ful prively two harneys hath he dight, 1630
Bothe suffisaunt and mete to darreyne
The bataille in the feeld bitwix hem tweyne.
And on his hors, allone as he was born,
He carieth al this harneys him biforn;
And in the grove, at tyme and place y-set, 1635
This Arcite and this Palamon ben met.

Tho chaungen gan the colour in hir face;
Right as the hunter in the regne of Trace,
That stondeth at the gappe with a spere,
Whan hunted is the leoun or the bere, 1640
And hereth him come russhing in the greves,
And breketh bothe bowes and the leves,
And thinketh, 'heer cometh my mortel enemy,
With-oute faile, he moot be deed, or I;
For outher I mot sleen him at the gappe, 1645
Or he mot sleen me, if that me mishappe:'
So ferden they, in chaunging of hir hewe,
As fer as everich of hem other knewe.

Since, however, you are a noble knight and wish to fight in combat for her, I give you my word of honour I shall not fail you tomorrow; and no one will know that I come here prepared like a knight. I shall bring sufficient armour for you, and you can choose the best for yourself and leave the worst for me. Not only that, but this very night I shall bring you a sufficiency of food and drink, and clothes for your bedding. If it turns out that you win my lady and slay me here in this wood, as far as I am concerned you can keep her.' 'I agree to that,' said Palamon; and so, as each of them had pledged his faith, they separated till the morning.

O Cupid, you have lost all goodwill! O Kingdom that will have no equal with you! Truly is it said that you will suffer no government or rival gladly. Arcite and Palamon found that so.

Arcite rode at once to the town and the next day before it was daylight, he prepared very secretly two sets of armour, both sufficient and fit for a fight by combat between the two of them.

And he rode forth alone on his horse with all the equipment before him. Then Arcite and Palamon met at the time and place appointed.

The colour of their faces changed just like those of the hunters in the Kingdom of Thrace do who stand at the gap with a spear when they hear a lion or a bear that is being hunted come rushing in the grove and breaking both the boughs and the leaves. The hunter thinks, 'Here comes my deadly enemy. There is nothing for it but either he or I must die. I must either kill him in the gap or, if things turn out badly for me, he must kill me.' So the change in the colour of the two combatants betrayed what each knew about the other.

Ther nas no good day, ne no saluing;
But streight, with-outen word or rehersing,   1650
Everich of hem halp for to armen other,
As freendly as he were his owne brother;
And after that, with sharpe speres stronge
They foynen ech at other wonder longe.
Thou mightest wene that this Palamoun   1655
In his fighting were a wood leoun,
And as a cruel tygre was Arcite:
As wilde bores gonne they to smyte,
That frothem whyte as foom for ire wood.
Up to the ancle foghte they in hir blood.   1660
And in this wyse I lete hem fighting dwelle;
And forth I wol of Theseus telle.

  The destinee, ministre general,
That executeth in the world over-al
The purveyaunce, that God hath seyn biforn.   1665
So strong it is, that, though the world had sworn
The contrarie of a thing, be ye or nay,
Yet sometyme it shal fallen on a day
That falleth nat eft with-inne a thousand yere.
For certeinly, our appetytes here,   1670
Be it of werre, or pees, or hate, or love,
Al is this reuled by the sighte above.
This mene I now by mighty Theseus,
That for to honten is so desirous,
And namely at the grete hert in May,   1675
That in his bed ther daweth him no day,
That he nis clad, and redy for to ryde
With hunte and horn, and houndes him bisyde.

For in his hunting hath he swich delyt,
That it is al his joye and appetyt   1680
To been him-self the grete hertes bane:
For after Mars he serveth now Diane.
  Cleer was the day, as I have told er this,
And Theseus, with alle joye and blis,
With his Ipolita, the fayre quene,   1685
And Emelye, clothed al in grene,
On hunting be they riden royally.
And to the grove, that stood ful faste by,
In which ther was an hert, as men him tolde,
Duk Theseus the streighte wey hath holde.   1690

There was no 'Good day' or any greeting, but immediately without any conversation or parley, each of them helped to arm the other in as friendly a fashion as if he was his own brother. Then they thrust at each other for an amazingly long time with strong, sharp spears. You would have thought Palamon was a mad lion fighting and Arcite a cruel tiger. Fighting up to the ankles in blood, they struck at each other like wild boars which froth with white foam from raving anger. So I shall leave them fighting in this way and I shall tell you about Theseus.

Destiny, master of Fate, who brings everything in the world to pass, the Providence that God has foreseen, is so powerful that, though this world has sworn the contrary of something by a mere 'Yes' or 'No,' yet one day there occurs a thing which will not happen again in a thousand years. Certainly, our desires here on earth, whether in peace or war, hate or love, are completely ruled by the powers above. An illustration of this can be seen with mighty Theseus who is so fond of hunting, and especially of hunting the great stag in May, that no day dawns to find him in his bed, for at that time he is dressed and ready to ride with the huntsmen and the horn, and the hounds beside him.

Indeed, he takes such a delight in his hunting that it is his whole joy and desire to be the mortal enemy of the great stag; for, instead of Mars, he now serves Diana.

As I have told you earlier, the day was extremely fine and Theseus with his fair Queen Hippolyta, and Emily, dressed entirely in green, rode very joyfully and happily to the hunt in true royal fashion. Duke Theseus made his way direct to a grove nearby because he had been informed a stag could be found there.

And to the launde he rydeth him ful right,
For thider was the hert wont have his flight,
And over a brook, and so forth on his weye.
This duk wol han a cours at him, or tweye,
With houndes, swiche as that him list comaunde. 1695
  And whan this duk was come un-to the launde,
Under the sonne he loketh, and anon
He was war of Arcite and Palamon,
That foughten breme, as it were bores two;
The brighte swerdes wenten to and fro 1700
So hidously, that with the leeste strook
It seemed as it wolde felle an ook;
But what they were, no-thing he ne woot.
This duk his courser with his spores smoot,
And at a stert he was bitwix hem two, 1705
And pulled out a swerd and cryed, 'ho!
Namore, up peyne of lesing of your heed.

By mighty Mars, he shal anon be deed,
That smyteth any strook, that I may seen!
But telleth me what mister men ye been, 1710
That been so hardy for to fighten here
With-outen juge or other officere,
As it were in a listes royally?'
  This Palamon answerde hastily
And seyde: 'sire, what nedeth wordes mo? 1715
We have the deeth deserved bothe two.
Two woful wrecches been we, two caytyves,
That been encombred of our owne lyves;
And as thou art a rightful lord an juge,
Ne yeve us neither mercy ne refuge, 1720
But slee me first, for seynte charitee;
But slee my felawe eek as wel as me.

Or slee him first; for, though thou knowe it lyte,
This is thy mortal fo, this is Arcite,
That fro thy lond is banished on his heed, 1725
For which he hath deserved to be deed.
For this is he that cam un-to thy gate,
And seyde, that he highte Philostrate.
Thus hath he japed thee ful many a yeer,
And thou has maked him thy chief squyer; 1730
And this is he that loveth Emelye.

As he wanted to have one or two runs at him with his hounds in the way he considered best, he rode straightway over a brook to the clearing where the stag would usually run right across his path.

When he reached the clearing, the Duke looked around as well as he could in the sun and at once noticed Arcite and Palamon fighting furiously like two wild boars. Their shining swords flashed to and fro so fearfully that the least stroke seemed as if it would fell an oak, but he did not have the slightest idea who they were. The Duke struck his spurs into his horse and, with a bound, was between the two of them. He pulled out his sword and cried, 'Ho! No more of this, or you will lose your heads!

By mighty Mars, the one who strikes another blow in my presence will be killed on the spot. Tell me what kind of men you are who are so bold as to fight here without an umpire or any other officer, as if it should be a royal list?'

Palamon quickly answered him. 'Sire, what further explanation do you need? Both of us deserve to die. We are two wretched creatures, two despicable fellows, who are weary of life. You are an impartial judge and lord, so give us neither mercy nor refuge; but, for Holy Love kill me first and kill my companion as well.

Otherwise, kill him first for, though you are little aware of it, this is Arcite, your deadly enemy, who was banished from your territory on pain of death. He deserves to die on that score alone. He is the person who came to your gate and said he was called Philostrate. He has deceived you in this way for many years and you even made him your chief squire. He is the man who loves Emily.

For sith the day is come that I shal dye,
I make pleynly my confessioun,
That I am thilke woful Palamoun,
That hath thy prison broken wikkedly.   1735
I am thy mortal fo, and it am I
That loveth so hote Emelye the brighte,
That I wol dye present in hir sighte.
Therfore I axe deeth and my juwyse;
But slee my felawe in the same wyse,   1740
For bothe han we deserved to be slayn.'
  This worthy duk answerde anon agayn,
And seyde, 'This is a short conclusioun:
Youre owne mouth, by your confessioun,
Hath dampned you, and I wol it recorde,   1745
It nedeth noght to pyne yow with the corde.
Ye shul be deed, by mighty Mars the rede!'

  The quene anon, for verray wommanhede,
Gan for to wepe, and so did Emelye,
And alle the ladies in the companye.   1750
Gret pitee was it, as it thoughte hem alle,
That ever swich a chaunce sholde falle;
For gentil men they were, of greet estat,
And no-thing but for love was this debat;
And sawe hir blody woundes wyde and sore;   1755
And alle cryden, bothe lasse and more,
'Have mercy, lord, up-on us wommen alle!'
And on hir bare knees adoun they falle,
And wolde have kist his feet ther-as he stood,
Til at the laste aslaked was his mood;   1760
For pitee renneth sone in gentil herte.

And though he first for ire quook and sterte,
He hath considered shortly, in a clause,
The trespas of hem bothe, and eek the cause:
And al-though that his ire hir gilt accused,   1765
Yet in his reson he hem bothe excused;
As thus: he thoghte wel, that every man
Wol helpe him-self in love, if that he can,
And eek delivere him-self out of prisoun;
And eek his herte had compassioun   1770
Of wommen, for they wepen ever in oon;

I also confess to you quite openly that, as the day for me to die has come, I am that miserable Palamon, your relentless enemy, who has wickedly broken from your prison and who loves the lovely Emily so ardently that I prefer to die before her eyes. I beg for death and my doom; but, as we both deserve to be killed, kill my companion in the same way as me.'

The noble Duke did not hesitate to reply. 'This is a quick end to things. What you have said, freely confessed, has condemned you and I believe your story. I need not torture you with the rope, for, by mighty Mars, you shall surely die.'

The Queen at once wept womanly tears, and so did Emily and all the ladies in the company. They all thought it was a great pity that such an eventuality should ever come about, for, apart from the fact that they were noble men of high rank, they had merely quarrelled about love. While they saw their blood-stained wounds, huge and grievous, all the people present, both great and small, cried, 'Lord have mercy on all us women!' Immediately they fell down on their bare knees and kissed his feet where he was standing; till, at last his anger abated (for pity soon flows from a noble heart).

Although at first he had trembled and quivered with rage, he quickly gave thought to the wrongs they had commited and the reason for them. His anger told him they had done wrong but reason prevailed upom him, as he realized that every man, if he could, would further his own love affairs even to the extent of escaping from prison. His heart too took pity on the women, who were constantly weeping.

And in his gentil herte he thoghte anoon,
And softe un-to himself he seyde: 'fy
Up-on a lord that wol have no mercy,
But been a leoun, bothe in word and dede,   1775
To hem that been in repentaunce and drede
As wel as to a proud despitous man
That wol maynteyne that he first bigan!
That lord hath litel of discrecioun,
That in swich cas can no divisioun,   1780
But weyeth pryde and humblesse after oon.'
And shortly, whan his ire is thus agoon,
He gan to loken up with eyen lighte,
And spak thise same wordes al on highte:—

'The god of love, a! *benedicite*,   1785
How mighty and how greet a lord is he!
Ayeins his might ther gayneth none obstacles,
He may be cleped a god for his miracles;
For he can maken at his own gyse
Of everich herte, as that him list devyse.   1790
Lo heer, this Arcite and this Palamoun,
That quitly weren out of my prisoun,
And mighte han lived in Thebes royally,
And witen I am hir mortal enemy,
And that hir deeth lyth in my might also;   1795
And yet hath love, maugree hir eyen two,
Y-broght hem hider bothe for to dye!
Now loketh, is nat that an heigh folye?
Who may been a fool, but-if he love?
Bihold, for Goddes sake that sit above,   1800
Se how they blede! be they noght wel arrayed?

Thus hath hir lord, the god of love, y-payed
Hir wages and hir fees for hir servyse!
And yet they wenen for to been ful wyse
That serven love, for aught that may bifalle!   1805
But this is yet the beste game of alle,
That she, for whom they han this jolitee,
Can hem ther-for as muche thank as me:
She woot namore of al this hote fare,
By God, than woot a cokkow or an hare!   1810
But al mot been assayed, hoot and cold;

He meditated in his heart and quietly said to himself, Fie upon a lord who is not prepared to show any mercy and will act like a lion both in word and deed not only to a proud, haughty individual who persists in pursuing the course he initiated but also to persons who are frightened and repentant. The lord who can make no distinction in such an affair and who values pride and humility in the same measure shows little discretion. Briefly, when his anger had so passed away, he looked up with a gleam in his eyes and exclaimed aloud:

'All praise to the God of Love! What a mighty powerful lord he is! No obstacles avail against his might! For these miracles alone he can be called a God, for, in his own way, he can make of every heart whatever he pleases to fashion. Standing here before me are Arcite and Palamon who were free of my prison and could have lived royally in Thebes. Although they knew that I was their deadly enemy and had the power of life or death over them in my hands, yet, despite what they could not help seeing, Love has brought them to this place to die. Now, don't you think this is the height of folly? Only a lover can be a fool. Yet, for the sake of God who rules above see how they bleed! They are well dressed too!

In this way their lord, the God of Love, has paid their wages and their fees for serving him; and they still think that those who serve Love are wise enough to meet any eventuality that may happen. But the biggest joke of it all is that she, for whom they have this sport, can be as indebted to them as I, for, by God, she knows no more about this wild conduct than a cuckoo or a hare. But all temperaments, both hot and cold, must be put to the test.

A man mot been a fool, or yong or old;
I woot it by my-self ful yore agoon:
For in my tyme a servant was I oon.
And therfore, sin I knowe of loves peyne,   1815
And woot how sore it can a man distreyne,
As he that hath ben caught ofte in his las,
I yow foryeve al hoolly this trespas,
At requeste of the quene that kneleth here,
And eek of Emelye, my suster dere.   1820
And ye shul bothe anon un-to me swere,
That never-mo ye shul my contree dere,
Ne make werre up-on me night ne day,
But been my freendes in al that ye may;
I yow foryeve this trespas every del.'   1825
And they him swore his axing fayre and wel,
And him of lordshipe and of mercy preyde,
And he hem graunteth grace, and thus he seyde:

'To speke of royal linage and richesse,
Though that she were a quene or a princesse,   1830
Ech of yow bothe is worthy, doutelees,
To wedden whan tyme is, but nathelees
I speke as for my suster Emelye,
For whom ye have this stryf and jelousye;
Ye woot your-self, she may not wedden two   1835
At ones, though ye fighten ever-mo:
That oon of yow, al be him looth or leef,
He moot go pypen in an ivy-leef,
This is to seyn, she may not now han bothe,
Al be ye never so jelous, ne so wrothe.   1840
And for-thy I yow putte in this degree,
That ech of yow shal have his destinee
As him is shape; and herkneth in what wyse;
Lo, heer your ende of that I shal devyse.

My wil is this, for plat conclusioun,   1845
With-outen any replicacioun,
If that yow lyketh, tak it for the beste,
That everich of yow shal gon wher him leste
Frely, with-outen raunson or daunger;
And this day fifty wykes, fer ne ner,   1850
Everich of yow shal bringe an hundred knightes,
Armed for listes up at alle rightes,
Al redy to darreyne hir by bataille.

A man either young or old, must be a fool sometimes – I knew that myself a long time ago, for in my time I too have been a lover. Well, then, as I am familiar with Love's pain and have had experience how sorely it can afflict a person – I should say it is like one who has been caught in his own snares – I completely forgive you this wrong, as the Queen kneeling here and my dear sister, Emily, beseech it. You must, however, swear to me on this spot that you will be my friends in every way you can and that you will never again harm my country not make war upon me, by night or day. If you do, I shall forgive every part of your wickedness.' They promised him faithfully and sincerely that they would do what he asked and begged for his lordship's mercy. Then he granted them his grace and said:

'As regards your royal birth and wealth, both of you, I agree, are persons worthy to wed her, when the time is opportune, even if she were a queen or a princess; but nevertheless – I am, of course, speaking on behalf of my sister, Emily, for whom you have this jealous strife – you yourselves are aware that, even if you fight for ever, she cannot marry two men at the same time. One of you, whether he likes it or not, must go and whistle on an ivy leaf. In other words, however jealous or angry you may be, she cannot have the both of you at the same time. I can do this much for you. Each one of you will have his fate as ordained. Now, listen what fashion it will take, for here is the upshot of the plan I have devised for you.

After due consideration, my decision – and it admits of no discussion, so if you like it, you might as well take it for the best – is that each of you may go wherever he wishes, freely, without ransom or personal danger. Fifty weeks from this day, neither more nor less, each of you shall bring a hundred knights, armed in every way for tournaments, all ready to strive for her by battle.

And this bihote I yow, with-outen faille,
Up-on my trouthe, and as I am a knight,   1855
That whether of yow bothe that hath might,
This is to seyn, that whether he or thou
May with his hundred, as I spak of now,
Sleen his contrarie, or out of listes dryve,
Him shal I yeve Emelya to wyve,   1860
To whom that fortune yeveth so fair a grace.
The listes shal I maken in this place,
And God so wisly on my soule rewe,
As I shal even juge been and trewe.
Ye shul non other ende with me maken,   1865
That oon of yow ne shal be deed or taken.
And if yow thinketh this is wel y-sayd,
Seyeth your avys, and holdeth yow apayd.
This is your ende and your conclusioun.'

  Who loketh lightly now but Palamoun?   1870
Who springeth up for joye but Arcite?
Who couthe telle, or who couthe it endyte,
The joye that is maked in the place
Whan Theseus hath doon so fair a grace?
But doun on knees wente every maner wight,   1875
And thanked him with al her herte and might,
And namely the Thebans oft sythe.
And thus with good hope and with herte blythe
They take hir leve, and hom-ward gonne they ryde
To Thebes, with his olde walles wyde.   1880

Part 3

I trowe men wolde deme it necligence,
If I foryete to tellen the dispence
Of Theseus, that goth so bisily
To maken up the listes royally:
That swich a noble theatre as it was,   1885
I dar wel seyn that in this world ther nas.
The circuit a myle was aboute,
Walled of stoon, and diched al with-oute.
Round was the shap, in maner of compas,
Ful of degrees, the heighte of sixty pas,   1890
That, whan a man was set on o degree,
He letted nat his felawe for to see.

I promise you this faithfully, upon my word of honour as a knight, whichever of you has the power, that is to say if he or you can with his hundred knights slay his adversary, as I said just now, or drive him out of the lists, I shall give Emily as wife to whomsoever fortune shows so fair a grace. I shall arrange for the tournaments to be held here in this place and, as surely as God will have compassion on my soul, I shall be an impartial and true judge. You shall make no other agreement with me until one of you will be dead or taken captive. If you consider this arrangement satisfactory, let me know what you think about it and regard yourselves at peace. This is my final decision for you.'

Who but Palamon can be happy now? Who but Arcite can spring up for sheer joy? Who can tell or write about the happiness created in the place when Theseus has granted them so fair a favour? All kinds of people, and especially the Thebans, went down on their knees and thanked him profusely from their very heart and soul. And so, with good hope and light hearts, they took their leave and rode homewards to Thebes with its large, old walls.

Part 3

I suppose people will consider it negligence on my part if I forget to tell you about the expense incurred by Theseus who went about so busily to arrange for the tournaments in a royal style. It was such a splendid amphitheatre that I dare maintain that there was not one like it in this world. Its circumference was about a mile, walled with stone and ditched completely outside: and its shape was rounded in the style of a circle with many steps to the height of sixty paces, so that when one person was seated on any step he did not hinder the view of another spectator.

   Est-ward ther stood a gate of marbel whyt,
West-ward, right swich another in the opposit.
And shortly to concluden, swich a place 1895
Was noon in erthe, as in so litel space;
For in the lond ther nas no crafty man,
That geometrie or ars-metrik can,
Ne purtreyour, ne kerver of images,
That Theseus ne yaf him mete and wages 1900
The theatre for to maken and devyse.
And for to doon his ryte and sacrifyse,
He est-ward hath, up-on the gate above,
In worship of Venus, goddesse of love,
Don make an auter and an oratorie; 1905
And west-ward, in the minde and in memorie
Of Mars, he maked hath right swich another,
Tha coste largely of gold a fother.

And north-ward, in a touret on the wal,
Of alabastre whyt and reed coral 1910
An oratorie riche for to see,
In worship of Dyane of chastitee,
Hath Theseus don wroght in noble wyse.
  But yet hadde I foryeten to devyse
The noble kerving, and the portreitures, 1915
The shap, the countenaunce, and the figures,
That weren in thise oratories three.
  First in the temple of Venus maystow see
Wroght on the wal, ful pitous to biholde,
The broken slepes, and the sykes colde; 1920
The sacred teres, and the waymenting;
The fyry strokes of the desiring,
That loves servaunts in this lyf enduren;
The othes, that hir covenants assuren;

Plesaunce and hope, desyr, fool-hardinesse, 1925
Beautee and youthe, bauderie, richesse,
Charmes and force, lesinges, flaterye,
Dispense, bisynesse, and jelousye,
That wered of yelwe goldes a gerland,
And a cokkow sitting on hir hand; 1930

In the East was a gate of white marble and directly in the West, in the opposite wall, was another one like it. To sum up, considering the short time taken to construct it, there was no such other place on earth; for there was in the country no craftsman, who knew geometry or arithmetic, painter or sculptor to whom Theseus did not give food and wages when they were engaged in building or designing the theatre. Above the gate in the East for the worship of Venus, the Goddess of Love, he had an altar and an oratory made for performing the rites and sacrifices; and in the West in memory of Mars he made another in the same style and that one cost many a cartload of gold.

In the North, in a turret on the wall, Theseus had an oratory of white alabaster and red coral constructed, wrought in excellent style. This was in honour of Diana's chastity and was magnificent to look upon.

But I had forgotten to describe the noble carvings and the paintings, the shapes, the faces and the figures that were in these three oratories.

First, in the temple of Venus you could have seen painted on the wall a pitiful scene, the broken sleeps and the cold sicknesses, the devoted tears, the lamentations, the fiery strokes and yearning that the servants of Love endure in this life, the oaths to keep pacts.

Pleasure and Hope, Desire, Foolhardiness, Beauty and Youth, Jollity, Riches, Charms and Power, Lies, Flattery, Expenditure, Business and Jealousy that wore a garland of marigolds and had a cuckoo sitting on her hand;

Festes, instruments, caroles, daunces,
Lust and array, and alle the circumstaunces
Of love, whiche that I rekne and rekne shal,
By ordre weren peynted on the wal,
And mo than I can make of mencioun.   1935
For soothly, al the mount of Citheroun,
Ther Venus hath hir principal dwelling,
Was shewed on the wal in portreying,
With al the gardin, and the lustinesse.
Nat was foryeten the porter Ydelnesse,   1940
Ne Narcisus the faire of yore agon,
Ne yet the folye of king Salamon,
Ne yet the grete strengthe of Hercules –
Th'enchauntements of Medea and Circes –
Ne of Turnus, with the hardy fiers corage,   1945
The riche Cresus, caytif in servage.

Thus may ye seen that wisdom ne richesse,
Beautee ne sleighte, strengthe, ne hardinesse,
Ne may with Venus holde champartye;
For as hir list the world than may she gye.   1950
Lo, alle thise folk so caught were in hir las.
Til they for wo ful ofte seyde 'allas!'
Suffyceth heer ensamples oon or two,
And though I coude rekne a thousand mo.

  The statue of Venus, glorious for to see,   1955
Was naked fleting in the large see,
And fro the navele doun all covered was
With wawes grene, and brighte as any glas,
A citole in hir right hand hadde she,
And on hir heed, ful semely for to see,   1960
A rose gerland, fresh and wel smellinge;
Above hir heed hir dowves flikeringe.
Biforn hir stood hir sone Cupido,
Up-on hir shuldres winges hadde he two;
And blind he was, as it is ofte sene;   1965
A bowe he bar and arwes brighte and kene.
  Why sholde I noght as wel eek telle yow al
The portreiture, that was up-on the wal
With-inne the temple of mighty Mars the rede?

Feasts, musical instruments, songs, dances, happiness and dress and all the conditions of Love, of which I took note, and many more than I can mention were depicted in order on the wall. Further, Mount Cithaeron, where Venus has her principal residence, was shown in painting on the wall with all the garden and its delights. Nor was the porter, Idleness, forgotten nor fair Narcissus of years gone by nor even the foolishness of King Solomon nor even the great strength of Hercules, the enchantments of Medea and Circe, nor the bold, fierce courage of Turnus nor the rich Croesus who was wretched in servitude.

In the same style you could have seen that Wisdom or Riches, Beauty or Craft, Strength or Courage could not share the field with Venus, for she guided the world at her pleasure. Indeed, all these were so enmeshed in her net that they continually sighed sadly. These one or two examples are enough for this description but I could, however, repeat a thousand more.

The statue of Venus, a glorious sight, was naked, floating in the wide sea, and from the navel downwards it was completely covered with green waves shining like glass. She held a harp in her right hand and, on her head, was a garland of roses, fresh and sweet-smelling, a magnificent sight. Her doves fluttered about above her head and in front of her stood her son, Cupid, with two wings on his shoulders and carrying a bow and shining, sharp arrows. He was blind, as illustrations often show.

Why should I not tell you as well about the paintings on the wall inside the Temple of mighty Mars the red?

Al peynted was the wal, in lengthe and brede,   1970
Lyk to the estres of the grisly place,
That highte the grete temple of Mars in Trace,
In thilke colde frosty regioun,
Ther-as Mars hath his sovereyn mansioun.
  First on the wal was peynted a foreste,   1975
In which ther dwelleth neither man ne beste,
With knotty knarry bareyn treës olde
Of stubbes sharpe and hidous to biholde;
In which ther ran a rumbel and a swough,
As though a storm sholde bresten every bough: 1980
And downward from an hille, under a bente,
Ther stood the temple of Mars armipotente,
Wroght al of burned steel, of which thentree
Was long and streit, and gastly for to see.

And ther-out came a rage and such a vese,   1985
That it made al the gates for to rese.
The northren light in at the dores shoon,
For windowe on the wal ne was ther noon,
Thurgh which men mighten any light discerne.
The dores were alle of adamant eterne,   1990
Y-clenched overthwart and endelong
With iren tough; and, for to make it strong,
Every piler, the temple to sustene,
Was tonne-greet, of iren bright and shene.

  Ther saugh I first the derke imagining   1995
Of felonye, and al the compassing;
The cruel ire, reed as any glede;
The pykepurs, and eek the pale drede;
The smyler with the knyf under the cloke;
The shepne brenning with the blake smoke;   2000
The treson of the mordring in the bedde;
The open werre, with woundes al bibledde;
Contek, with blody knyf and sharp manace;
Al ful of chirking was that sory place.
The sleere of him-self yet saugh I ther,   2005
His herte-blood hath bathed al his heer;
The nayl y-driven in the shode a-night;
The colde deeth, with mouth gaping upright.
Amiddes of the temple sat meschaunce,
With disconfort and sory countenaunce.   2010

The entire wall was painted throughout its length and breadth like the frightful place called the great Temple of Mars in Thrace in that cold, frosty region where Mars has his principal mansion.

First on the wall was painted a forest in which neither man nor beast dwelt, with its knotty, gnarled, barren old trees, with stumps that were sharp and extremely dreadful to see. Through it ran a rumbling and swooning noise as though a storm was going to break every bough, and downward on a hill under a grassy slope stood the Temple of Mars, mighty in arms, wrought wholly of burnished steel, the entrance of which was long, narrow and of dreadful aspect.

From it issued such a strong raging blast that it caused all the gate to shake. The northern light shone through the doors, for in the wall there was no window through which any light could be seen. The doors were made entirely of everlasting adamant, clamped across and lengthwise with tough iron to strengthen them while every pillar, to uphold the Temple, was as huge as a cask and was made of beautiful bright iron.

There I first saw the dark imagination of Wickedness and the way it was brought to pass, cruel anger like red-hot coal, the pickpocket and also pale fear, the hypocrite with his knife hidden under his cloak, the sheepfold burning with black smoke, treasonous murder in one's own bed, open warfare with all its wounds smeared in blood, strife with bloody knife and direct threat. That unhappy place was chockfull of screaming. I saw there too the suicide, the blood of his heart bathing all his hair, the nail driven into his temple at night and cold death with his mouth agape in the air. Amidst his temple sat Calamity showing discomfiture on his melancholy expression.

Yet saugh I woodnesse laughing in his rage;
Armed compleint, out-hees, and fiers outrage.
The careyne in the bush, with throte y-corve:
A thousand slayn, and nat of qualm y-storve;
The tiraunt, with the prey by force y-raft;   2015
The toun destroyed, ther was no-thing laft.
Yet saugh I brent the shippes hoppesteres;
The hunte strangled with the wilde beres:
The sowe freten the child right in the cradel;
The cook y-scalded, for al his longe ladel.   2020
Noght was foryeten by th'infortune of Marte;
The carter over-riden with his carte,
Under the wheel ful lowe he lay adoun.

Ther were also, of Martes divisioun,
The barbour, and the bocher, and the smith   2025
That forgeth sharpe swerdes on his stith.
And al above, depeynted in a tour,
Saw I conquest sittinge in greet honour,
With the sharpe swerde over his heed
Hanginge by a sotil twynes threed.   2030
Depeynted was the slaughtre of Julius,
Of grete Nero, and of Antonius;
Al be that thilke tyme they were unborn,
Yet was hir deeth depeynted ther-biforn,
By manasinge of Mars, right by figure;   2035
So was it shewed in that portreiture
As is depeynted in the sterres above,
Who shal be slayn or elles deed for love.
Suffyceth oon ensample in stories olde,
I may not rekne hem alle, thogh I wolde.   2040

  The statue of Mars up-on a carte stood,
Armed, and loked grim as he were wood;
And over his heed ther shynen two figures
Of sterres, that been cleped in scriptures,
That oon Puella, tha other Rubeus.   2045
This god of armes was arrayed thus:—
A wolf ther stood biforn him at his feet
With eyen rede, and of a man he eet;
With sotil pencel was depeynt this storie,
In redoutinge of Mars and of his glorie.   2050

I also saw Madness laughing in his rage, armed Complaint, Hue and Cry and fierce Outrage, the corpse with his throat cut in the bush, a thousand slain and not dead as the result of disease, the tyrant with the prey that he has forcibly torn away and the town destroyed without any survivors. There I saw fire among the dancing ships, the huntsmen strangled by wild boars, the sow devouring the child even in the cradle and the cook scalded in spite of his long ladle. Nor was the charioteer run over by his chariot forgotten in the misfortunes of Mars. He lay prostrate under its wheel.

There were also in the division caused by Mars the barber, the butcher and the smith who forges sharp swords on his anvil. In a tower depicted above all the rest I saw Conquest sitting in great honour with the sharp sword hanging by a finely-entwined thread over his head. The murders of Julius, of great Nero and of Antony were depicted, although these men were still unborn at that time; yet their deaths were so accurately portrayed beforehand by the influence of Mars, even in the astrological figure, that it was represented in their illustrations just as it set out in the stars above, even to the extent as to who would be slain or who would die for Love. These are enough examples of old stories but, even if I wished, I could not name them all.

The Statue of Mars, armed and grim-looking, as if he was mad, stood on a chariot and over his head gleamed two illustrations of stars that have been called in books Puella and Rubeus. The God of War was dressed in this fashion, and before him stood a wolf with red eyes and it was eating a man. This story was represented by a clever instrument in honour of Mars and his glory.

Now to the temple of Diane the chaste
As shortly as I can I wol me haste,
To telle yow al the descripcioun.
Depeynted been the walles up and doun
Of hunting and of shamfast chastitee.   2055
Ther saugh I how woful Calistopee,
Whan that Diane agreved was with here,
Was turned from a womman til a bere,
And after was she maad the lode-sterre;
Thus was it peynt, I can say yow no ferre;   2060
Hir sone is eek a sterre, as men may see.
Ther saugh I Dane, Y-turned til a tree,
I mene nat the goddesse Diane,
But Penneus doughter, which that highte Dane.

Ther saugh I Attheon an hert y-maked,   2065
For vengeaunce that he saugh Diane al naked;
I saugh how that his houndes have him caught,
And freten him, for that they knewe him naught.
Yet peynted was a litel forther-moor,
How Atthalante hunted the wilde boor,   2070
And Meleagre, and many another mo,
For which Diane wroughte him care and wo.
Ther saugh I many another wonder storie,
The whiche me list nat drawen to memorie.
This goddesse on an hert ful hye seet,   2075
With smale houndes al aboute hir feet;
And undernethe hir feet she hadde a mone,
Wexing it was, and sholde wanie sone.

In gaude grene hir statue clothed was,
With bowe in honde, and arwes in a cas.   2080
Hir eyen caste she ful lowe adoun,
Ther Pluto hath his derke regioun.
A womman travailinge was hir biforn,
But, for hir child so longe was unborn,
Ful pitously Lucyna gan she calle,   2085
And seyde, 'help, for thou mayst best of alle.'
Wel couthe he peynten lyfly that it wroghte,
With many a florin he the hewes boghte.
    Now been thise listes maad, and Theseus,
That at his grete cost arrayed thus   2090
The temples and the theatre every del,
Whan it was doon, him lyked wonder wel.

Now, I shall hurry as fast as I can to the Temple of Diana to give you a full description of it. Everywhere the walls were depicted with scenes of hunting and modest chastity. There I saw how wretched Callisto was changed from a woman into a bear when Diana was displeased with her and how she was later transformed into the North Star. I can only tell you that she was depicted in this way and that, as you can see for yourselves, her son is also a star. I also saw Daphne turned into a tree – Of course, I refer to the daughter of Peneus who was also called Daphne and not to the goddess, Diana.

There I also saw Actaeon turned into a stag out of vengeance for seeing Diana completely naked. I saw how his hounds caught and devoured him because they did not recognize him. Still another representation a little farther off was the story showing how Atalanta hunted the wild boar, and Meleager and many others for whom Diana had brought trouble and misery. I saw there many other wonderful stories which I do not wish to recall at present.

This goddess sat high on a stag with small hounds all about her feet and a moon which was waxing but would soon wane.

With a bow and a sheath of arrows in her hand, she was dressed entirely in green and cast her eyes down low towards the place where Pluto has his dark region.

Before her was a woman in childbirth, but because her child was so long unborn she kept calling very pitifully upon Lucina, 'Help me, for you best of all can do so!' He who had represented this scene could depict lifelikeness brilliantly, for he had bought the colours for many florins.

When these lists had been constructed and Theseus had finished equipping the temples and every part of the amphitheatre in this manner at great personal expense, he was immensely delighted with what had been done.

But stinte I wol of Thesius a lyte,
And speke of Palamon and of Arcite.
  The day approcheth of hir retourninge,   2095
That everich sholde an hundred knightes bringe,
The bataille to darreyne, as I yow tolde;
And til Athénes, hir covenant for to holde,
Hath everich of hem broght an hundred knightes
Wel armed for the werre at alle rightes.   2100
And sikerly, ther trowed many a man
That never, sithen that the world bigan,
As for to speke to knighthod of hir hond,
As fer as God hath maked see or lond,
Nas, of so fewe, so noble a companye.   2105

For every wight that lovede chivalrye,
And wolde, his thankes, han a passant name,
Hath preyed that he mighte ben of that game;
And wel was him, that ther-to chosen was.
For if ther fille to-morwe swich a cas,   2110
Ye knowen wel, that every lusty knight,
That loveth paramours, and hath his might,
Were it in Engelond, or elles-where,
They wolde, hir thankes, wilnen to be there.
To fighte, for a lady, *ben'cite!*   2115
It were a lusty sighte for to see.

  And right so ferden they with Palamon.
With him ther wenten knightes many oon;
Som wol ben armed in an habergeoun,
In a brest-plat and in a light gipoun;   2120
And somme woln have a peyre plates large;
And somme woln have a Pruce sheld, or a targe;
Somme woln ben armed on hir legges weel,
And have an ax, and somme a mace of steel.
Ther nis no newe gyse, that it nas old.   2125
Armed were they, as I have you told,
Everich after his opinioun.
  Ther maistow seen coming with Palamoun
Ligurge him-self, the grete king of Trace;
Blak was his berd, and manly was his face.   2130
The cercles of his eyen in his heed,
They gloweden bitwixe yelow and reed:
And lyk a griffon loked he aboute,
With kempe heres on his browes stoute;

But I must leave Theseus for a time and tell you about Palamon and Arcite.

The day approached for their return, when each had to bring a hundred knights to contest the fight, as I have told you; and, true to their promise, each one brought to Athens a hundred knights, splendidly equipped in every way for the battle. When it came to a matter of speaking of the martial dexterity of knighthood, indeed many people thought that never, since the creation of the world, as far as God had made sea or land, was there such a noble company consisting of so few men.

Every knight who loved chivalry and desired to gain surpassing fame had begged that he might take part in that sport. Indeed, he was a lucky person to be selected, for, if any thing similar should take place again tomorrow, you realize that every happy knight in England or elsewhere who loves passionately and has the knightly ability would desire strongly to participate in it. To fight on behalf of a lady – Praise be! It was a fine sight!

Many a knight marched forth with Palamon. Some preferred to be clad in a small coat of mail, a breastplate and a light tunic; some preferred to wear a pair of large steel plates and some had a Prussian shield or buckler; some preferred to be well-protected about their legs and have an axe, and some a mace of steel. I can assure you that there is nothing new which was not in existence long ago. Each, as I have told you, was equipped according to his personal taste.

There you could have seen Lycurgus, the mighty King of Thrace, with his black beard and manly face, accompanying Palamon. His eyelashes glowing between yellow and red, shaggy hairs on his huge eye-brows, he glared around him like a griffin.

His limes grete, his braunes harde and stronge,   2135
His shuldres brode, his armes rounde and longe.
And as the gyse was in his contree,
Ful hye up-on a char of gold stood he,
With foure whyte boles in the trays.
In-stede of cote-armure over his harnays,   2140
With nayles yelwe and brighte as any gold,
He hadde a beres skin, col-blak, for-old.
His longe heer was kembd bihinde his bak,
As any ravenes fether it shoon for-blak:
A wrethe of gold arm-greet, of huge wighte,   2145
Upon his heed, set ful of stones brighte,
Of fyne rubies and of dyamaunts.

Aboute his char ther wenten whyte alaunts,
Twenty an mo, as grete as any steer,
To hunten at the leoun or the deer,   2150
And folwed him, with mosel faste y-bounde,
Colers of gold, and torets fyled rounde.
An hundred lordes hadde he in his route
Armed ful wel, with hertes sterne and stoute.
  With Arcita, in stories as men finde,   2155
The grete Emetreus, the king of Inde,
Up-on a stede bay, trapped in steel,
Covered in cloth of gold diapred weel,
Cam ryding lyk the god of armes, Mars.

His cote-armure was of cloth of Tars,   2160
Couched with perles whyte and rounde and grete.
His sadel was of brend gold newe y-bete;
A mantelet upon his shuldre hanginge
Bret-ful of rubies rede, as fyr sparklinge.
His crispe heer lyk ringes was y-ronne,   2165
And that was yelow, and glitered as the sonne.
His nose was heigh, his eyen bright citryn,
His lippes rounde, his colour was sangwyn,
A fewe fraknes in his face y-spreynd,
Betwixen yelow and somdel blak y-meynd,   2170
And as a leoun he his loking caste.
Of fyve and twenty yeer his age I caste.
His berd was wel bigonne for to springe;
His voys was as a trompe thunderinge.

His limbs were large, his muscles hard and strong, his shoulders broad and his arms rounded and long. He sat aloft in a golden chariot drawn by four white bulls in the traces. Instead of coat-armour, he wore over his equipment a very old, coal-black bear skin with yellow claws shining like gold. His long hair, shining black like a raven's feathers, was combed behind his back, and on his head he wore a golden wreath, as thick as a man's arm, of great weight and set completely with bright stones, fine rubies and diamonds.

Around his chariot ran twenty or more white wolf-hounds, as powerful as any steer and suitable for hunting the lion or the deer. They wore golden collars and rings filed round and were tightly muzzled. He had with him in his company a hundred lords fully armed and with hearts stern and stout.

The old stories tell us that the great Demetrius, the King of India, accompanied Arcite. Just like Mars, the God of War, he came riding on a bay horse with steel trappings, covered with a beautifully ornamented cloth of gold.

His coat-armour was made of the cloth of Tatars, inlaid with large, round, white pearls; his saddle was only recently embossed with burnished gold; and his small cloak, brimful of red rubies sparkling like a flame, hung over his shoulder. His crisp hair, in clustered curls was yellow and glittered like the sun. He had a prominent nose, bright-yellow eyes and a fresh complexion but there were a few freckles, a mixture of yellow and black, spread over his face. He glared around like a lion. He was about twenty-five years of age, I suppose. His beard was already well on the way to growing thick and his voice resembled a thundering trumpet.

Up-on his heed he wered of laurer grene   2175
A gerland fresh and lusty for to sene.
Up-on his hand he bar, for his deduyt,
An egle tame, as eny lilie whyt.
An hundred lordes hadde he with him there,
Al armed, sauf hir heddes, in al hir gere,   2180
Ful richely in alle maner thinges.
For trusteth wel, that dukes, erles, kinges,
Were gadered in this noble companye,
For love and for encrees of chivalrye.
Aboute this king ther ran on every part   2185
Ful many a tame leoun and lepart.
And in this wyse thise lordes, alle and some,
Ben on the Sonday to the citee come
Aboute pryme, and in the toun alight.

   This Theseus, this duk, this worthy knight,   2190
Whan he had broght hem in-to his citee,
And inned hem, everich in his degree,
He festeth hem, and dooth so greet labour
To esen hem, and doon hem al honour,
That yet men weneth that no mannes wit   2195
Of noon estat ne coude amenden it.
The minstralcye, the service at the feste,
The grete yiftes to the moste and leste,
The rich array of Theseus paleys,
Ne who sat first ne last up-on the deys,   2200
What ladies fairest been or best daunsinge,
Or which of hem can dauncen best and singe,
Ne who most felingly speketh of love:
What haukes sitten on the perche above.
What houndes liggen on the floor adoun: 2205
Of al this make I now no mencioun;
But al th'effect, that thinketh me the beste;
Now comth the poynt, and herkneth if yow leste.
   The Sonday night, er day bigan to springe,
When Palamon the larke herde singe,   2210
Although it nere nat day by houres two,
Yet song the larke, and Palamon also.
With holy herte, and with an heigh corage
He roos, to wenden on his pilgrimage
Un-to the blisful Citherea benigne,   2215
I mene Venus, honurable and digne.

On his head he wore a garland of green laurel, fresh and pleasant to look at, while he carried a tame, lily-white eagle in his hand for personal pleasure. A hundred knights accompanied him to that place and all of them were richly armed, save for their heads, with the proper equipment and all sorts of armour. You can well believe that dukes, earls and kings were collected in this company for the sheer love and better renown of chivalry. Around this king ran many tame lions on all sides. So this was the style in which these lords, one and all, came to the city on a Sunday about the first hour of the day. Here they alighted.

When the noble Theseus had escorted them into his city and had accommodated them, each man according to his rank, he feasted them and did all he could to make them comfortable and pay them all the respect you could imagine. I assure you that he did this so well that the ingenuity of man of any rank, could not better it.

The minstrelsy; the service at the feast; the great gifts to the highest and lowest in rank; the rich deckings of Theseus's palace; neither he who had the seat of honour nor he who sat lowest upon the dais; who were the most beautiful ladies nor those who could sing and dance best; nor those who could speak most sincerely of love; what hawks sat above on the perch; what dogs were lying down on the floor – I think I can make no mention of these things but only tell you what I think best. As we are now coming to the chief point, please listen carefully.

During the Sunday night, even before the dawn of day, Palamon heard the lark singing and so, although day did not dawn for another two hours, Palamon joined the lark in his singing. With a devout heart and high courage, he left his bed to make his pilgrimage to the blessed, kindly Citherea, that is, of course, the honourable and worthy Venus.

And in hir houre he walketh forth a pas
Un-to the listes, ther hir temple was,
And doun he kneleth, and with humble chere
And herte soor, he seyde as ye shul here.   2220
  'Faireste of faire, o lady myn, Venus,
Doughter to Jove and spouse of Vulcanus,
Thou glader of the mount of Citheroun,
For thilke love thou haddest to Adoun,
Have pitee of my bittre teres smerte,   2225
And tak myn humble preyer at thyn herte.
Allas! I ne have no langage to telle
Th'effectes ne the torments of myn helle;
Myn herte may myne harmes nat biwreye;
I am so confus, that I can noght seye.   2230

But mercy, lady bright, that knowest weel
My thought, and seest what harmes that I feel,
Considere al this, and rewe up-on my sore,
As wisly as I shal for evermore,
Emforth my might, thy trewe servant be,   2235
And holden werre alwey with chastitee;
That make I myn avow, so ye me helpe.
I kepe noght of armes for to yelpe,
Ne I ne axe nat to-morwe to have victorie,
Ne renoun in this cas, ne veyne glorie   2240
Of pris of armes blowen up and doun,
But I wolde have fully possessioun
Of Emelye, and dye in thy servyse;
Find thou the maner how, and in what wyse.

I recche nat, but it may bettre be,   2245
To have victorie of hem, or they of me,
So that I have my lady in myne armes.
For though so be that Mars is god of armes,
Your vertu is so greet in hevene above,
That, if yow list, I shal wel have my love.   2250
Thy temple wol I worshipe evermo,
And on thyn auter, wher I ryde or go,
I wol don sacrifice, and fyres bete.
And if ye wol nat so, my lady swete,
Than preye I thee, to-morwe with a spere   2255
That Arcita me thurgh the herte bere.

And, at the time dedicated to her, he took a short walk to the lists where her Temple was situated. Here he knelt down and, with a humble expression and pained heart, he uttered these words:–

'O, my lady Venus, fairest of the fair, daughter of Jupiter and spouse of Vulcan, the one who gladdens Mount Cithaeron, for the sake of the love you bore Adonis, take pity on the grief of my bitter tears and let my humble prayer enter your heart. Alas! I neither have the language to describe the consequences or the torments of my hell nor can my heart disclose my wounds. Indeed, I am so bewildered I can hardly speak.

But, my beautiful lady, who knows well what I think and can see what I suffer, please have mercy on me. Meditate upon my desires and, if you will have compassion on my pain, I promise that for evermore I shall, as far as it lies in my power, be your true servant and wage perpetual war against Chastity. I make that vow to you, so please help me. I do not make war so that I can boast about it nor do I beg for victory tomorrow. It is not my desire to win far-reaching renown in this tournament or vain glory in reputation of arms to be noised abroad but I must gain complete possession of Emily and liberty to die in your service. Please find the manner and means of bringing this about.

It may not be absolutely essential but it would be better if I gained the victory over my adversaries or they over me, so long as I can have my lady in my arms. Though Mars is the god of War, your influence is so powerful in heaven above that, if you wish, I can easily win my love. If you grant me this, I shall worship your temple ever more and on your altar, whatever the circumstances, I shall perform sacrifices and kindle fires. If you cannot do so, my sweet lady, then I beseech you that Arcite will pierce me through with a spear tomorrow.

Thanne rekke I noght, whan I have lost my lyf,
Though that Artica winne hir to his wyf.
This is th'effect and ende of my preyere,
Yif me my love, thou blisful lady dere.'   2260
  Whan th'orisoun was doon of Palamon,
His sacrifice he dide, and that anon
Ful pitously, with alle circumstaunces,
Al telle I noght as now his observaunces.
But atte last the statue of Venus shook,   2265
And made a signe, wher-by that he took
That his preyere accepted was that day.
For thogh the signe shewed a delay,
Yet wiste he wel that graunted was his bone;
And with glad herte he wente him hoom ful sone.   2270

  The thridde houre inequal that Palamon
Bigan to Venus temple for to goon,
Up roos the sonne, and up roos Emelye,
And to the temple of Diane gan hye .
Hir maydens, that she thider with hir ladde,   2275
Ful redily with hem the fyr they hadde,
Th'encens, the clothes, and the remenant al
That to the sacrifyce longen shal;
The hornes fulle of meth, as was the gyse;
Ther lakked noght to doon hir sacrifyse.   2280
Smoking the temple, ful of clothes faire,
This Emelye, with herte debonaire,
Hir body wessh with water of a welle;

But how she dide hir ryte I dar nat telle,
But it be any thing in general;   2285
And yet it were a game to heren al;
To him that meneth wel, it were no charge:
But it is good a man ben at his large.
Hir brighte heer was kempt, untressed al;
A coroune of grene ook cerial   2290
Up-on hir heed was set ful fair and mete.
Two fyres on the auter gan she bete,
And dide hir thinges, as men may biholde
In Stace of Thebes, and thise bokes olde.
Whan kindled was the fyr, with pitous chere   2295
Un-to Diane she spak, as ye may here.

I do not care if Arcite should gain her for his wife after I have been killed. I have no more to ask but, my blessed, dear lady, please give me my love.'

When his prayer was concluded, Palamon performed his sacrifice immediately, very dutifully in all respects, although I shall not tell you about his observances at present; but, after he had finished, the Statue of Venus shook and gave a sign whereby Palamon understood that his prayer that day was accepted. Though there was some delay before the sign was given, he was well aware that his request was granted so he quickly went home with a light heart.

At the third hour, the unequal hour, when Palamon had prepared to go to the Temple of Venus, Emily arose at sun-rise and hastened to the Temple of Diana. She lacked nothing for the performing of her rites, as the maidens accompanying her had the fire all ready with them and took as well the incense, the robes, the customary horns of mead and all the other paraphernalia appertaining to the sacrifice. While the incense was burning in the Temple draped with beautiful hangings, Emily lightheartedly washed her body with water from a well.

But I dare not describe how she performed that, lest I should put it in too common terminology but I assure you it would be a pleasure for you to hear about it. It would not give offence to any person of good intent but it is best to describe such things in general terms. Everything was unloosened, her glistening hair combed properly and a crown of evergreen holm-oak was set beautifully and neatly upon her head. She then kindled two fires on the altar and made her offerings in the manner described in Statius of Thebes and the ancient books. When the fire was kindled, with a pitiful expression she spoke to Diana, as I shall tell you.

'O chaste goddesse of the wodes grene,
To whom both heven and erthe and see is sene,
Quene of the regne of Pluto derk and lowe,
Goddesse of maydens, that myn herte has knowe   2300
Ful many a yeer, and woost what I desire,
As keep me fro thy vengeaunce and thyn ire,
That Attheon aboughte cruelly.
Chaste goddesse, wel wostow that I
Desire to been a mayden al my lyf,   2305
Ne never wol I be no love ne wyf.
I am, thou woost, yet of thy companye,
A mayde, and love hunting and venerye,
And for to walken in the wodes wilde,
And noght to been a wyf, and be with childe.   2310
Noght wol I knowe companye of man.

Now help me, lady, sith ye may and can,
For tho thre formes that thou hast in thee.
And Palamon, that swich love to me,
And eek Arcite, that loveth me so sore,   2315
This grace I preye thee with-oute more,
As sende love and pees bitwixe hem two;
And fro me turne awey hir hertes so,
That al hir hote love, and hir desyr,
And al hir bisy torment, and hir fyr   2320
Be queynt, or turned in another place;
And if so be thou wolt not do me grace,
Or if my destinee be shapen so,
That I shal nedes have oon of hem two,
As sende me him that most desireth me.   2325

Bihold, goddesse of clene chastitee,
The bittre teres that on my chekes falle.
Sin thou are mayde, and keper of us alle,
My maydenhede thou kepe and wel conserve,
And whyl I live a mayde, I wol thee serve.'   2330
    The fyres brenne up-on the auter clere,
Whyl Emelye was thus in hir preyere;
But sodeinly she saugh a sighte queynte,
For right anon oon of the fyres queynte,
And quiked agayn, and after that anon   2335
That other fyr was queynt, and al agon;

'O chaste Goddess of the green woods, who always looks upon the heaven, earth and sea, Queen of the dark, infernal Kingdoms of Pluto, the Goddess of maidens, whom my heart has known for many a year, you know my desire to be protected from your vengeance and anger which Actaeon paid for so cruelly. Chaste Goddess, you know that I desire to be a maiden all my life and that I have no wish to fall in love or be a wife. You know that I am still a maiden of your company who loves hunting and walking in the wild woods and that I do not wish to be a wife or be with child. I do not desire to know the company of man.

Now, my lady, please help me, for, by those three forms you have in yourself, you are well able to do so. I seek only this favour in the matter of Palamon who entertains such deep love for me and Arcite who loves me so ardently – bring love and peace between the two of them and turn away their hearts from me in such a manner that all their passionate desire, love and all their anxious worries and their fire will be quenched or devoted to some one else. If it is not your wish to grant me any favour or if it is so ordained by fate that I must needs accept one of these two as my husband, give me the one who desires me most.

I beg of you to look upon the bitter tears that fall on my cheeks, Goddess of Chastity, and, as you are the maiden and guardian of us all, please protect and carefully preserve my maidenhood. If you grant me this request, I promise you that during all my life as a maiden I shall serve you.'

While Emily was at her prayers, the fires burnt brightly upon the altar but suddenly she saw a curious sight. Immediately one of the fires went out but revived again; then, the other fire was quenched and disappeared altogether.

And as it queynte, it made a whistelinge,
As doon thise wete brondes in hir brenninge,
And at the brondes ende out-ran anoon
As it were blody dropes many oon;   2340
For which so sore agast was Emelye,
That she was wel ny mad, and gan to crye,
For she ne wiste what it signifyed;
But only for the fere thus hath she cryed,
And weep, that it was pitee for to here.   2345
And ther-with-al Diane gan appere,
With bowe in hond, right as an hunteresse,
And seyde: 'Doghter, stint thyn hevinesse.
Among the goddes hye it is affermed,
And by eterne word write and confermed,   2350
Thou shalt ben wedded un-to oon of tho
That han for thee so muchel care and wo;
But un-to which of hem I may nat telle.

Farwel, for I ne may no lenger dwelle.
The fyres which that on myn auter brenne   2355
Shul thee declaren, er that thou go henne,
Thyn aventure of love, as in this cas.'
And with that word, the arwes in the cas
Of the goddesse clateren faste and ringe,
And forth she wente, and made a vanisshinge;   2360
For which this Emelye astoned was,
And seyde, 'What amounteth this, allas!
I putte me in thy proteccioun,
Diane, and in thy disposicioun.'
And hoom she gooth anon the nexte weye.   2365
This is th'effect, ther is namore to seye.

The nexte houre of Mars folwinge this,
Arcite un-to the temple walked is
Of fierse Mars, to doon his sacrifyse,
With alle the rytes of his payen wyse.   2370
With pitous herte and heigh devocioun,
Right thus to Mars he seyde his orisoun:
'O stronge god, that in the regnes colde
Of Trace honoured art, and lord y-holde,
And hast in every regne and every lond   2375
Of armes al the brydel in thyn hond,
And hem fortunest as thee list devyse,
Accept of me my pitous sacrifyse.

As the fire was quenched, it whistled just like wet brands do when they burn and at the tip of the burning log many drops like blood ran forth. Emily was so frightened at this sight that she almost went mad and began weeping, as she did not understand what the sign meant. Although she cried merely from fear, she wept so bitterly that it was pitiful to hear. At once Diana, just like a huntress, appeared with bow in hand and said, 'Cease your grief, my daughter. It is confirmed among the gods on high and written and established by eternal word that you will be wedded unto one of these who have endured so much care and suffered so much misery on your behalf; but I cannot divulge unto you to which of them you will be joined.

Farewell now, for I can remain here no longer. The fires on my altar will reveal to you, before you depart from here, what fortune in love you will have in this affair.' When she had finished speaking, the arrows in the Goddess's quiver rattled and rang suddenly; forth she went and vanished. At this Emily grew amazed. 'Alas!' she cried. 'What does this signify? I am, Diana, entirely yours and in your protection.' She went home by the nearest route. These are the main points of this episode, so I shall say no more about it.

At the next hour of Mars following this Arcite walked to the Temple of fierce Mars to perform his sacrifice with all the rites of the pagan style. With imploring heart and deep devotion he addressed this morning prayer to Mars.

'O mighty God who are honoured and considered lord in the cold region of Thrace and who has in every kingdom and in every land the sway of arms in your power and who grants fortune to people as you wish to ordain, please accept from me my piteous sacrifice.

If so be that my youthe may deserve,
And that my might be worthy for to serve   2380
Thy godhede, that I may been oon of thyne,
Than preye I thee to rewe up-on my pyne.
For thilke peyne, and thilke hote fyr,
In which thou whylom brendest for desyr,
Whan that thou usedest the grete beautee   2385
Of fayre yonge fresshe Venus free,
And haddest hir in armes at thy wille,
Al-though thee ones on a tyme misfille
Whan Vulcanus had caught thee in his las,
And fond thee ligging by his wyf, allas!   2390
For thilke sorwe that was in thyn herte,
Have routhe as wel up-on my peynes smerte.

I am yong and unkonning, as thou wost,
And, as I trowe, with love offended most,
That ever was any lyves creature;   2395
For she, that dooth me al this wo endure,
Ne reccheth never wher I sinke or flete.
And wel I woot, er she me mercy hete,
I moot with strengthe winne hir in the place;
And wel I woot, withouten help or grace   2400
Of thee, ne may my strengthe noght availle.
Than help me, lord, to-morwe in my bataille,
For thilke fyr that whylom brente thee,
As wel as thilke fyr now brenneth me;
And do that I to-morwe have victorie.   2405
Myn be the travaille, and thyn be the glorie!

Thy soverein temple wol I most honouren
Of any place, and alwey most labouren
In thy plesaunce and in thy craftes stronge,
And in thy temple I wol my baner honge,   2410
And alle the armes of my companye;
And evere-mo, un-to that day I dye,
Eterne fyr I wol biforn thee finde.
And eek to this avow I wol me binde:
My berd, myn heer that hongeth long adoun,   2415
That never yet ne felte offensioun
Of rasour nor of shere, I wol thee yive,
And been thy trewe servant whyl I live.
Now lord, have routhe up-on my sorwes sore,
Yif me victorie, I aske thee namore.'   2420

If you consider that my youth so deserves and my ability is worthy of serving your goodness so that I may become one of your true followers, then I beseech you to take pity on my sorrow. This I beg for the sake of that same pain and ardent fire with which you once burnt with desire when you used the beauty of fair, young, fresh, free Venus and had her at your own will in your arms. I admit that it did misfire once when Vulcan caught you in his snare and, alas, found you lying by his wife! For the sake of that very sorrow that was in your heart, have mercy too on my grievous pain.

You know well that I am young and inexperienced and I believe that Love, always the most vital part of any creature, has wounded me; for she who has caused me to endure all this misery cares not whether I live or die. I am well aware that I must win her by sheer might in the lists before she will become well-disposed towards me but I also realize that my strength will not avail me unless I have your help or favour. Then, my lord, for the sake of that same passion that consumed you and now consumes me, please help me and bring it about that I shall gain the victory tomorrow. Let mine be the labour but to you the glory shall accrue.

Of all places I shall principally honour your temple and I shall always strive for your pleasure and your manual arts; in your Temple I shall hang my banner and all the arms of my company; and I shall place eternal fire before you for evermore till the day of my death. I swear that I shall bind myself to these promises. I shall dedicate to you my beard and my long-hanging hair, neither of which has yet felt the cut of razor or shears, and I shall be your faithful servant for life. Now, my lord, take pity on my grievous sorrows and grant me victory. I seek no more.'

The preyere stinte of Arcita the stronge,
The ringes on the temple-dore that honge,
And eek the dores, clatereden ful faste,
Of which Arcita som-what him agaste.
The fyres brende up-on the auter brighte,   2425
That it gan al the temple for to lighte;
And swete smel the ground anon up-yaf,
And Arcita anon his hand up-haf,
And more encens in-to the fyr he caste,
With othere rytes mo; and atte laste   2430
The statue of Mars bigan his hauberk ringe.
And with that soun he herde a murmuringe
Ful lowe and dim, that sayde thus, 'Victorie';
For which he yaf to Mars honour and glorie.
And thus with joye, and hope wel to fare,   2435
Arcite anon un-to his inne is fare,
As fayn as fowel is of the brighte sonne.

And right anon swich stryf ther is bigonne
For thilke graunting, in the hevene above,
Bitwixe Venus, the goddesse of love,   2440
And Mars, the sterne god armipotente,
That Jupiter was bisy it to stente;
Til that the pale Saturnus the colde,
That knew so manye of aventures olde,
Fond in his olde experience an art,   2445
That he ful sone hath plesed every part.
As sooth is sayd, elde hath greet avantage;
In elde is bothe wisdom and usage;
Men may the olde at-renne, and noght at-rede.
Saturne anon, to stinten stryf and drede,   2450
Al be it that it is agayn his kynde,
Of al this stryf he gan remedie fynde.

'My dere doghter Venus,' quod Saturne,
'My cours, that hath so wyde for to turne,
Hath more power than wot any man.   2455
Myn is the drenching in the see so wan;
Myn is the prison in the derke cote;
Myn is the strangling and hanging by the throte;
The murmure, and the cherles rebelling,
The groyning, and the pryvee empoysoning: 2460
I do vengeance and pleyn correccioun
Whyl I dwelle in the signe of the Leoun.

When the prayers of the mighty Arcite were concluded, the rings that hung on the Temple door, and even the doors themselves, rattled for a long time and Arcite grew somewhat frightened of the noise. At the same time the fires burnt so brightly on the altar that they lit up all the Temple and the ground gave forth a sweet smell. Arcite at once lifted up his hand and cast more incense into the fire and performed other rites as well. At last he heard not only the sound of the Statue of Mars rattling his chain-mail but also a very low, soft murmur which whispered, 'Victory!' When he had recognized this sign, he showed honour and glory to Mars and then, with the happy hope of success, Arcite went immediately to his inn, as happy as a bird in the brilliant sunshine.

Straightway in the heavens above such strife over that award was created between Venus, the Goddess of Love, and the stern Mars, mighty in arms, that Jupiter grew anxious to stop it. At last pale, cold Saturn, who knew so many events of old time, found from his long experience a means by which he soon satisfied both parties. It is, indeed, a great truth that age holds a big advantage, for both wisdom and experience are found in age. One can outrun but not outwit the aged. Although it was contrary to his nature, Saturn soon discovered the remedy for all this quarrelling and was instrumental in stopping the strife and fear.

'My dear daughter, Venus,' Saturn said, 'My course that covers so many aspects has more power than any individual can guess. Under my influence is the drowning in the pale sea; mine is the prison in the dark dungeon; and mine is the strangling and hanging by the throat, the discontent of the rebellious serfs and the secret poisoning. While I dwell in the sign of the Lion, I am responsible for both vengeance and open correction.

'Myn is the ruine of the hye halles,
The falling of the toures and of the walles
Up-on the mynour or the carpenter.   2465
I slow Sampsoun in shaking the piler;
And myne be the maladyes colde,
The derke tresons, and the castes olde;
My loking is the fader of pestilence.
Now weep namore, I shal doon diligence   2470
That Palamon, that is thyn owne knight,
Shal have his lady, as thou hast him hight.
Though Mars shal helpe his knight, yet nathelees
Bitwixe yow ther moot be som tyme pees,
Al be ye noght of o complexioun,   2475
That causeth al day swich divisioun.
I am thin ayel, redy at thy wille;
Weep thou namore, I wol thy lust fulfille.'

  Now wol I stinten of the goddes above,
Of Mars, and of Venus, goddesse of love,   2480
And telle yow, as pleynly as I can,
The grete effect, for which that I bigan.

Part 4

Greet was the feste in Athenes that day,
And eek the lusty seson of that May
Made every wight to been in swich plesaunce,   2485
That al that Monday justen they and daunce,
And spenden it in Venus heigh servyse.
But by the cause that they sholde ryse
Erly, for to seen the grete fight,
Unto hir reste wente they at night.   2490
And on the morwe, whan that day gan springe,
Of hors and harneys, noyse and clateringe
Ther was in hostelryes al aboute;
And to the paleys rood ther many a route
Of lordes, up-on stedes and palfreys.   2495
Ther maystow seen devysing of herneys
So uncouth and so riche, and wroght so weel
Of goldsmithrie, of browding, and of steel;
The sheeldes brighte, testers, and trappures;
Gold-hewen helmes, hauberks, cote-armures.   2500

Mine is the ruin of grand halls, the falling of towers and walls upon the miner and the carpenter – I slew Samson while he was shaking the pillar – and under my influence are the cold diseases, dark treasons and old plots. My glance is the source of pestilence. Now weep no more for I shall see to it that your own knight, Palamon, shall win his lady just as you have promised him. Mars shall help his knight but, nevertheless, I shall bring about peace between you at some time; even so that peace will not be the kind that sees fresh dissensions all day long. I am your grandfather, always ready to perform your will. I shall bring to pass what you desire, so weep no more.'

Now I shall tell you no more about the gods above, of Mars or Venus, the Goddess of Love. Instead I shall tell you, as simply as I can, the great ending to the story I have begun.

Part 4

Great was the feast-making in Athens on that day; and the pleasant season of May brought such happiness to every one that all tilted and danced all that Monday and devoted time to the devout service of Venus. As they had to arise early to see the great fight, they retired to their beds that night. When dawn came the next day, everywhere could be heard the noise and clattering of horses and armour in the inns and of many a company of lords riding on horseback to the palace. There could be seen designs of armour so strange, so rich and so elaborately wrought by the skill of gold-smiths, both of embroidery and steel, bright shields, head-pieces and trapping helmets forged from gold, coats of mail, coat-armours.

Lordes in paraments on hir courseres,
Knightes of retenue, and eek squyeres
Nailinge the speres, and helmes bokelinge,
Gigginge of sheeldes, with layneres lacinge;
Ther as need is, they weren no-thing ydel;   2505
The fomy stedes on the golden brydel
Gnawinge, and faste the armurers also
With fyle and hamer prikinge to and fro;
Yemen on fote, and communes many oon
With shorte staves, thikke as they may goon;   2510
Pypes, trompes, nakers, clariounes,
That in the bataille blowen blody sounes;
The paleys ful of peples up and doun,
Heer three, ther ten, holding hir questioun,
Divyninge of thise Theban knightes two.   2515

Somme seyden thus, somme seyde it shal be so;
Somme helden with him with the blake berd,
Somme with the balled, somme with the thikke-herd:
Somme sayde, he loked grim and he wolde fighte;
He hath a sparth of twenty pound of wighte.   2520
Thus was the halle ful of divyninge,
Longe after that the sonne gan to springe.
  The grete Theseus, that of his sleep awaked
With minstralcye and noyse that was maked,
Held yet the chambre of his paleys riche,   2525
Til that the Thebane knightes, bothe y-liche
Honoured, were into the paleys fet.
Duk Theseus was at a window set,
Arrayed right as he were a god in trone
The peple preesseth thider-ward ful sone   2530
Him for to seen, and doon heigh reverence,
And eek to herkne his hest and his sentence.

  An heraud on a scaffold made an ho,
Til al the noyse of peple was y-do;
And whan he saugh the peple of noyse al stille,   2535
Tho showed he the mighty dukes wille.
  'The lord hath of his heigh discrecioun
Considered, that it were destruccioun
To gentil blood, to fighten in the gyse
Of mortal bataille now in this empryse;   2540
Wherfore, to shapen that they shul not dye,
He wol his firste purpos modifye.

Lords in rich array on their steeds, knights of retinues, squires nailing the spears and buckling helmets, the fitting of shields and the lacing of straps. Wherever anything was needed, no one was idle. There were frothing steeds champing on their bits and, close by, were armourers rushing to and fro with file and hammer, yeomen on foot and many commoners packed as closely together as was possible for walking, and pipers, trumpets, battle-drums and clarions that blow the bloody sounds of battle. The palace was crowded everywhere with people, three here, ten there, all discussing various issues and making guesses about the capabilities of the two Theban knights.

Some were saying this, others were saying that; some supported the knight with the black beard, others took the side of the bald fellow; some favoured the one with the thick hair – a number maintained that he looked fierce, especially as he held a battle-axe some twenty pounds in weight. So the hall buzzed with guessing long after the sun arose.

When the mighty Theseus was awakened by the minstrelsy and noise that was being made, he remained in the room in his beautiful palace until the Theban knights, similarly honoured, were fetched to the palace. As Duke Theseus, dressed as if he was a god on his throne, sat at a window, the people pressed towards the palace very early to see him, pay their respects to him and to listen to his orders and decree.

A herald on a scaffold proclaimed 'Ho!' till the people ceased creating a noise; and, when he saw that silence prevailed, he announced the mighty Dukes's will: -

'In his deep wisdom the lord has deemed it would be mere slaughter for men of noble blood to fight in the fashion of mortal battle in this tourney. Therefore, to ensure that they will not die, he wishes to modify his original purpose.

No man therfor, up peyne of los of lyf,
No man shot, ne pollax, ne short knyf
Into the listes sende, or thider bringe;   2545
Ne short swerd for to stoke, with poynt bytinge,
No man ne drawe, ne bere it by his syde.
Ne no man shal un-to his felawe ryde
But o cours, with a sharp y-grounde spere;
Foyne, if him list, on fote, him-self to were.   2550
And he that is at meschief, shal be take,
And noght slayn, but be broght un-to the stake
That shal ben ordeyned on either syde;
But thider he shal by force, and ther abyde.
And if so falle, the chieftayn be take   2555
On either syde, or elles slee his make,
No lenger shal the turneyinge laste.
God spede yow; goth forth, and ley on faste.
With long swerd and with maces fight your fille.
Goth now your wey; this is the lordes wille.'   2560

   The voys of peple touchede the hevene,
So loude cryden they with mery stevene:
'God save swich a lord, that is so good,
He wilneth no destruccioun of blood!'
Up goon the trompes and the melodye.   2565
And to the listes rit the companye
By ordinaunce, thurgh-out the citee large,
Hanged with cloth of gold, and nat with sarge.
Ful lyk a lord this noble duk gan ryde,
Thise two Thebanes up-on either syde;   2570
And after rood the quene, and Emelye,
And after that another companye
Of oon and other, after hir degree.

And thus they passen thurgh-out the citee,
And to the listes come they by tyme.   2575
It nas not of the day yet fully pryme,
Whan set was Theseus ful riche and hye,
Ipolita the quene and Emelye,
And other ladies in degrees aboute.
Un-to the seetes presseth al the route   2580
And west-ward, thurgh the gates under Marte,
Arcite, and eek the hundred of his parte,
With baner reed is entred right anon;

No knight then, on pain of death, shall bring here into the lists any kind of arrow, pole-axe or short knife. No knight shall draw or carry by his side any short sword that can stab with a keen point. No knight shall ride towards his opponent on his course except with his sharp sword pointing towards the ground. If one wishes, one can thrust on foot for personal defence but the knight who may be in danger, though he is not slain, must be brought to the special enclosure that will be fixed by both sides – he may even be brought there forcibly – and he must remain there.

If it should come about that the leader or either side should be taken or else his rival slain, the tourney will last no longer. Now God speed you! Go and fight hard! Fight to your satisfaction with long sword and mace. The lord wishes that you now begin.'

The people shouted so loudly in their excitement that the noise reached the heavens. 'God save such a lord who is so good that he will not allow bloodshed!'
Up went the trumpets and the martial music began; by decree, the company rode to the lists throughout the city draped with cloth of gold, not serge.
The noble Duke rode very much like the lord he was with the two Thebans on each side of him; the Queen and Emily rode immediately after them, then another company of various people one after the other according to their rank.

In this order they passed throughout the city and arrived punctually at the lists. It was not yet six in the morning when Theseus, in rich array and high-positioned, took his seat with Queen Hipployta, Emily and all the other ladies on the steps about him. After all the crowd had thronged to the seats, Arcite and a hundred of his knights, carrying a red banner, entered from the West gates beneath the Temple of Mars.

And in that selve moment Palamon
Is under Venus, est-ward in the place,   2585
With baner whyt, and hardy chere and face.
In al the world, to seken up and doun,
So even with-outen variacioun,
Ther nere swiche companyes tweye.
For ther nas noon so wys that coude seye,   2590
That any hadde of other avauntage
Of worthinesse, ne of estaat, ne age,
So even were they chosen, for to gesse.
And in two renges faire they hem dresse.
Whan that hir names rad wer everichoon,   2595
That in hir nombre gyle were ther noon,
Tho were the gates shet, and cryed was loude:
'Do now your devoir, yonge knightes proude!'

  The heraudes lefte hir priking up and doun;
Now ringen trompes loude and clarioun;   2600
Ther is namore to seyn, but west and est
In goon the speres ful sadly in arest;
In goth the sharpe spore in-to the syde.
Ther seen men who can juste, and who can ryde;
Ther shiveren shaftes up-on sheeldes thikke;   2605
He feleth thurgh the herte-spoon the prikke.
Up springen speres twenty foot on highte;
Out goon the swerdes as the silver brighte.
The helmes they to-hewen and to-shrede;
Out brest the blood, with sterne stremes rede.   2610
With mighty maces the bones they tobreste.

He thurgh the thikkeste of the throng gan threste.
Ther stomblen stedes stronge, and doun goth al.
He rolleth under foot as dooth a bal.
He foyneth on his feet with his tronchoun,   2615
And he him hurtleth with his hors adoun.
He thurgh the body is hurt, and sithen y-take,
Maugree his heed, and broght un-to the stake,
As forward was, right ther he moste abyde;
Another lad is on that other syde.   2620
And som tyme dooth hem Theseus to reste,
Hem to refresshe, and drinken if hem leste.
Ful ofte a-day han thise Thebanes two
Togidre y-met, and wroght his felawe wo;
Unhorsed hath ech other of hem tweye.   2625

At the same time, Palamon, with a bold appearance and manner, entered from the Eastern quarter of the amphitheatre beneath the Temple of Venus with a white banner. Even if you had searched everywhere in the world, you would never have found two such other companies so equally matched. Indeed, no one present was so wise that he could judge which side held the advantage in worth, rank or age over the other, as they had been selected so evenly, so I should say on the spur of the moment. Then they arranged themselves most orderly in two ranks.

When the name of every knight had been called to see that there was no deceit in their numbers, the gates were closed and a loud proclamation was made, 'Now, you young, proud knights, do your duty!'

The heralds ceased trotting around, and the clarions rang out. All I can say now is that on the east and west the spears entered very earnestly into position and the sharp spur went into the horse's side. There you could have seen men who could tilt and ride, shafts splintered upon the thick shields – the victim felt the stab through his chest. Spears sprang up, twenty feet in the air; out flashed the swords shining like silver; helmets were hewn and broken in pieces; and strong streams of red blood gushed forth, and bones were burst asunder by the mighty maces.

One knight thrust through the thickest part of the throng where strong steeds stumbled and fell; one rolled under foot like a ball; another lashed on foot with his club and pushed his opponent down with his horse. Another was pierced through the body and later taken and, despite his efforts, was brought to the special enclosure of the opposing side. According to the agreement he had to remain there. Then another of the other side was led to the enclosure. Now and then Theseus made them take a rest and take a drink if they felt like it. Very often during that day the two Thebans clashed and wrought havoc on each other; and each of them had unhorsed the other on two occasions.

Ther nas no tygre in the vale of Galgopheye,
Whan that hir whelp is stole, whan it is lyte,
So cruel on the hunte, as is Arcite
For jelous herte upon this Palamoun:
Ne in Belmarye ther nis so fel leoun,   2630
That hunted is, or for his hunger wood,
Ne of his praye desireth so the blood,
As Palamon to sleen his fo Arcite.
The jelous strokes on hir helmes byte;
Out renneth blood on both hir sydes rede.   2635
 Som tyme an ende ther is of every dede;
For er the sonne un-to the reste wente,
The stronge king Emetreus gan hente
This Palamon, as he faught with Arcite,
And made his swerd depe in his flesh to byte;   2640
And by the force of twenty is he take
Unyolden, and y-drawe unto the stake.

And in the rescous of this Palamoun
The stronge king Ligurge is born adoun;
And king Emetreus, for al his strengthe,   2645
Is born out of his sadel a swerdes lengthe,
So hitte him Palamon er he were take;
But al for noght, he was broght to the stake.
His hardy herte mighte him helpe naught;
He moste abyde, whan that he was caught   2650
By force, and eek by composicioun.
 Who sorweth now but woful Palamoun,
That moot namore goon agayn to fighte?
And whan that Theseus had seyn this sighte,
Un-to the folk that foghten thus echoon   2655
He cryde, 'Ho! namore, for it is doon!

I wol be trewe juge, and no partye.
Arcite of Thebes shal have Emelye,
That by his fortune hath hir faire y-wonne.'
Anon ther is a noyse of peple bigonne   2660
For joye of this, so loude and heigh withalle,
It semed that the listes sholde falle.
 What can now faire Venus doon above?
What seith she now? what dooth this quene of love?
But wepeth so, for wanting of hir wille,   2665
Til that hir teres in the listes fille;

There was no tiger in the Vale of Gargaphie, when its small whelp has been stolen, that could compare with Arcite who was so terrible on the hunt and nursed such a jealous heart for Palamon; again, there was no such fierce lion hunted in Ben-Marin as Palamon with his mad hunger or desire for blood to slay his foe. The jealous strokes bit on their helmets and blood gushed forth from both the sides of the victim.

Every event must come to an end at some time or other and, before the sun had gone to rest, the powerful King Demetrius seized Palamon as he was fighting with Arcite and made his sword bite deeply into his flesh. Through the efforts of twenty knights of the opposition, he was captured and, although he refused to surrender, he was dragged to the enclosure.

Not only was the mighty King Lycurgus borne down when he was trying to rescue Palamon but King Demetrius also, despite all his strength, was thrown a sword's length out of his saddle. It was all in vain, however, because he was still brought to the enclosure where, through force and also according to the agreement, he had to remain after his capture. His bold heart could not extricate him from the situation.

The wretched Palamon was now extremely sorrowful that he could no longer join battle. When Theseus noticed what had happened, he shouted to all the fighters, 'Ho! No more! It is all over.

I must be a true, impartial judge. Arcite of Thebes, who has had the good fortune to win her fairly, shall have Emily.'

At once the spectators began to shout for sheer joy but so noisy and loud was the applause that it seemed as if the lists would fall.

What could the fair Venus do in the heavens about this? What could the Queen of Love do or say? She could do nothing but weep till her tears filled the lists.

She seyde: 'I am ashamed, doutelees,'
Saturnus seyde: 'Doghter, hold thy pees.
Mars hath his wille, his knighte hath al his bone,
And, by myn heed, thou shalt ben esed sone.'   2670
   The trompes, with the loude minstralcye,
The heraudes, that ful loude yolle and crye,
Been in hir wele for joye of daun Arcite.
But herkneth me, and stinteth now a lyte,
Which a miracle ther bifel anon.   2675
   This fierse Arcite hath of his helm y-don,
And on a courser, for to shewe his face,
He priketh endelong the large place,
Loking upward up-on this Emelye;
And she agayn him caste a freendlich yë,   2680
(For wommen, as to speken in comune,
They folwen al the favour of fortune);
And she was al his chere, as in his herte.

Out of the ground a furie infernal sterte,
From Pluto sent, at requeste of Saturne,   2685
For which his hors for fere gan to turne,
And leep asyde, and foundred as he leep;
And, er that Arcite may taken keep,
He pighte him on the pomel of his heed,
That in the place he lay as he were deed   2690
His brest to-brosten with his sadel-bowe.
As blak he lay as any cole or crowe,
So was the blood y-ronnen in his face.
Anon he was y-born out of the place
With herte soor, to Theseus paleys.   2695
Tho was he corven out of his harneys,
And in a bed y-brought ful faire and blyve,
For he was yet in memorie and alyve,
And alway crying after Emelye.

   Duk Theseus, with al his companye,   2700
Is comen hoom to Athenes his citee,
With alle blisse and greet solempnitee.
Al be it that this aventure was falle,
He nolde noght disconforten hem alle.
Men seyde eek, that Arcite shal nat dye;   2705
He shal ben heled of his maladye.

'I am well and truly ashamed,' she cried.

'Daughter,' replied Saturn, 'be calm, Mars has had his wish and his knight has gained his whole prayer; but, nevertheless, I swear by my life that you will soon be recompensed.'

The trumpeters with their loud minstrelsy and the heralds who had shouted and yelled loudly were greatly delighted with Lord Arcite. Now, listen to me and wait to hear what miracle happened straight after that.

Fierce Arcite had unloosened his helmet and was riding on his courser along the length of the spacious lists to show his face to the spectators. All the time he kept looking up at Emily and she, in return, threw him friendly glances (for women, generally speaking, all follow the grace of Fortune), showing that she was entirely his in countenance as well as heart.

An infernal fury, sent by Pluto at the request of Saturn, leapt out of the ground, making his horse shy for fear and prance aside, stumbling as he jumped. Before Arcite could take any precautions, he was pitched so heavily on the crown of his head that he lay still on the spot as if he was dead, his breast broken by his saddle-bow, looking as black as a piece of coal or a crow as the blood had run into his head. At once he was carried from the place to Theseus's palace, his heart sorely wounded. There he was cut free from his armour and carried very quickly to bed, for he was still conscious and constantly calling for Emily.

Duke Theseus returned home to his city of Athens with his company amid intense enthusiasm and with great glory. Although this accident had happened, he did not wish to upset everybody as he was told that Arcite would not die but would even be healed of his injuries.

And of another thing they were as fayn,
That of hem alle was ther noon y-slayn,
Al were they sore y-hurt, and namely oon,
That with a spere was thirled his brestboon. 2710
To othere woundes, and to broken armes,
Some hadden salves, and some hadden charmes;
Fermacies of herbes, and eek save
They dronken, for they wolde hir limes have.
For which this noble duk, as he wel can, 2715
Conforteth and honoureth every man,
And made revel al the longe night,
Un-to the straunge lordes, as was right.

Ne ther was holden no disconfitinge,
But as a justes or a tourneyinge; 2720
For soothly ther was no disconfiture,
For falling nis nat but an aventure;
Ne to be lad with fors un-to the stake
Unyolden, and with twenty knightes take.
O persone allone, with-outen mo, 2725
And haried forth by arme, foot, and to,
And eek his stede driven forth with staves,
With footmen, bothe yemen and eek knaves,
It nas aretted him no vileinye,
Ther may no man clepen it cowardye. 2730

  For which anon duk Theseus leet crye,
To stinten alle rancour and envye,
The gree as wel of o syde as of other,
And either syde y-lyk, as otheres brother;
And yaf hem yiftes after hir degree, 2735
And fully heeld a feste dayes three;
And conveyed the kinges worthily
Out of his toun a journee largely.
And hoom wente every man the righte way.
Ther was namore, but 'far wel, have good day!' 2740
Of this bataille I wol namore endyte,
But speke of Palamon and of Arcite.
  Swelleth the brest of Arcite, and the sore
Encreesseth at his herte more and more.
The clothered blood, for any lechecraft, 2745
Corrupteth, and is in his bouk y-laft,
That neither veyne-blood, ne ventusinge,
Ne drinke of herbes may ben his helpinge.

Another fact that pleased every one was that no one person had been killed, though some were grievously hurt and one particularly so as his breast-bone had been pierced by a spear. To help heal some of the wounds and broken arms a few of the wounded used certain doctorings, others applied charms or cures made from fresh herbs or even drank sage, for they were anxious to retain their limbs. In recognition of this the noble Duke comforted and honoured every knight as well as he could and all that night he provided entertainment, as was only fitting, for the strange lords.

Nor was there any rout kept, except what was usual for such jousts and tournaments. Truly no rout had been witnessed that day for falling is a mere accident while the misfortune of being taken and led to the enclosure by the efforts of twenty knights, and the victim refusing to surrender – one person only, no more, harried towards that place wholly by force of arms and his steed also driven there by footmen with sticks and yeomen and knaves – that could not be considered shameful in any way and no one whatsoever could call it cowardice.

To make sure that all the hatred and spite should cease, Duke Theseus announced that one side had done as well as the other and that each side should be treated as if they were the other's brothers. He presented gifts to them according to their rank, held a full three days' feast for them and, when he escorted the kings a days' journey from his town in royal fashion, saw to it every one went home on the right road. There was no more to it except, 'Farewell' and 'Have a good day.' I shall tell no more about this fight but talk only of Palamon and Arcite.

Arcite's breast swelled and the pain increased immensely in his heart. Despite all surgical skill, the clotted blood corrupted and, as it was left in his body, neither the blood of his veins nor the cupping and drinking of herbs could relieve him.

The vertu expulsif, or animal,
Fro thilke vertu cleped natural   2750
Ne may the venim voyden, ne expelle.
The pypes of his longes gonne to swelle,
And every lacerte in his breste adoun
Is shent with venim and corrupcioun.
Him gayneth neither, for to gete his lyf,   2755
Vomyt upward, ne dounward laxatif;
Al is to-brosten thilke regioun,
Nature hath now no dominacioun.
And certeinly, ther nature wol nat wirche,
Far-wel, phisyk! go ber the man to chirche!   2760
This al and som, that Arcita mot dye,
For which he sendeth after Emelye,
And Palamon, that was his cosin dere;
Than seyde he thus; as ye shul after here.

'Naught may the woful spirit in myn herte   2765
Declare o poynt of alle my sorwes smerte
To yow, my lady, that I love most;
But I biquethe the service of my gost
To yow aboven every creature,
Sin that my lyf may no lenger dure.   2770
Allas, the wo! allas, the peynes stronge,
That I for yow have suffred, and so longe!
Allas, the deeth! allas, myn Emelye!
Allas, departing of our companye!
Allas, myn hertes quene! allas, my wyf!   2775
Myn hertes lady, endere of my lyf!

What is this world? what asketh men to have?
Now with his love, now in his colde grave
Allone, with-outen any companye.
Far-wel, my swete fo! myn Emelye!   2780
And softe tak me in your armes tweye,
For love of God, and herkneth what I seye.
  I have heer with my cosin Palamon
Had stryf and rancour, many a day a-gon,
For love of yow, and for my jelousye.   2785

As the excellent animal virtue which is extracted from the virtue called Natural could neither remove nor expel the poison, the pipes of his lungs swelled and every muscle in his chest and below that region was destroyed by poison and gangrene. All that part of the body was broken to pieces so vomiting and laxative downwards could not help him to sustain his life. Nature had no power there, for Nature simply could not work. Farewell, physic! Go and carry the man to the churchyard! The point is that Arcite could not avoid dying so he sent for Emily and his dear cousin, Palamon. Then he uttered to them these words, as you shall hear.

'The grievous spirit in my heart cannot declare to you, my dearly beloved lady, one word about all the pains of my sorrows. Even so, I bequeath to you the service of my spirit, rather than to any one else, as my life can last no longer. Alas my misery! Alas my excruciating pain that I have suffered so long for you! Alas the death! Alas my Emily! Alas for the separation of our company! Alas the queen of my heart! Alas my wife, the lady of my heart who has brought about my death!

What do men desire in this cold world? One moment they are with their love, the next they are alone in their cold grave without any company! Farewell, my sweet foe, my Emily! For the love of God, take me gently in your arms and listen to what I have to say.

For many a day gone by I have hated and struggled with my cousin, Palamon, out of jealous love for you.

And Jupiter so wis my soule gye,
To speken of a servant proprely,
With alle circumstaunces trewely,
That is to seyn, trouthe, honour, and knighthede,
Wisdom, humblesse, estaat, and heigh kinrede, 2790
Fredom, an al that longeth to that art,
So Jupiter have of my soule part,
As in this world right now ne knowe I non
So worthy to ben loved as Palamon,
That serveth yow, and wol don al his lyf. 2795
And if that ever ye shul been a wyf,
Foryet nat Palamon, the gentil man.'
And with that word his speche faille gan,
For from his feet up to his brest was come
The cold of deeth, that hadde him overcome. 2800

And yet more-over, in his armes two
The vital strengthe is lost, and al ago.
Only the intellect, with-outen more,
That dwelled in his herte syk and sore,
Gan faillen, when the herte felte deeth, 2805
Dusked his eyen two, and failled breeth.
But on his lady yet caste he his yë;
His laste word was, 'mercy, Emelye!'
His spirit chaunged hous, and wente ther,
As I cam never, I can nat tellen wher, 2810
Therfor I stinte, I nam no divinistre;
Of soules finde I nat in this registre,
Ne me ne list thilke opiniouns to telle
Of hem, though that they wryten wher they dwelle.
Arcite is cold, ther Mars his soule gye; 2815
Now wol I speken forth of Emelye.

Shrighte Emelye, and howleth Palamon,
And Theseus his suster took anon
Swowninge, and bar hir fro the corps away.
What helpeth it to tarien forth the day, 2820
To telle how she weep, bothe eve and morwe?
For in swich cas wommen have swich sorwe,
Whan that hir housbonds been from hem ago,
That for the more part they sorwen so,
Or elles fallen in swich maladye, 2825
That at the laste certeinly they dye.

Now I beg wise Jupiter to guide my soul speak truly of a lover, truly with all the circumstances of truth, honour, chivalry, wisdom, humility, rank, high birth, freedom and all the qualities that belong to that art. Jupiter may have a part of my soul if I do not know that in this world at this moment there is no one so worthy to be loved as Palamon who serves and will continue to serve you all his life. If you will ever be a wife, do not forget this noble man, Palamon.' With these words his speech failed him and the coldness of death that had overcome him spread from his feet up to his breast.

The vital power was already lost and departed from his arms; his mental powers and the faculties that dwelt in his sick, sore heart failed him when his heart felt the touch of death; his eyes grew dark; and his breath became weaker. He still looked upon his lady and his last words were, 'Have mercy on me, Emily.' His spirit changed homes and went to some place but I do not know its situation as I never came from there. I am no diviner so I shall say no more about it. As I cannot find 'the place of souls' in the Register, I prefer not to express the opinions of others, even though they may have sent word where they dwell. Arcite, however, must have been cold in the place where Mars guided him. Now I shall tell you about Emily.

Emily shrieked, Palamon howled for grief and Theseus had to carry his swooning sister away from the corpse. What is the point of wasting time in telling you how she wept morning and evening, for, as you know, in such circumstances women suffer such sorrow when their husbands have departed from them that, in most cases, they grieve so deeply or lapse into such sickness that they are sure to die in the end.

Infinite been the sorwes and the teres
Of olde folk, and folk of tendre yeres,
In al the toun, for deeth of this Theban;
For him ther wepeth bothe child and man; 2830
So greet a weping was ther noon, certayn,
Whan Ector was y-broght, al fresh y-slayn,
To Troye; allas! the pitee that was ther,
Cracching of chekes, rending eek of heer.
'Why woldestow be deed,' thise wommen crye, 2835
'And haddest gold y-nough, and Emelye?'
No man mighte gladen Theseus,
Savinge his olde fader Egeus,
That knew this worldes transmutacioun,
As he had seyn it chaungen up and doun, 2840
Joye after wo, and wo after gladnesse:
And shewed hem ensamples and lyknesse.

'Right as ther deyed never man,' quod he,
'That he ne livede in erthe in som degree,
Right so ther livede never man,' he seyde, 2845
'In al this world, that some tyme he ne deyde.
This world nis but a thurghfare ful of wo,
And we ben pilgrimes, passinge to and fro;
Deeth is an ende of every wordly sore.'
And over al this yet seyde he muchel more 2850
To this effect, ful wysly to enhorte
The peple, that they sholde hem reconforte.

Duk Theseus, with al his bisy cure,
Caste now wher that the sepulture
Of good Arcite may best y-maked be, 2855
And eek most honurable in his degree.
And at the laste he took conclusioun,
That ther as first Arcite and Palamoun
Hadden for love the bataille hem bitwene,
That in that selve grove, swote and grene, 2860
Ther as he hadde his amorous desires,
His compleynt, and for love his hote fires,
He wolde make a fyr, in which th'office
Funeral he mighte al accomplice;
And leet comaunde anon to hakke and hewe 2865
The okes olde, and leye hem on a rewe
In colpons wel arrayed for to brenne;

The grief and tears of both the young and old in the whole town were extremely bitter because of this Theban's death and both child and adult grieved for him. I can assure you that, even when Hector, just killed, was brought to Troy, definitely there could not have been such lamentation. Alas the pity that was there! Alas the scratching of cheeks and the rending of hair! 'Why did you have to die?' cried the women. 'You had gold enough and Emily as well.' No man could comfort Theseus except his aged father, Egeus, who was well aware of the changes in this world, for he had seen it alter, up and down, joy succeeding trouble and trouble succeeding gladness and of such a variety of Fortune he quoted several instances.

'Just as no man ever died,' he said, 'who has not lived on earth with some rank even so no man ever lived in all this world but he had to die at some time. This world is nothing but a thoroughfare full of trouble and we are pilgrims passing to and fro. Death is the end of all worldly sorrow.' He said much more to this effect and wisely exhorted the people to comfort themselves anew.

Despite his anxious care Duke Theseus now pondered where a burial place, the most honourable for a knight of the rank of the good Arcite, could best be situated. After some consideration he decided on the place where Arcite and Palamon had first fought between themselves over the issue of love, that same sweet, green grove where he had experienced his amorous desires, his trouble and his ardent love passions. This was the place where he intended to build a pyre on which all the funeral rites could be performed. He commanded the old oaks to be hacked down and hewn and the logs placed in a row, ready for burning.

His officers with swifte feet they renne
And ryde anon at his comaundement.
And after this, Theseus hath y-sent   2870
After a bere, and it al over-spradde
With cloth of gold, the richest that he hadde.
And of the same suyte he cladde Arcite;
Upon hes hondes hadde he gloves whyte;
Eek on his heed a croune of laurer grene,   2875
And in his hond a swerd ful bright and kene.
He leyde him bare the visage on the bere,
Therwith he weep that pitee was to here.
And for the peple sholde seen him alle,
Whan it was day, he broghte him to the halle,   2880
That roreth of the crying and the soun.

  Tho cam this woful Theban Palamoun,
With flotery berd, and ruggy asshy heres,
In clothes blake, y-dropped al with teres;
And, passing othere of weping, Emelye,   2885
The rewfulleste of al the companye.
In as muche as the service sholde be
The more noble and riche in his degree,
Duk Theseus leet forth three stedes bringe,
That trapped were in steel al gliteringe,   2890
And covered with the armes of daun Arcite.
Up-on thise stedes, that weren grete and whyte,
Ther seten folk, of which oon bar his sheeld,
Another his spere up in his hondes heeld;
The thridde bar with him hos bowe Turkeys,   2895
Of brend gold was the cas, and eek the harneys;
And riden forth a pas with sorweful chere
Toward the grove, as ye shul after here.

The nobleste of the Grekes that ther were
Upon hir shuldres carieden the bere,   2900
With slakke pas, and eyen rede and wete,
Thurgh-out the citee, by the maister-strete,
That sprad was al with blak, and wonder hye
Right of the same is al the strete y-wrye.
Up-on the right hond wente old Egeus,   2905
And on that other syde duk Theseus,
With vessels in hir hand of gold ful fyn,
Al ful of hony, milk, and blood, and wyn;

His officers hurried about everywhere and obeyed his orders instantly. Theseus then sent for a bier and had it completely spread with the richest cloth of gold he possessed and he dressed Arcite with the same cloth. He wore white gloves on his hands, a crown of green laurel on his head and carried a sharp shining sword in his hands. When Theseus had placed him, his face uncovered, on the bier, he wept so bitterly that it was pitiful to hear him. Further, when day came, so that all the people could see him, he brought the body to the hall that resounded with the noise of crying.

Then came the heart-broken Theban, Palamon, with flowing beard and shaggy, ash-strewn hair, dressed in black clothes dripping with his tears; and Emily, the most sorrowful of all the company, weeping even more bitterly than the rest. With the object of making the funeral rites nobler and more imposing and most suitable for one of his rank, Duke Theseus ordered three steeds, glittering in their trappings wrought completely of silver and carrying the arms of Lord Arcite, to be led forth. On these three fine white steeds sat horsemen, one of whom carried his shield, another held his spear in his hand and the third carried with him his Turkish bow, the quiver and equipment all of burnished gold; then, the horsemen rode with dejected countenance at footpace towards the grove, as you shall hear.

The noblest of the Greeks present, with inflamed, tear-stained eyes, carried the bier upon their shoulders at a slow pace throughout the city, draped everywhere with black cloth, along the main street that was covered with the same stuff to a great height. On the right hand of the bier walked Egeus and on the other was Duke Theseus both bearing very fine gold vessels full of honey, milk, blood and wine in their hands.

Eek Palamon, with ful greet companye;
And after that cam woful Emelye,   2910
With fyr in honde, as was that tyme the gyse,
To do th'office of funeral servyse.
  · Heigh labour, and ful greet apparaillinge ·
Was at the service and the fyr-makinge,
That with his grene top the heven raughte,   2915
And twenty fadme of brede the armes straughte;
This is to seyn, the bowes were so brode.
Of stree first ther was leyd ful many a lode.
But how the fyr was maked up on highte,
And eek the names how the treës highte,   2920
As ook, firre, birch, asp, alder, holm, popler,
Wilow, elm, plane, ash, box, chasteyn, lind, laurer,
Mapul, thorn, beech, hasel, ew, whippel-tree,
How they weren feld, shal nat be told for me;

Ne how the goddes ronnen up and doun,   2925
Disherited of hir habitacioun,
In which they woneden in reste and pees,
Nymphes, Faunes, and Amadrides;
Ne how the bestes and the briddes alle
Fledden for fere, whan the wode was falle;   2930
Ne how the ground agast was of the light,
That was nat wont to seen the sonne bright;
Ne how the fyr was couched first with stree,
And than with drye stokkes cloven a three,
And than with grene wode and spycerye,   2935
And than with cloth of gold and with perrye,
And gerlandes hanging with ful many a flour,
The mirre, th'encens, with al so greet odour;

Ne how Arcite lay among al this,
Ne what richesse aboute his body is;   2940
Ne how that Emelye, as was the gyse,
Putte in the fyr of funeral servyse;
Ne how she swowned whan men made the fyr,
Ne what she spak, ne what was hir desyr;
Ne what jeweles men in the fyr tho caste,   2945
Whan that the fyr was greet and brente faste;
Ne how som caste hir sheeld, and som hir spere,
And of hir vestiments, whiche that they were,
And cuppes ful of wyn, and milk, and blood,
Into the fyr, that brente as it were wood;   2950

Palamon accompanied them with a very large company and then came the unfortunate Emily, bearing fire in her hand, as people used to do at that time when the funeral rites were performed.

Great labour and very intensive preparations were involved in the service and the making of the fire which reached to the heavens with its green tops and whose boughs were so broad that its arms stretched twenty fathoms across. Many a load of straw was first laid on the pyre but as to the method of making the towering fire and also the names of the trees – oak, fir, birch, aspen, alder, holm, poplar, willow, elm, plane, ash, box, chestnut, lime-tree, laurel, maple, thorn, beech, hazel, yew, cornel-tree – it is not for me to describe how they were hewn;

occupatio

nor how the gods deprived of their habitation, the place where they dwelt in restful peace, ran up and down, nymphs, fauns and hama-dryads: nor how all the animals and birds fled from fear when the wood was felled; nor how the ground, which was not accustomed to seeing the bright sun, was terrified of the light; nor how the fire was laid first with straw, then with dry sticks cleft into three pieces, then with green wood and spices, then with gold cloth, many precious stones and garlands bedecked with many flowers, the myrrh and the incense, all with such a sweet perfume;

nor how Arcite lay among all this; nor what riches surrounded his body; nor how Emily, in the fashion then prevailing, placed the funeral fire among them; nor how she swooned when the men lit the fire nor what she said or wished; nor what jewels were cast into the huge, fiercely burning fire; nor how some men cast their shields, others their spears, others clothes of all kinds, cups full of wine, milk and blood, into the fire that was burning furiously;

Ne how the Grekes with an huge route
Thryës riden al the fyr aboute
Up-on the left hand, with a loud shoutinge,
And thryës with her speres clateringe;
And thryës how the ladies gonne crye;   2955
Ne how that lad was hom-ward Emelye;
Ne how Arcite is brent to asshen colde;
Ne how that liche-wake was y-holde
Al thilke night, ne how the Grekes pleye
The wake-pleyes, ne kepe I nat to seye;   2960
Who wrastleth best naked, with oille enoynt,
Ne who that bar him best, in no disjoynt.
I wol nat tellen eek how that they goon
Hoom til Athenes, whan the pley is doon;
But shortly to the poynt than wol I wende,   2965
·And maken of my longe tale an ende. ·

   By processe and by lengthe of certeyn yeres
Al stinted is the moorning and the teres.
Of Grekes, by oon general assent,
Than sēmed me ther was a parlement   2970
At Athenes, up-on certeyn poynts and cas;
Among the whiche poynts y-spoken was
To have with certeyn contrees alliaunce,
And have fully of Thebans obeisaunce.
For which this noble Theseus anon   2975
Leet senden after gentil Palamon,
Unwist of him what was the cause and why;
But in his blake clothes sorwefully
He cam at his comaundemente in hye.
Tho sente Theseus for Emelye.   2980

Whan they were set, and hust was al the place,
And Theseus abiden hadde a space
Er any word cam from his wyse brest,
His eyen sette he ther as was his lest,
And with a sad visage he syked stille,   2985
And after that right thus he seyde his wille.
   'The firste moevere of the cause above,
Whan he first made the faire cheyne of love,
Greet was th'effect, and heigh was his entente;
Wel wiste he why, and what ther-of he mente;   2990

nor how a huge crowd of the Greeks rode thrice around the fire moving in a circle from the left, shouting aloud and rattling their spears; nor how the ladies cried; nor how Emily was led homewards; nor how Arcite was burnt to cold ashes; nor how the vigil was kept all that night; nor how the Greeks celebrated it with funeral games; nor need I tell you who wrestled naked best, anointed with oil; nor who naturally behaved best. Again, I shall not tell you how they returned home at the end of the games, for I must come to my point quickly so that I can conclude my story.

After the long progress of several years, all the mourning and tears of the Greeks were ended by common consent. I believe that a Parliament was then summoned to consider certain problems and events and that among the issues discussed was one to make an alliance with certain countries and to obtain the complete obedience of the Thebans. Although the noble Palamon did not know the cause of the matter, Theseus sent for him with this object in view. Even so he came in haste on Theseus's orders, still dressed in black clothes. Theseus then sent for Emily.

When they had settled down and the place was quiet, Theseus hesitated a time before he uttered any word from his wise breast. He looked at the place he desired, then with a sad face and a quiet sigh, he announced his purpose.

'When the Prime Mover of all courses first created the fair chain of Love, he had a strong reason behind his lofty intention and he knew well why he had made it.

For with that faire cheyne of love he bond
The fyr, the eyr, the water, and the lond
In certeyn boundes, that they may nat flee;
That same prince and that moevere,' quod he,
'Hath stablissed, in this wrecched world adoun,   2995
Certyne dayes and duracioun
To al that is engendred in this place,
Over the whiche day they may nat pace,
Al mowe they yet tho dayes wel abregge;
Ther needeth non auctoritee allegge,   3000
For it is preved by experience,
But that me list declaren my sentence.

Than may men by this ordre wel discerne,
That thilke moevere stable is and eterne.
Wel may men knowe, but it be a fool,   3005
That every part deryveth from his hool.
For nature hath nat take his beginning
Of no party ne cantel of a thing,
But of a thing that parfit is and stable,
Descending so, til it be corrumpable.   3010
And therfore, of his wyse purveyaunce,
He hath so wel biset his ordinaunce,
That speces of thinges and progressiouns
Shullen enduren by successiouns,
And nat eterne be, with-oute lyë: 3015
This maistow understonde and seen at yë.

  'Lo the ook, that hath so long a norisshinge
From tyme that it first biginneth springe,
And hath so long a lyf, as we may see,
Yet at the laste wasted is the tree.   3020
  'Considereth eek, how that the harde stoon
Under our feet, on which we trede and goon,
Yit wasteth it, as it lyth by the weye.
The brode river somtyme wexeth dreye.
The grete tounes see we wane and wende.   3025
Than may ye see that al this thing hath ende.
  'Of man and womman seen we wel also,
That nedeth, in oon of thise termes two,
This is to seyn, in youthe or elles age,
He moot ben deed, the king as shal a page;   3030
Som in his bed, som in the depe see,
Som in the large feeld, as men may se;

By that fair chain of Love he bound the fire, air, water and land in sure limits so that they could not escape. In this miserable world,' he continued, 'that same Prince, that very Mover, has fixed certain days and durations for all who are born into it and, although they can easily shorten those days, they cannot pass over the day he has fixed. No authority was needed to lay this down as it has already proved by experience but I merely wish to express my opinion about it.

People can clearly see by this order of things that the Mover is firmly established. Again, one can easily see, unless he is a fool, that every part is derived from the whole, for Nature has not taken its origin in any part or portion of anything but only in some things that is perfect and stable and that will deteriorate in a certain way until it is corruptible. And so, by his wise providence, he has arranged it so perfectly that types and progressions of things shall endure by successive examples and still not be everlasting. You can see that at a glance.

'Look at the oak which from the time it first began to spring up has been so long a-growing and, as we can see, endures so long. Yet, in the end, the tree decays.

'Consider also the hard stone beneath our feet on which we tread and walk. It wastes away even as it lies on the road. The broad river sometimes dries up and the great towns we can see decrease and increase. So you can see that every thing must come to an end.

'Among men and women we can also see too that one of two terms is necessary, that is youth or age, for all must die, the king like the page, some in bed, some in the deep sea and, as you know, others in the open fields.

Ther helpeth noght, al goth that ilke weye.
Thanne may I seyn that al this thing moot deye.
What maketh this but Jupiter the king? 3035
The which is prince and cause of alle thing,
Converting al un-to his propre welle,
From which it is deryved, sooth to telle.
And here-agayns no creature on lyve
Of no degree availleth for to stryve. 3040
  'Thanne is it wisdom, as it thinketh me,
To maken vertu of necessitee,
And take it wel, that we may nat eschue,
And namely that to us alle is due.
And who-so gruccheth ought, he dooth folye, 3045
And rebel is to him that al may gye.

And certeinly a man hath most honour
To dyen in his excellence and flour,
Whan he is siker of his gode name;
Than hath he doon his freend, ne him, no shame. 3050
And gladder oghte his freend ben of his deeth,
Whan with honour up-yolden is his breeth,
Than whan his name apalled is for age;
For al forgeten is his vasselage.
Than is it best, as for a worthy fame, 3055
To dyen whan that he is best of name.
The contrarie of al this is wilfulnesse.
Why grucchen we? why have we hevinesse,
That good Arcite, of chivalrye flour
Departed is, with duetee and honour, 3060
Out of this foule prison of this lyf?

Why grucchen heer his cosin and his wyf
Of his wel-fare that loved hem so weel?
Can he hem thank? nay, God wot, never a deel,
That bothe his soule and eek hem-self offende, 3065
And yet they mowe hir lustes nat amende.
  'What may I conclude of this longe serie,
But, after wo, I rede us to be merie,
And thanken Jupiter of al his grace?
And, er that we departen from this place, 3070
I rede that we make, of sorwes two,
O parfyt joye, lasting ever-mo;
And loketh now, wher most sorwe is herinne,
Ther wol we first amenden and biginne.

Nothing avails. All must go the same way. I tell you every thing must die. To tell the truth, who is the cause of this but Jupiter, the King who is the prime cause of every thing, even turning it to its own source from which it has been derived. And no living creature of any degree is strong enough to struggle against it.

'Then I think it is up to our wisdom to make a virtue of necessity and accept what we cannot avoid, and especially what is due to us all, cheerfully. The person who grumbles about it is acting foolishly and is rebellious against Him who can guide us all.

Certainly a person enjoys widespread honour to die in the excellence of his prime when he is sure of gaining a fine reputation, for at that time he will have caused no shame to his friend or himself. Indeed, his friend ought to be better pleased if he should die when his breath is given up with honour than when his good name is weakened through old age and all his prowess has been forgotten. Then, to gain everlasting fame, it is best to die when one is at the height of one's reputation.

To do the opposite of this is sheer wilfulness. Why do we grumble? Why are we so sad that the good Arcite, the flower of chivalry, has died with reverence and honour and has left this foul prison of life?

Why do we begrudge his cousin here and his wife who loved him so well of his good name? Can he show them gratitude? No, God knows, not a bit. Not only do you injure both his soul and himself but also you are not able to do any good for your desires.

'How can I conclude this long series of arguments except to advise you that after trouble you must be happy and thank Jupiter for his favour? Before we go from here, I advise that we should make perfect happiness from two sorrows, a happiness that will last for ever. We can now see where the greatest misfortune lies in this affair so we shall begin to put things right in that quarter.

'Suster,' quod he, 'this is my fulle assent,   3075
With al th'avys heer of my parlement,
That gentil Palamon, your owne knight,
That serveth yow with wille, herte, and might,
And ever hath doon, sin that ye first him knewe,
That ye shul, of your grace, up-on him rewe,   3080
And taken him for housbonde and for lord:
Leen me your hond, for this is our acord.
Lat see now of your wommanly pitee.
He is a kinges brother sone, pardee;
And, though he were a povre bacheler,   3085
Sin he hath served yow so many a yeer,
And had for yow so greet adversitee,
It moste been considered, leveth me;
For gentil mercy oghte to passen right.'

   Than seyde he thus to Palamon ful right: 3090
'I trowe ther nedeth litel sermoning
To make yow assente to this thing.
Com neer, and tak your lady by the hond.'
Bitwixen hem was maad anon the bond,
That highte matrimoine or mariage,   3095
By al the counseil and the baronage.

And thus with alle blisse and melodye
Hath Palamon y-wedded Emelye.
And God, that al this wyde world hath wroght,
Sende him his love, that hath it dere a-boght.   3100
For now is Palamon in alle wele,
Lyvyng in blisse, in richesse, and in hele;
And Emelye him loveth so tendrely,
And he hir serveth al-so gentilly,
That never was ther no word hem bitwene   3105
Of jelousye, or any other tene.
Thus endeth Palamon and Emelye;
And God save al this faire companye! – Amen.

Here is ended the Knightes Tale.

'Sister,' he said, 'the full agreement taken wholly on the advice of my Parliament, is that noble Palamon your own knight, who serves you with his will, heart and might, and has done so ever since you first knew him, shall have the pity of your tender nature and that you shall take him as your lord and husband. As this is our agreement, I want you to give me your hand, so that you can show us an example of a woman's compassion. Indeed, he is the son of a King's brother and – even if he were a poor bachelor, it would be the same – he has served you for so many years and has suffered such great trouble on your behalf that we should remember that tender mercy ought to have more influence that strict justice.'

Then, quite rightly, he said to Palamon, 'I think there is little need for me to make sermons to have you agree to this proposal. Come nearer and take your lady by the hand.' The bond called matrimony or marriage was immediately made between them by all the Council and barons.

And so, with great happiness and music-making, Palamon was wedded to Emily. God who created this whole wide world sent love to him who dearly bought it, for Palamon then lived in great joy, happiness, wealth and health. Emily loved him so dearly and he, in return served her so nobly that there was never any word of jealousy or any other trouble between them.

So ends the story of 'Palamon and Emily' and may God save all this fine company.

Amen.

Chaucer's grammar

It should not be forgotten that, in point of time, Chaucer stands about midway between the days of King Alfred, who died in 899, and our own. We would therefore expect the language he wrote to represent a transitional stage between Old English and Modern English, and this is in fact what we find. There were a number of quite distinct dialects of Middle English in Chaucer's time, and it was partly owing to his prestige that his own speech gained ultimately the mastery; that, and the importance of London. Old English (sometimes still called Anglo-Saxon) was a fully inflected language, closely resembling Modern German in the variety and complexity of its terminations. Modern English has very few inflections, and those it has are very simple to learn. Chaucer's inflections are far fewer than those of King Alfred, though more than our own. What we shall see is that a very large number of the inflections of Old English are represented in Chaucer by the single letter -e, which is as a rule pronounced; in Modern English we often write the -e but do not pronounce it. This is not a complete account of Chaucerian inflection, but it will be a guide to much of his grammar and much of his versification. Some of the inflections in Old English were made by changing the root vowels in both nouns and verbs, and these changes are mostly preserved in Chaucer. But even so, as early as the poet's time, there was a tendency to get rid of irregular or anomalous forms, and to require all words to conform to pattern. We shall now indicate the normal accidence of Middle English as shown in Chaucer's work; the abnormalities will be pointed out in the notes on particular words.

Nouns

There is no standard termination for the nominative and accusative singular. The dative singular is unchanged or ends in -e, and all other cases, singular and plural, end in -es. As sometimes the nominative and accusative end in -e, it must be remembered that a final -e is not a sure sign of the dative singular of a noun. Sometimes also the -es becomes -s in a long word.

Some words have plurals in -en or -n; these are survivals of Old English nouns which had plurals in -an; we still have 'oxen' in Modern English, and a few others.

Prepositions all take the dative case.

Adjectives

A few adjectives end normally in -e in the nominative and accusative singular, but most end in a consonant. In the plural all adjectives end in -e. But when an adjective is preceded by a demonstrative or a possessive adjective, such as 'the', 'his', 'your', it has an -e in all cases, both singular and plural. This form in -e is called the 'weak' form; the uninflected singular is called 'strong'.

The comparatives end in -er, and the superlatives in -este. The ancestors of the modern irregular comparisons are, naturally, found in Chaucer.

Pronouns

These are so like the Modern English pronouns that we shall not need to say much about them. We shall not, however, find forms corresponding to our 'its', 'their' and 'them'. Instead we shall find 'his' used for persons and things, 'hir' (which is easily confused with 'hir', which means 'her') and 'hem' respectively. Sometimes the pronoun 'thou' is attached to the verb when used in an interrogative sentence. We find 'maistow' for 'mayst thou'.

The plural of 'that' is 'tho', not 'those'.

The relatives show the greatest differences from the modern pronouns. Our 'who' is not relative in Chaucer, but interrogative. We find that 'that' is the chief relative if followed by 'he', 'his', or 'him' after an interval of a few words. 'That ... he' will be translated by 'who'; 'that ... his' by 'whose'; and 'that ... him' by 'whom'. 'Whiche' is used as a relative in the singular and plural, for persons and things. We still say: 'Our Father, Which are in Heaven ...'. 'Whose' and 'whom' can be used as relatives, although 'who' cannot. 'Which?' means 'of what kind?' When 'what' is used interrogatively it means 'why?'

The chief indefinite pronoun is 'man', or 'men'. It acts like the French *on* (or the German *man*), and should as a rule be translated by 'one', 'anyone'.

Verbs

These are either strong or weak, according to the method of formation of the past tense and past participle (again as in German). Change of vowel characterizes a strong verb; addition of -ede, -de, or -te to form past tense, and of -ed, -d, or -t to form past participle indicates a weak verb.

The conjugations of typical strong and weak verbs are shown below.

		Strong: to singen	Weak: to maken
Indic. pres. singular	1	singe	make
	2	singest	makest
	3	singeth	maketh
plural 1,2,3		singe(n)	make(n)

Subj. pres. singular	1 singe		make
	2 singe		make
	3 singe		make
	plural 1,2,3 singe(n)		make(n)

Indic. past singular	1 song, sang		made
	2 song(e)		madest
	3 song, sang		made, maked
	plural 1,2,3 songe(n)		made(n), makede(n)

Subj. past singular	1 songe		made
	2 songe		made
	3 songe		made
	plural 1,2,3 songe(n)		made(n)

Imperative	singular	sing	make
	plural	singeth, singe	maketh, make

Participles	present	singing(e)	making(e)
	past	ysonge(n)	ymaked, maad

Infinitive	present	singe(n)	make(n)

There is a tendency for a final -n to drop off.

Adverbs

Many adverbs resemble the weak adjective, having the -e ending; others add -ly or -liche to the adjective. Those in the first group lose their -e eventually, and give us the phenomenon of adjectives and adverbs of the same form in Modern English: e.g. He runs fast, He is a fast runner.

Chaucer's pronunciation

Chaucer's English is the East Midland dialect. For a considerable time before the Conquest the language of government and literature had been West Saxon, the dialect of King Alfred's capital, Winchester. After the Conquest the French language predominated in ruling, educated and, therefore, literary circles, the various dialects of English being restricted to the uneducated. Gradually, however, in the fourteenth century the English language took over from the French language as the language of the state, government and literature, and it was the East Midland dialect of London and the Home Counties, where lay the seats of court, government and the universities, that became the standard.

This Standard English was the combination of the Old English, or Anglo-Saxon, and French, and this is reflected in Chaucer's vocabulary and pronunciation. In Chaucer we find the beginning of English literature as we now know it; the acceptance of an English language, with Saxon and French words blended into an 'English tongue', understood by all people. Chaucer's works were probably intended to be read aloud to an audience – at Court or to friends. If we can learn to read Chaucer with as near the original pronunciation as possible, the wit, beauty and humour will become clearer; and at the same time the meaning of many of those words made difficult for us by archaic spelling will be clarified. A good guide is to pronounce the words of French origin as if they were French, and words of Anglo-Saxon origin as if they were German.

It would be easier, and more fun, to learn the pronunciation of Chaucer's English by listening to gramophone records of Chaucer's poetry in what is considered to be the original pronunciation. Several recordings have been made of modern scholars reading Chaucer. We particularly recommend the reading of the Prologue to The Canterbury Tales (Argo, PLP 1001) mentioned at the end of the Bibliography, p. 6. However, it will be helpful to study the following table, which indicates approximately Chaucer's pronunciation:

Vowels

Words of English origin

Short vowels

'a' pronounced like 'a' in French *placer*; but not like 'a' in English 'cat'.

'e' pronounced like 'e' in Modern English 'men'.

'i' pronounced like 'i' in 'pin'. 'y' is often written for 'i', and has the same sound as 'i'.

'o' pronounced like 'o' in 'not'. Before letters written with a number of short strokes, like 'm, n,' and especially a combination of these two, 'o' is written for 'u', but should be pronounced like 'u', as for example, in 'comen, love, somer, monk'.

'u' pronounced like 'u' in 'pull', or like 'oo' in 'soot'; but not like 'u' in 'duke'.

Long vowels

It is often possible to recognize a long vowel by its being duplicated in writing. For example 'taak' contains a long 'a'; 'sooth' contains a long 'o'.

'a' pronounced like 'a' in 'father'.

'e' pronounced like 'e' acute or like 'e' grave in French. Only a knowledge of the origin of the words in Old English can guide the reader to distinguish between the close and open sounds, as they are called, in Chaucer; but the former sound is usually represented in Modern English by 'ee', and the latter by 'ea'. Modern English 'need' had a close vowel in Old English, where it was spelt 'nēd'; Modern English 'mead', a meadow, was 'mēd' in Old English with an open vowel. As an indication that these two vowels had distinct sounds, we may note that Chaucer very rarely makes them rhyme.

'i' (often written 'y'), pronounced like 'ee' in 'feel'.

'o' pronounced either like 'o' in 'so', or like 'a' in 'call'. Chaucer recognizes the different pronunciations just as he distinguishes the two long 'e' sounds. In Modern English the former sound is represented by 'oo', as in 'soon' while the latter is like the vowel sound in 'note'.

'u' pronounced like 'oo' in 'soon'.

Diphthongs

'ai, ei, ay', and 'ey' pronounced like the diphthong in 'day', though some authorities believe they were sounded like 'i' in 'line'.

'au, aw' pronounced like 'ou' in 'house'; but not before the combination '-ght' like the 'o' in 'not'.

'eu, ew' pronounced like 'ew' in 'few'.

'oi, oy' pronounced like 'oy' in 'boy'.

'ou, ow' pronounced like 'u', or like 'au, aw'.

In words of French origin

Such of these words as had already become part and parcel of the everyday speech would obey the rules for the pronunciation of English vowel sounds; the others would retain the vowels of the French language, which were sounded much as they are today.

In unaccented syllables

The final '-e' so common at the end of a line and elsewhere is sounded like the second syllable of the word 'china'.

Consonants

The consonants had generally the same pronunciation as they have today, with certain slight modifications.

There were no silent consonants, unless, as some scholars believe, the 'g' before 'n' is not sounded.

'kn' is pronounced as in Modern German.

'gg' is pronounced like the 'dge' in Modern English 'ridge'.

'gh' as in Modern German may be either palatal or guttural, according to whether it is preceded by a palatal or a guttural vowel.

'ng' is sounded as in southern English 'fin-ger', not as in 'sing-er'.

'th' (initial) is sounded as in 'thin', not as in 'then'.

'ch' in words of both English and French origin is pronounced like the 'ch' of Modern English 'choose'.

'w' before 'r' is pronounced like a rapidly sounded 'oo'.

'h' in words of French origin and in words like 'he, him', which are rarely emphasized, is silent; but in most words of English origin an initial 'h' is sounded. Where the metre demands that a final '-e' should be elided before an 'h', that 'h' is silent.

Final 'f' is founded as 'f', and not as 'v'.

Final 's' is sounded as 's', and not as 'z'.

Chaucer's use of the final -e

It is important to say something about the function of the final -e found at the end of many words in Chaucer's verse. At the beginning of the fourteenth century these were generally sounded as separate syllables, but by the end of the century they were coming into disuse. In Chaucer's verse the final -e may represent an inflexional change in a noun, an adjective, or a verb; or it may be what is left of a word-ending in Old

English. There are many explanations of this termination, and the following rules usually apply in Chaucer:

1 The final -e is usually sounded, except when

(a) it is slurred over before a word beginning with a vowel (e.g. Of deerne love he koude and of solas): before certain words beginning with 'h'; any part of the verb to have (e.g. a clerk-hadde litherly biset his while); the adverbs heer, how, and a silent 'h' as in honour, him and hem (e.g. For for no cry hir maide koude him calle).

(b) it is sometimes cropped in some words in common use as were, wolde.

2 The final -e should always be sounded at the end of a line.

Chaucer's versification

Chaucer's verse is not difficult to read. As Professor Manly remarks, 'The general principles of stress and movement in Chaucer's language and in his verse-patterns are, so far as we can discover, essentially the same as for present English.' The main difference is that a great many of Chaucer's words end in an unstressed final -e, -en, or -es. It has already been mentioned that the final -e of any Chaucerian line must always be pronounced (as the final -a is pronounced in 'china'), together with many other final syllables within the line itself if the verse is to scan. Chaucer was a master crafts-man, with an ear for subtle rhythm, and in practice many final syllables were either slurred or suppressed altogether.

The *Knight's Tale* is written throughout in what are called heroic, or decasyllabic, couplets. Each line has ten syllables, normally, and the lines rhyme in pairs. These ten syllables are divided into five groups of two, known as feet. In most lines an unaccented syllable begins the foot, and is followed by an accented one. Such a line is No. 893

Thĭs dúk, ŏf whóm Ĭ mákĕ ménciŏún.

Note that 'make' has two syllables and that 'mencioun' has three. The second line of the couplet is 'scanned' similarly

Whĕn hé wăs cóm(e) ălmóst ŭntó thĕ tóun

except that the 'e' in 'come' is elided in front of the 'a' of 'almost'.

A long poem, and the *Knight's Tale* is 2,250 lines long, accented regularly as are lines 893 and 894, would almost certainly send listeners to sleep, and it was for hearers, not readers, that Chaucer was writing, for the art of printing was not common in England till a century or so after his time. Among the devices he adopted to vary the monotony of his verses was that of an extra syllable, lightly accented, at the end of both lines of a couplet. Lines 863 and 864 illustrate this expedient, for 'sónnĕ' and 'wónnĕ' are dissyllables. Further examples are to be noticed in lines 903 and 904, and indeed throughout the poem. Sometimes his line has nine syllables only.

In every decasyllabic line there is a pause known as a caesura: it is found normally after the fourth or fifth syllable and sometimes indicated by a comma in printed editions. In line 893, however, it follows the second syllable: in line 906 it follows the seventh. In this way also variety is introduced, and must have been welcome to the listeners.

Textual notes

The character of the Knight from the Prologue to *The Canterbury Tales*, lines 43–78

43. **worthy** Respected, notable, distinguished. (Do not translate as *worthy*.)

44–5. **that . . . he** Who.
to ryden out To join a military expedition.

46. **freedom** Liberality.
curtesye Courtly conduct.

47. **his lordes werre** Possibly the Hundred Years' war, or perhaps a kind of crusade.

48. **therto** In addition, moreover. It does not refer to 'werre' in 47.

49. **as wel . . . as** Not only . . . but also.
hethenesse Heathen lands.

51–66. He had campaigned against the Turks in the Eastern Mediterranean, against the Moors in the Western Mediterranean, and against the heathen of North-easter Europe.

51. Alexandria was captured by Christian knights in 1365.

53. **the bord bigonne** Taken the head of the table, a place of honour.

53–60. **Pruce** is Prussia, **Lettow**, Lithuania; **Ruce**, Russia; **Gernade** is Granada in Spain; **Algezir,** Algeciras, a Moorish stronghold in Southern Spain, taken in 1344.
Belmarye Now Benmarin, is in Southern Morocco.
Lyeys and **Satalye** Now Ayas and Adalia respectively, were important ports of Asia Minor and opposite Cyprus: they were captured by the Christian knights in 1367 and 1361 respectively.
The Grete See Is the Mediterranean.
Tramyssene Is in Western Algeria, and **Palatye**, now Balat, is in Asia Minor. The Knight was indeed a far-travelled man.

71. **maner wight** Kind of person, person at all.

74. **hors were** Horses were.

78. **pilgrimage** Journey to Canterbury to give thanks for a safe return.

'Who shal telle the firste tale'? – lines 822 to 858

822. The host of the Tabard had suggested that on the way to Canterbury and back each member of the party should tell two tales, and that the pilgrim who told what was by common consent the best tale should have a supper at the Tabard when they had returned to London. They retired to rest and were called at daybreak to begin the journey.
A-morwe In the morning.
whan that When.

823. **oure aller cok** The one who roused us all, as the cock is supposed to believe that he rouses the sun.

826. **the wateryng of Saint Thomas** This is a brook by the second milestone from London on the Old Kent Road. Here the pilgrims would water their horses. St Thomas is St Thomas à Becket.

·827. **bigan his hors areste** Stopped his horse.

830. If what is sung in the morning agrees with what was sung at night.

832. 'As I hope always to be able to drink wine or ale' – a mild oath.

839. **cometh neer** Come nearer.
neer Is comparative of **neh,** meaning nigh.

840. The two clerical members of the party seem to have drawn back.

847. **as was resoun** As was only right.

849. **what nedeth** What is the need of.

851. **as he that wys was** As one who was wise.

The Knight's Tale – lines 859 to 3108

The nine Latin words, from the poem known as *The Thebaid* by
the Latin poet Statius who wrote at the end of the first century
AD, may be translated: 'and now [nearing] his native land in a
chariot decked with laurel, [Theseus] after his hard battles
against the Scythians ...'

860. **duk** This title was introduced into England as part of the
feudal system; translate by 'ruler' or 'lord'.

Theseus Is a character from romance and not from history. He
is said to have killed the Minotaur, a monster with a man's body
but a bull's head; to have become King of Athens, and joined an
expedition to Thebes in Central Greece. Later he overcame the
Amazons and married their Queen Hippolyta (see line 868).
Chaucer apologizes to his readers – or perhaps we should say that
the Knight apologizes to his hearers as they went along the road
to Canterbury – for not telling us more about him before
introducing him as a leading personage in his tale. He figures
also in Shakespeare's *Midsummer Night's Dream*.

865. **what with** With.

chivalrye Knightly exploits.

866. **regne of Femenye** Kingdom of the women, i.e. of the
Amazons.

867. **Scithia** A district north of the Black Sea.

870. **solempnitee** Pomp, ceremony. Be on your guard against
translating words found in Chaucer by their apparent equivalent
in English. In the course of centuries words in a living language
are apt to change their meaning.

875–84. Boccaccio, to whose *Teseide* Chaucer is indebted for much
of the story he puts into the mouth of the Knight, gives at some
length the details the Knight is omitting (see line 885).

for the nones A phrase meaning 'for the occasion', often used by
Chaucer to complete a line, but without any special significance,
as here, where, however, it makes a rhyme for **Amazones**.

886–7. A brief glance into the countryside through which the
pilgrims were already riding.

889. **nat letten ... noon** A double negative is very commonly

found in Chaucer and his contemporaries. As it happened, it was
the Knight who told the longest tale of them all.

890. **felawe** The word had a more definite meaning than has the
word 'fellow' today. It meant 'member of the party', or 'comrade'.

891. **the soper** Was the prize offered to the teller of the best tale,
the rest of the company contributing to the cost of the meal. It
was to be taken on the return to London at the Tabard Inn, from
which they had set out. The Host was to decide who had acquitted
himself – or herself – best.

892. **ther I lefte** The Knight had digressed after line 874.
ther Where.

895. **his moste pryde** At the height of his pride, as victor.

896. **caste...asyde** Looked from side to side. Notice the vividness
and detail of Chaucer's description.

898. **ladies** The word suggests their high rank.
tweye and tweye Two by two.

901. **nis** Is not. Similarly, in line 875, **nere** Were not.

903. **nolde never** A double negative, for emphasis. 'They would
not stop at all.' (See line 922 etc.)

904. **henten** Is a present indicative. The tense increases the
vividness of the description.

909. **offended** Injured, hurt, ill-treated. The word is more
emphatic than it is today.

910. **telleth** Here the word is a plural imperative. A verb in *-eth*
might also be third person singular indicative, as is **greveth** in
line 917.

914. **to seen and here** The final *-n* in **seen** is used to avoid an
awkward hiatus between **see** and **and** and to secure euphony.

917. **noght** Not at all does your glory grieve us. The word is
emphatic.

920. **gentilesse** Noble nature, kindness, courtesy.

921. **lat thou falle** Do you permit to fall.

923. **that she nath been** Who has not been.
nath Ne + hath.

925–6. false Fickle, untrustworthy: gives no assurance to any condition of life to be prosperous always.

927. t'abyden: To await.
presence Being present, i.e. arrival.

928. Clemence The Goddess of Mercy.

930. might Power.

931. I wrecche Wretched as I am now.

932. King Capaneus was one of the Seven who marched against Thebes, Theseus being another. An account of the expedition was written by Statius, from whom a few words are prefixed to the *Knight's Tale*.

933. starf p.t. of *sterven*, to die. The word nowadays refers to death by hunger, though in some dialects it still means to die of cold, or to be very cold.

936. alle All of us.

938. Creon The tyrant of Thebes, against whom the famous Seven marched.

945. by noon assent On any consideration. The four negatives in this and the next line indicate the strength of Creon's refusal and the horror felt by the widows.

949. gruf Prostrate, face downwards.

950. mercy Pity, compassion.

952. The effect of the appeal of the women is shown vividly in the actions of Theseus; notice throughout the whole of this text the liveliness of Chaucer's narrative.

954. him thoughte It seemed to him. Do not translate by 'he thought'.

955. mat Downcast. The word is the same as 'mate' as used in chess. That a word of Persian origin should be found in English of the fourteenth century indicates how far the game had spread westward. 'Checkmate' means 'the king is helpless', 'check' being a corruption of the word 'shah' or king.

958. in ful good entente With the utmost goodwill.

960–1. Do his utmost to wreak vengeance upon the tyrant Creon.

964. **as he that hadde** As one who had.

967. **to Thebes-ward** Towards Thebes.

968. **go ne ryde** Literally, walk or ride.
neer Nearer.

970. **on his wey** On his journey towards Thebes.

974. **rit** Rides, another vivid present tense after a series of preterites.

975. **Mars** Was the Roman god of war.

977. **feeldes** Fields through which he passed on his way.

978. **the pennon** Was attached to the head of the lance as an indication of the standing of the owner.

979. **y-bete** The exact meaning of this word is in dispute; it may mean 'stamped', or possibly 'embossed' or 'embroidered'.

980. **the Minotaur** Consumed youths and girls sent by the Athenians to Crete until it was slain by Theseus.

984. **alighte faire in a feeld** dismounted in the very field.

990. **wall, sparre and rafter** The phrase suggests the completeness of the destruction. Compare 'lock, stock and barrel.'

994. **it were** It would be. Notice the Knight's anxiety to get to the really important parts of his story. Chaucer is avoiding the mass of detail which his source, Boccaccio's poem, was encumbered with. Boccaccio's poem was 9,896 lines long; Chaucer's, 2,250.

996. **brenninge** Cremation of the bodies.

1000. The Knight again insists on his desire to tell the story without a load of unnecessary detail.

1003. **stille** Quietly.

1004. **as him leste** As it pleased him.

1007. **pilours** Pillagers engaged in some crude form of salvaging.

1010. **thrugh-girt** Pierced through. The verb *girden* is represented in the present-day English 'to gird at', meaning 'pierce through with invective, or scoffing'.

1011. **two yonge knightes** We are here introduced to the 'two noble kinsmen' round whose fortunes the story centres.

by and by side by side.

1012. **bothe in oon armes** Wearing the same coat of arms. Chaucer has assumed that these warriors of so long ago wore coats-of-arms as did noblemen in his own day. He lacked historical perspective.

1013–14. **that oon ... that other** The one ... the other.

1015. **quike** Alive. We retain the word in the phrase 'the quick and the dead'.

1019. They were cousins, their mothers being sisters.

1020–1. Had dragged them out and carried them.
softe Gently.

1029. 'For the term of his natural life; what more need be said?'

1032. **may no gold hem quyte** No gold may ransom them.

1035. As Emelye is to be the heroine of the story, although a passive one, it is right that she should now be described. Otherwise, with Theseus living in 'joye and in honour' and with the others in prison, the action of the story might seem to have come to an end. It may well be assumed that the heroine would still be of surpassing beauty, although 'yeer by yeer' have passed since we first heard of her in line 972.

1041. **she was arisen** The subject of the sentence is 'Emelye' in line 1035. Why has Chaucer repeated it in 'she'?

1045. **do thyn observaunce** do your homage to the delights of spring.

1048. **for to devyse** To describe (her).
fresh Brightly.

1051. **at the sonne upriste** 'Sonne' is in the possessive case, and 'upriste' is governed by 'at' – hence, at the rising of the sun.

1052. **as hir liste** As was pleasing to her.

1053. **party** Probably 'some ... others ...'

1055. **hevenly** Is an adverb. 'Divinely as an angel.'

1057. **dongeoun** The word does not mean 'dungeon', but 'tower'. To avoid confusion, the word is spelt 'donjon' in modern English when a tower is intended.

1060. **evene joynant** Closely adjoining.

1061. **hadde hir pleyinge** Was amusing herself, taking her pleasure.

1065. **romed** Wandered. See also lines 1069, 1071 etc.

1071. **goth** Goes, walks, strides – but in his prison in the tower.

1072. **compleyning of** Bewailing.

1074. **aventure or cas** A common phrase: 'as luck would have it'.

1077. The name is spelt here with a final -*a* to provide a rhyme with the next line.

1082. **on to see** To look at. Arcite puts Palamon's exclamation down to misery at his imprisonment.

1083. **crydestow** Did you cry out.

1088. Saturn is always supposed to have an evil effect on men and women. See lines 2663–2691.

1089. **we hadde it sworn** A difficult clause, probably meaning 'although we had sworn to take our ill-fortune without repining'. Line 1084 points to some such meaning as this.

1090. They had been born under an evil star.

1092. **seyde ageyn** Replied.
of this opinion As regards your statement.

1094. **veyn imaginacioun** mistaken notion.

1097. **that wol my bane be** An adjectival clause with no noun to connect it with.
bane Death.

1099. **romen** Not 'roaming', but 'roam' – an infinitive, meaning 'wander'.

1101. **noot wher** Do not know whether.

1102. **Venus** Is the Goddess of Love. See line 2221, where Palamon prays again to Venus for her help.

1105. **yow ... transfigure** Transform yourself, show yourself in another form.

1107. **that we may scapen** In the word 'we,' he includes Arcite in his petition.

1110. **our linage** Our noble birth. See line 1018.

1112. **gan espye** Espied, noticed.

gan Is used as an auxiliary verb to form the past tense.

1119. **in the yonder place** Over there, i.e. in the garden.

1121. **atte leeste weye** At the very least.

1122. **I nam but deed** I am as good as dead.

1125. **whether seistow this** Do you say this?

whether Is used to ask a question which has two possible answers.
'Do you speak in earnest or in jest?'

1126. **by my fey** On my honour.

1127. **me list** It pleases me.

ful yvele Scarcely at all.

pleye To jest.

1133. **to dyen in the peyne** Even if we should be tortured to death.

1134. **departe** Separate. 'Till death us do part' in the marriage service was originally 'till death us *depart*', or separate.

1137. **forthren me** Further my interests.

1141. **artow of my conseil** You agree with my opinion.

1142. **been about** Are purposing.

1143. The emphasis is on *my* and *I*.

1147. **counseil** Counsellor, advisor.

1152. **spak ageyn** Replied.

proudly Arrogantly, haughtily.

1154. **utterly** Emphatically.

1155. *par amour* With true love.

first er thow First, before you did.

1157. Palamon had declared this in line 1101, and decided he had seen the Goddess Venus. Arcite then contended that his rival loved a goddess, whereas he himself loved a woman.

1163. **the olde clerk** Referred to was Boethius, who had written in his *De Consolatione Philosophiae*, 'Who can lay down a law for lovers?' Quite early in his literary career, Chaucer had translated Boethius.

1164. 'Who shall lay down laws for a lover to obey?'

1165. **by my pan** By my brain-pan, that is, by my reckoning.

1167. **positif lawe** A legal enactment.
swich decree Such a law.

1168. **in ech degree** In every rank of life.

1169. **maugre his heed** In spite of his intelligence. *Amor Vincit Omnia* was on the brooch of the Prioress, who was presumably listening to the story the Knight was telling.

1170. **should be deed** Cost him his life.

1172. 'It is not likely that however long you live you will win her favour.'

1176. **us ... raunsoun** No ransom benefits us.

1178. **hir part was noon** They got no share in it at all.

1181–2. At the king's court each man looks after himself.

1183. **if thee list** If it pleases you.

1188. The Knight again suggests he is pressed for time. After all, each of the pilgrims is to tell four tales before they complete the double journey they are just beginning.

1189. **but to th' effect** To sum it all up.

1192. **felawe** A friend of Theseus since their boyhood. The classical writers, however, say they did not become friends till Theseus had conquered the Amazons.

1195. **to pleye** To enjoy himself.

1200. The story as told by Ovid is that the two 'dukes' went to Hades together in an unsuccessful attempt to rescue Proserpina.

1201. **list me nat to wryte** A strange slip on Chaucer's part, for he had put the story into the mouth of the Knight was was *telling* it along the road to Canterbury. It was not a matter of *writing* at all.

1203. **yeer by yere** Year by year. There were several ways in which a word might be pronounced in Chaucer's time. As he wanted a rhyme for 'preyere' in the next line, he chose the dissyllabic spelling and pronunciation of 'yere' for the final word of this line, while using the monosyllabic 'yeer' also, after the word 'Thebes'.

1207. **wher ... over-al** Wherever he liked.

1208. 'In such a way as I shall explain.' There were restrictions imposed by Theseus to Arcite's free movements.

1209. **forward ... t'endite** The agreement, to put it clearly.

1210. **him Arcite** That Arcite, his captive Arcite. The words 'him' and 'Arcite' are in apposition, referring to the same person.

1216. **remedye ne reed** Means or course of action; nothing else for it.

1217. **taketh** Let him take.
spedde Hurry. (*lit* hurried.)

1218. **to wedde** As a pledge that he will keep away.

1222. **wayteth** Seeks an opportunity.
prively In secret.

1225. **me shape** Destined for me.

1226. **purgatorie** The place of spiritual purifying after death and of preparation for heaven.
helle The place of punishment for the wicked after death.

1231. **only the sighte** The mere sight.

1235. **aventure** Affair, mischance.

1237. 'In prison? Indeed, no; but in Paradise!'
paradys The abode of the blessed. (He continues the use of terms of Christian theology.)

1238. 'Certainly fortune has thrown the dice in your favour.'

1244–5. **bareyne ... grace** Lacking in all good fortune.

1249. 'It is best that I should die.'

1250. **my lust** My delight.

1254. **wel bettre** Far better gifts.

1255. **som man** This man.

1257. 'That man would gladly be out of prison.'

1258. **of his meynee** By his servants.

1259. 'An infinity of suffering arises from the matter of complaining of one's misfortune.'

1268. **namely I** And I in particular.

1272. **ther** Whereas.

1274. **I nam but deed** I am as good as dead.

1275. **up-on that other syde** On the other hand.

1279. **pure fettres** Very fetters.

1282. **al our stryf** All our quarrelling.
the fruyt is thine The advantage is yours.

1283. **now in Thebes** He is anticipating. See line 1355.
at thy large At large, at liberty.

1294. **sterve** Die.
cage Prison.

1301. **lyk ... the box-tree** A strange comparison. The word
'woodly' means 'madly'. An Elizabethan writer says 'the wood
of the box is yelowe and pale', and is possibly repeating some
earlier writer on trees; but no satisfactory explanation is so far
forthcoming.
asshen Refers to the ashes of a wood fire.

1303. **goddes** Gods, not goddess. See lines 1328, 1329, and 1332.

1305. **wryten** The final -*n* is introduced to avoid the awkward
sound of 'wryte' followed by 'in'. There are several examples of
this effort to preserve euphony.
athamaunt Adamant, an imaginary stone of impregnable
hardness.

1306. **parlement** Decree, decision.
graunt Promise.

1307. 'How much more valuable is mankind considered by you
than is a sheep?'

1313–14. 'What sort of considered plan is there in this
foreknowledge which torments the innocent and guiltless?'

1315–18. 'And yet this knowledge that man is bound to keep the
law of God, for God's own sake, increases my suffering. He must
restrain his own wishes, whereas a beast may indulge all his
desires.'

1326. 'Who has done many a true man harm.'

1327. **at his large** Perfectly free.

1328. **Saturne** The planet was supposed to have a banal influence on the human race. Refer to lines 1087–1091, and also lines 2453–2478. Here, however, the God Saturn is referred to.

1329. **Juno** Is said to have destroyed Thebes in anger at the conduct of Jupiter, her husband.

1332. **on that other syde** On the other hand.

1333. **him Arcite** See line 1210.

1335. **stille dwelle** To remain living.

1336. **forth I wol yow telle** Proceed to tell you more.

1338. **double wyse** Twofold.

1340. **mester** Occupation, business, situation to endure.

1343. **to ben deed** To be as good as dead.

1344. **upon his head** Upon pain of losing his life if he returns to Athens. See lines 1211–1215.

1347. The Knight turns to the rest of the pilgrims with his question.

1353. **demeth as yow liste** Form an opinion as seems right to you.

Part 2

1355. Chaucer now tells us something more of the fortunes of Arcite, before turning at line 1450 to deal with Palamon.

1360. **shal** Shall be.

1361. **him biraft** Taken from him.

1362. **wex** Became. In modern English the word frequently means 'become greater', in distinction from 'wane', meaning 'grow less'.

1364. **falwe** Pallid, colourless.

1371. **though men it herde** Although people heard it.

1374. **Hereos** Eros the Greek word for love, is thought to have become confused with the Greek word for hero, and hence its spelling.

1375. **malencolyk** The humours, fluids running through the body, may produce many kinds of mania, according to the medieval physiologists.

1376. **celle fantastyk** The seat of a sullen humour in the front part of the brain. It was supposed to produce melancholy.

1378. **habit and disposicioun** Behaviour and character.

1379. **daun Arcite** Daun is derived from the Latin Dominus: the Lord Arcite.

1380. **what** Why.

1385. **him thoughte** It seemed to him.
Mercurie The messenger of the gods, and himself the God of Dreams.

1386. **murye** Cheerful.

1387. **slepy yerde** Sleep-bringing wand.

1389. **as he took keep** As Arcite noticed.

1390. **Argus** The hundred-eyed servant of Juno, was lulled to sleep before, at Jupiter's command, Mercury slew him.

1392. **is thee shapen** Is prepared for thee.

1394. **smerte** Stings, incites.

1395. **right now** Now an Americanism.

1396. **ne ... nat** The double negative suggests a strong resolution.

1398. 'I count death as nothing so long as I die in her presence.'

1399. **caughte** Took up, seized.

1401. **al in another kinde** Completely changed.

1404. **of maladye** Through the illness.

1405. **bar him lowe** Acted humbly, kept himself to himself.

1407. **seen** Is an infinitive, used with 'mighte' in line 1405.

1411. **privitee and all his cas** His secret and all his affairs.

1412. **which** The squire.
povrely As a poor man.

1413. **the nexte way** The nearest way.

1416. **drawe** Draw water.

what so men wol devyse Whatever they ordered him.

1418. **fil in office** Got employment with.

chamberleyn Officer.

1419. **dwelling with** Employed in her household.

1420. **aspye of** Discover, find out.

1423. **for the nones** Indeed.

1428. **Philostrate** The word means 'laid low by love', or 'become humble for the sake of love'.

1433–4. 'It would be a kindness if Theseus would promote him.'

1436. **his vertu excercyse** Exercise his abilities.

1437–8. 'A report has spread about, not only of his doings but also of his courteous speech.'

1439. **taken him so neer** Taken him so intimately into his own service.

1442. 'And also people brought him his income from his own country, year by year.'

1444. **honestly** Fittingly, honourably.

slyly Prudently. The present day hint of something underhand did not present itself in Chaucer's time.

1447. **bar him so** Behaved, acted.

1448. **that Theseus hath derre** Whom Theseus considers more highly.

1452. **this seven yeer** For three of these years Arcite has been acting as the king's equerry – to use a modern term.

1453. **what for ...** For both sorrow and his affliction.

1455. **that** Whom.

1456. Notice the alliteration in the line.

1458. **perpetually** His was a life sentence.

1459. **ryme** Put into verse.

proprely Adequately.

1460. **it am not I** 'I am not the one.' Is it the Knight or Chaucer who speaks here?

1462. **in May** A month of rejoicing in Chaucer's time for the coming of spring and summer days and festivities. Note that the previous line also ends in the same word – may.

1463. **the thridde night** An exact date gives a sense of actuality to the story.

1465. **aventure or destinee** Chance or fate.

1468. **brak** Past tense, is followed by several verbs in the present, a device to make the incident more vivid.

1470. **so** Is followed in sense by the 'that' in line 1473.

1471. **clarree** A wine mixed with honey and spices.

1472. **Thebes** Strange to find this name again and in this connection.
opie Opium.
nercotikes Drugs to induce sleep.

1475. **faste** Quickly.

1476. **faste by** Very near.

1478. **til** To. More usual in northern than in midland or southern English.
faste Close.

1479. **dredful** Cautious.
stalketh Moves stealthily.

1480. **opinioun** Intention.

1484. To beg his friends to help him make war on Theseus.

1485. **outher ... or** Either ... or.

1487. **th'effect** The intention.
entente Purpose.
pleyn Obvious.

1489. **care** Anxiety, what he should fear, what would cause him trouble.

1490. The next six lines are often found in anthologies as showing Chaucer's delight in the springtime.

1493. **Phebus** The sun.

1499. **myrie** Not merry, but pleasant, delightful.

1500. **his observaunce** Customary greeting.

1501. **the poynt of his desyr** Namely, the purpose he had uppermost in his mind, the winning of Emelye.

1502. **sterting** Leaping, as a fire does.

1503. **him to pleye** To amuse himself, to occupy his mind.

1504. **were it** Perhaps.

1505. See lines 1478–87.

1506. **gan to holde** Began to take.
gan Not followed by to indicates a past tense.

1507. **greves** Here twigs, rather than the usual 'boughs'.

1509. **ageyn the sonne shene** Towards the bright sun.

1512. **som grene** A green garland, something green.

1514. **sterte** Leapt, plunged.

1516. **ther-as, by aventure** Where, by chance.
this Palamoun The word 'this' has the added notion of 'our hero' or 'the Palamon we have just been hearing about'. Note that the name is spelt here with a final -*oun* to rhyme with 'doun'.

1519. **no-thing** Not at all.

1520. **wolde have trowed it ful lite** Would hardly have believed it.

1521. 'But the truth was said, many a year ago, that a field has eyes and a wood has ears.'

1523. 'It is a good thing for a man to preserve some kind of balance, for we are continually meeting what we least expect to.'

1524. **unset stevene** An hour not pre-arranged.

1526. **al his sawe** All he was saying.

1529. **the roundel** See lines 1510–12. A roundel is a short poem of complicated construction.

1530. **a studie** A reverie, or 'brown study'; a state of mental abstraction.

1531. **thise lovers** Lovers in general.
queynte geres Strange fashion.

1534. **Friday** In Latin, is *dies Veneris*, or the day of Venus, who is described in line 1536 as 'gery' or inconstant. (The English word 'Friday' means the day of Freya, the Goddess of Love in northern mythology.)

1538. **changeth she array** She changes her dress.

1539. **al the wyke y-lyke** Like the rest of the week.

1543. In line 1329 Palamon makes a similar reference to Juno and her responsibility for the destruction of Thebes.

1546. **Cadme and Amphioun** Cadmus, son of a king of Phoenicia, was the reputed founder of Thebes. Amphioun was so skilful a musician that, when he played on the lyre which Hermes had given him, the stones with which Thebes was being fortified moved into their places of their own accord!

1551. **verray ligne** True descent.
stok royal Royal line.

1553. **he** Would have no place in a Modern English construction. Omit it in translation.
povrely In poverty.

1557. **highte** Be called.

1558. 'Not worth a farthing.'

1560. **al fordo** Quite destroyed.

1561. Palamon was listening to Arcite's complaint. An instance of irony, for Palamon was not in prison, but had actually escaped.

1565. **my trewe careful herte** My faithful troubled heart.

1566. **erst than my sherte** Even before my first garment was made – that is, before I was born. He was predestined to this death from babyhood.

1570. **mountance of a tare** That is, of no value at all.

1571. **to your plesaunce** To win your favour.

1574. **this Palamoun** i.e. our hero Palamon.

1578. **deed and pale** As pale as death.

1592. **astert by grace** Escaped by good fortune.

1593. **I drede noght** I doubt not.

1596. **this Arcite** Compare 'this Palamoun', line 1574, and elsewhere.

1599. **nere** Were it not.
wood Mad.

1603. 'So that thou shouldst escape dying at my hand.'

1604. **defye** Mistrust, do not honour.

1606. **verray fool** True fool, complete fool.

1610. **have heer my trouthe** Accept my word of honour.

1612. **as a knight** In knightly array.

1616. **clothes** Coverings.

1619. **as for me** As far as I am concerned.

1620. **I graunte it thee** I agree to your suggestion.

1622. 'When each of them had pledged his faith.'

1623. **out of alle charitee** Without any goodwill.

1624. 'That wilt have none equal to thee.'

1626. **his thankes** With goodwill, willingly.

1627. **wel finden that** Find that to be true.

1628. **anon** At once.

1631. **mete to darreyne** Suitable for the contest.

1633. **allone as he was born** i.e. he had no one with him.

1636. **ben met** Have met.

1638. **regne of Trace** Kingdom of Thrace, in Greece.

1639. **at the gappe** At the gap in the thicket.

1646. **if that me mishappe** If that misfortune be mine.

1650. **rehersing** Repeating the conditions.

1654. **wonder longe** For a remarkably long time.

1658. **gonne they to smyte** They began smiting one another.

1659. **ire wood** Mad anger.

1661. **lete hem fighting dwelle** Let them remain fighting.

1663. Fate the general functionary . . .

1667. **by ye or nay** One way or the other.

1669. **falleth nat eft** Happens not again.

1672. **sighte above** Providence.

1673. **by mighty Theseus** In the case of mighty Theseus.

1676. **ther daweth him** There dawns no day for him.

1681. **bane** Killer.

1682. **Diane** Diana, the Goddess of Hunting.

1687. **be they riden** Had they ridden.

1691. **launde** An open space between woods.

1694. **han a cours at him** Have a run at him.

1697. **under the sun** Shading his eyes from the sun's rays, towards the sun.

1703. 'Who they were he had no idea at all.'

1710. **mister men** Sort of men (O.F. *mester* means profession or trade.)

1715. **what nedeth** What need is there for.

1717. **caytyves** Wretched men.

1718. **encombered of** Weary of.

1721. **seynte charitee** Holy charity.

1725. **on his heed** Upon pain of losing his head if found in thy kingdom. (See line 1215.)

1736. **it am I** I am he.

1738. **present** At once.

1743. **a short conclusioun** A quick way of deciding the matter.

1746. **pyne you with the corde** That is, hang you.

1747. Theseus evidently intends to kill them at once with his sword, but is restrained by the tears of the ladies in the company.

1752. **chaunce sholde falle** Event – their execution – should happen.

1754. 'The quarrel was for love and nothing else.'

1756. **lasse and more** Of higher or lower rank. The incident recalls lines 919–21.

1761. **for pitee renneth sone in gentil herte** This sentiment has been called Chaucer's favourite one. It appears four times in his poems.

1765–9. His anger betrayed that they were guilty, but he realized that their faults were pardonable. Any man would take up arms on behalf of a loved one, and also to free himself from prison.

1771. **ever in oon** Always without ceasing, constantly.

1773–4. **fy up-on a lord** That lord is to be despised.

1777. **proud despitous man** Proud scornful man.

1778. 'Who will persist in the course he began.'

1780. **can no divisioun** Recognizes no difference.

1781. 'But considers pride and humility as of equal worth.'

1783. **gan to loken** Began to look. (Note – 'gan loken' would mean 'looked'.)

1784. **al on highte** Aloud.

1785. *benedicite* May he be blessed by all.

1787. **gayneth none obstacles** No obstacles can prevail.

1790. **as ... devyse** Whatever it pleases him to make.

1795. 'I have power over their life or death.'

1796. **maugree hir eyen two** In spite of what they could plainly see.

1799. 'It is a lover who is the real fool.'

1803. **for hir servyse** For their service to him.

1806. 'the best joke of all.'

1807. **jolitee** All this fun.

1808. 'can thank them for it as much as she thanks me.'

1809–10. 'She knows no more of all these wild goings-on than does a cuckoo or a hare; creatures living in these very woods.' (A cuckoo is traditionally a foolish bird, and a hare is always mad in March – though this is actually May.)

1814. **a servant** That is, a slave of the God of Love.

1826. **swore his axing** Swore to carry out what he asked them.

1828. It will be noticed from the light touches in this speech that Theseus has genuinely forgiven the two men.

1829. **to speke of** With regard to.

1837. **al ... leef** Whether it be distressing or joyful to him.

1838. **go pypen on an ivy-leef;** Whistle on an ivy-leaf – or do anything else quite useless – because his rival and not he has won the lady.

1841. **in this degree** Into this position.

1844. **your ende** The upshot so far as you are concerned.

1845. **plat conclusioun** Final decision.

1847. 'If it pleases you, accept it as the best solution of your problem.'

1849. 'Without any payment of ransom or any personal danger.'

1850. **fer ne ner** Neither later nor sooner.

1852. **at alle rightes** In every detail.
armed for listes Armed for a tournament.

1854. **bihote I yow** I promise you.

1856. **whether of yow bothe** Which of you two.

1860. 'To him will I give Emelye as his wife.' (**to wyve** does not mean 'to marry', as 'wyve' is a noun, not a verb.)

1863–4. 'And even as God shall show pity on my soul, so shall I be a fair judge and a true.'

1865–6. 'You shall make no other bargain with me than that one of you shall be dead or captured.'

1868. **holdeth yow apayd** Consider you have got your deserts.

1869. 'This is the end and decision, so far as you are concerned.'

1874. 'had been so gracious to them.'

1875. **every maner wight** Every kind of person.

1879. **gonne they ryde** They rode.

Part 3

1884. **maken up** Prepare.

1886. As Chaucer himself had been Clerk of the Works to King Richard II, we may assume that he was critical of Boccaccio's description of the construction of the 'listes' as found in the *Teseide*. Indeed, he modified some of the statements of the original and made certain additions.

1890. **degrees** Steps.

pas Paces or yards.

1892. 'He did not prevent his fellow from seeing.'

1896. **space** Time for its erection.

1897. **crafty** Skilful. Notice how the meaning of this word has deteriorated with the years.

1898. 'Who knows his geometry or arithmetic.'

1900. **that Theseus ne yaf him** To whom Theseus did not give.

1901. **devyse** Design.

1903. **hath ... don make an auter** Has had an altar made.

1906. **in the minde and in memorie** These words seem to have little or no meaning; probably some scribe copying a manuscript has been at fault. It is usually supposed that Chaucer may have written something meaning 'on the gate and in memory and honour'.

1908. **largely** With due ceremony.

fother Cartload. The splendour of the altar and oratory seems to have encouraged some exaggeration.

1912. **Dyane of chastitee** Diana, Protectress of chastity.

1913. **don wroght** Had made. Chaucer now proceeds to describe in great detail the characteristics of each of the temples.

1918. **maystow** A contraction of 'mayst thou'.

1920. **sykes colde** Sighs of hopelessness.

1921. **sacred teres** Tears of the devotees of Venus.

1923. **loves servaunts** Those who serve Venus.

1924. 'The oaths that confirm their promises.'

1926. **bauderie** Gaiety, mirth.

1929. **goldes** Marigolds.

1930. **cokkow** Cuckoo. Yellow has often been associated with jealousy, and a cuckoo is well-known for its habit of driving another bird off its own nest.

1932. **alle the circumstaunces** Accompaniments, characteristics.

1936. **soothly** Truly, indeed.

the mount of Citheroun Was sacred to Bacchus and the Nine Muses; it was on the island of Cythera that Venus had her dwelling, not on Mount Citheroun.

1939. **lustinesse** Delights, pleasures. The word in Chaucer's time had no unpleasant suggestion.

1940. **the porter Ydelnesse** Vanity or Indolence.

1941. **Narcisus** He did not return the love Echo had for him. In consequence he was caused to fall in love with his own reflection, and so pined to death.

1942. **the folye of King Salamon** Solomon, the son of David, King of Israel, was one whose amorous desires knew little restraint.

1943. **Hercules** After death he received almost divine honours, for he had devoted his great strength to the service of mankind; but he also was no constant lover.

1944. **Medea** Used her enchantments to help Jason to win the famous Golden Fleece. **Circe's** enchantments turned the companions of Ulysses into swine.

1945. **Turnus** Mentioned in the Aeneid, fought Aeneas to secure the love of Lavinia.

1946. **Cresus** The rich King of Lydia, wretched in slavery to Cyrus, King of Persia.

1948. **sleighte** Skill, cleverness.

1949. **holde champartye** Maintain any equality.

1950. **hir list** It pleases her.

1954. **and though** Although.

1959. **citole** A stringed instrument, possibly a sort of lyre or harp.

1967. Chaucer now proceeds to tell of the decorations inside the Temple of Mars.

1971. **estres** The interior.

1972. **the grete temple of Mars in Trace** This was sited under Mount Haemus, 'with snows eternal crowned'.

1983. **thentree** The entrance.

1984. **streit** Narrow (not straight).

1987. **northern light** The dull light from the north, as contrasted with that from the south.

1990. **adamant** A substance of impregnable hardness.

1991. **y-clenched** Riveted.
overthwart and endelong From side to side, and top to bottom.

1994. **tonne-greet** As huge as a tun, or barrel.

1995. **saugh I** It is surprising to find the first person pronoun here. It recurs several times in the Knight's account of this temple and that of Diana. His hearers could hardly suppose he had actually visited the places he is speaking of, especially as he is speaking of ancient times. The lines which follow are notable for their enumeration of the horrors found in the pavilion of the God of War.
imagining of felonye What a wicked man could imagine and carry out.

1998. **pale drede** Ghastly fear.

2000. **shepne** Cow-house. The word exists still in dialect as 'shippon'; it does not refer to sheep, but rather to shop or shed.

2002. **bibledde** covered with blood.

2004. **chirking** A strident noise, screaming.
sory Dreadful.

2007. **shode** Temple, parting of the hair.

2009. **temple** The Temple of Mars, which Chaucer is describing.
meschaunce Calamity. Many of the abstractions are now personified.

2011. **woodnesse** Madness.

2014. **nat ... y-storve** Not slain by disease.

2017. **shippes hoppesteres** Ships rocked by the waves.
(**hoppesteres** Means female dancers.)

brent Burned.

2019. **freten ... cradel** Devour ... in its very cradle.

2020. **for al** In spite of.

2021. **infortune of Marte** Malign influence of Mars.

2022. 'The charioteer run over by his own chariot.'

2024. **Martes divisioun** The sphere of influence of Mars. There seems some confusion between Mars, the God of War, and Mars, the planet. See later lines.

2025. **barbour** In the Middle Ages the barber was a crude surgeon and dentist, and so one who shed blood. The smith made knives, swords etc.

2028. **conquest sitting in greet honour** The reference is to Damocles, who was invited by his master to experience what Damocles so much envied, namely the chief position at a banquet. Over his head and suspended by a single hair was a naked sword.

2030. **sotil** Slight, thin.

2031–2. **Julius Caesar** Was stabbed by Brutus and the other conspirators in Rome.
Nero Killed himself after a revolt of his subjects, while **Mark Antony** committed suicide after his defeat in the sea-fight at Actium.

2033. A humorous insertion. The three just mentioned had not been born at the time Chaucer is telling about, but by the influence of Mars – he says – the manner of their deaths was shown as they were to be read by astrologers in the stars above.

2040. The Knight says he could have told of others who would die in battle or for love, but he has refrained.

2043. **figures of sterres** There has always been a craving to discover what the future holds for us. Among devices for this purpose was that of jotting down four rows of dots, without regarding how many dots each row contained. If on being counted a row was found to contain an odd number, that fact was recorded by a conspicuous dot placed separately. If the number was even, two dots were recorded, side by side. If by chance the four rows of conspicuous dots made this figure

an arrangement known as Rubeus – it was taken to mean
that Mars would help the enquirer, Rubeus meaning red. Should
the resulting figure be

to which the name of Puella is given here – Mars would also
avail. (It is thought, however, that this second arrangement
should be named Puer – the Boy – rather than Puella – the
Girl – who would naturally be aided by Venus; but the whole
matter is very obscure.) The 'figures of stars' would be the two
diagrams shown above.

2051. The third 'auter and oratorie', that of Diana, is now
described.

2055. **Diana** Was Goddess of Hunting – 'queen and huntress,
chaste and fair', wrote Ben Jonson.

2056. **Calistopee** Was changed into a bear by Diana on account
of her unchaste association with Jupiter, who as a kind of
compensation, changed her again into the constellation now
known as the Great Bear. (The **lode-sterre**, however, is in the
Little Bear.) Her son became the constellation Boötes.

2062. **Dane** Is Daphne. She prayed to be rescued from pursuit by
Apollo and was changed into a laurel.

2065. **Attheon** Or Acteon, chanced to see Diana bathing and was
thereupon changed into a hart. His own dogs then set upon him
and he was killed.

2069. **forther-moor** A little farther on.

2070. **Atthalante** Atalanta was renowned for her fleetness of foot.

2071. **Meleagre** Was associated with Atalanta in the hunting of
the wild boar of Calydon. Diana is said to have killed him as he
was held to be the father of Atalanta's child.

2074. me list nat It is not my pleasure.

2085. Lucyna gan she calle She called on Lucyna, the name Diana bore as helper of women in childbirth.

2087. he peynten lyfly that it wroghte The artist who painted it did it to the life.

2088. Something of an anticlimax suggesting that the artist had gone to some expense to procure the best paints. Florins were originally of gold, and were first coined in England in 1337; having a flower on the obverse side, the coin was known by the Latin word for a flower – florem. Silver florins were first coined in England in 1849.

2089. thise listes Chaucer began his account of the lists at line 1881.

been Are.

2092. him lyked wonder wel It pleased him wondrously well.

2095. Refer to lines 1845–1880 for a reminder of what instructions Palamon and Arcite had received from Theseus.

2098. hir ... holde Fulfilling their promise to Theseus.

2100. at alle rightes Exactly carrying out the stipulations they had to fulfil.

2103. knighthod of hir hond The knightly deeds done by their hands, their prowess in former days.

2105. of so fewe Considering how few there were, for there were only two hundred altogether.

nas Was not.

2107. his thankes Of his own free will.

a passant name Surpassing reputation.

2108. of that game One in that enterprise.

2109. wel was him Good fortune was to him, he was fortunate.

2110. 'If such an opportunity occurred tomorrow.'

2112. loveth paramours Loves passionately. Here 'paramours' has the force of an adverb.

2114. Chaucer's Knight's prophecy has been proved true over and over again in our history – and elsewhere.

2115. **ben'cite** A contraction of *benedicite* – praise be to God. (See line 1785.)

2117. **ferden they** Did they do.

2119. For the armour and equipment see the description of Knight himself – lines 73–76.
wol ben Chose to be.

2121. **peyre plates large** 'Peyre' and 'plates' are in apposition to one another and the word 'of' is therefore not required. The plates were worn over the habergeon as extra protection.

2122. **a Pruce sheld** A Prussian shield. A notable error in time: Theseus could not have seen such a shield. The Knight, however, as line 53 of the *General Prologue* mentions, had himself been in Prussia, so the fault on his lips may be pardoned if any of his hearers noticed it. Possibly line 2125 is his apology.

2124. **mace of steel** A heavy club, often with a spiked head.

2129. **Ligurge him-self** Lycurgus was a famous lawgiver in Sparta about 800 BC.

2133. **a griffon** Is an imaginary monster, with the body of a lion but with the legs, and from the shoulder to the head, of an eagle.

2142. **for-old** Very old. 'For-' is frequently used as an intensive prefix.

2156. **Emetreus, the king of Inde** Was the most notable figure on Arcite's side. He is an invention of Chaucer's and unknown to history.

2157. **trapped in steel** With steel trappings.

2158. **diapred** With the pattern consisting of lines crossing diamond-wise with the spaces filled up with parallel lines, leaves, dots etc.

2160. **cloth of Tars** A rich cloth of silk, probably of Eastern origin, and possibly deriving its name from Tartary.

2165. **lyk ringes was y-ronne** Clustered together in ringlets.

2168. **sangwyn** Fresh, ruddy.

2169. **y-spreynd** Scattered.

2170. **y-meynd** Mingled, mixed.

2171. **he his loking caste** He glared around.

2172. Two lines here rhyme with identical words. Chaucer seems to allow such rhymes if the two words concerned have different derivations, and meanings.

caste Here means calculate.

2181. **alle maner thinges** Every respect. 'Maner' and 'thinges' are in apposition.

2182. **trusteth wel** Be assured.

trusteth Is a plural imperative.

2185. **every part** All sides.

2187. **alle and some** One and all.

2188. **ben come** Are come, came, arrived.

2189. **in the toun alight** Dismounted in the town, i.e. Athens.

2190. **this duk** This illustrious monarch.

2191. **had broght hem** He met them before they had actually reached the 'toun'.

2192. **inned hem** Found them accommodation.

2193–4. 'Takes so much trouble to put them at their ease, to show them every respect.'

2195. 'That even now it is thought that the skill of no one of whatever rank could improve on it.'

2206. **of al this make I now no mencioun** Chaucer is not going into the details which Boccaccio indulged in. The Knight who is telling the tale to the pilgrims along the road to Canterbury must not take up too much of the time; there are many others who may wish to compete for the prize for the best story. These considerations provide Chaucer with an excellent reason for avoiding unnecessary matter. That he did so is a tribute to his artistry.

2211. **it nere nat day** It were not yet day.

2215. **the blisful Citherea** Venus: but see line 1936.

2217. **in hir houre** In the time dedicated to her. Thomas Tyrwhitt (1730–86), the first editor of Chaucer, has a long note in

explanation of the hours belonging to the different deities, whose
names appear in this order: Saturn, Jupiter, Mars, Sun, Venus,
Mercury, Moon. The first hour of each day belonged to the
planet to which the day 'belonged', the next hour to the next
planet on the list, and so on. As Palamon got up on Sunday night,
two hours before Monday began – and Monday belonged to the
Moon – he rose during that part of the day or night dedicated
to Venus, who comes two places before the Moon in the list.
Fittingly then he prayed to Venus at that hour. We are told that
Emelye rose at sunrise on Monday, so that her rising coincided
with the hour devoted to the Moon Goddess, namely Diana. (See
line 2274.) Arcite – line 2367 – rose three hours later when
Mars would be the ruling deity.

a pas At walking pace.

2223. **glader** One who makes glad; gladdener.

2224. **Adoun** Is Adonis. He was loved by Venus, and such was
her grief at his death that he was allowed by the gods to spend
half the year in the upper world.

2229. **biwreye** Disclose, reveal. The word appears in the
authorised version of the Bible; 'thy speech bewrayeth thee' was
said to Peter at the time of the trial of Jesus.

2230. **can noght seye** Can hardly speak.

2231. **mercy** Have mercy.
bright Gracious, beautiful.

2232. **what ... feel** What sufferings I endure.

2237. **so ye me helpe** If you will help me. Here, as elsewhere, we
should expect the singular pronoun, **thou**.

2238. **kepe noght** Do not care.

2240–1. 'Nor vain glory proclaimed because of my reputation in the
fight.'

2242. **fully** Completely, entirely.

2249. **vertu** Power, influence.

2252. **ryde or go** Ride or walk. The phrase also has the sense
of 'whatever happens'.

2253. **bete** Kindle, provide fuel for.

2256. **bere** Pierce.

2258. **to his wyf** For his wife.

2259. **th'effect** Point, intention, purpose.

2263. **with alle circumstaunces** With all due ceremony.

2264. Again the Knight wishes to hurry on with his story.

2266–7. **he took ... accepted was** He understood that his prayer was heard favourably.

2268. **shewed a delay** These words suggest that after all, everything was well for Palamon.

2270. 'He took himself home forthwith.'

2271. **houre inequal** Tyrwhitt comments that in the astrological system 'the day from sunrise to sunset, and the night from sunset to sunrise, being each divided into twelve hours, it is plain that the hours of the day and night were never equal except just at the equinoxes'.

2273. **up roos the sonne** See note to line 2217.

2274. **gan hye** Hastened – not 'began to hasten'.

2277. **the clothes** The robes required by the ritual of the sacrifice.

2278. **longen shal** Are essential.

2279. **meth** Mead, a drink made of honey.
hornes Vessels used in ritual.

2281. **smoking the temple** The temple being now filled with incense.

2285. 'Unless it be generally, without detail.'

2286. **it were a game** It would be a pleasure, a delight.

2287. 'To one whose mind is clean it would be of no real consequence.'

2288. 'But it is good for a man to be at liberty to please himself in the matter of what he says.'

2289. **kempt** Well combed, and quite loose.

2290. 'A crown of evergreen holm-oak.'

2293. 'Carried out the ritual, as you may see in the Thebiad of Statius.' The two lines at the beginning of the tale are from Statius who is the earliest authority for the story itself. He does not, however, describe this incident.

2295. **pitous chere** Devout bearing.

2297. **wodes grene** Diana was Goddess of Hunting as well as of Chastity.

2298. **is sene** Lies open.

2299. **Diana** Was also, under the name of Proserpina, the Queen of Pluto, God of the Underworld.

2300. **that ... knowe** Who hast known my heart.

2302. **as keep me** Pray keep me.

2303. **Attheon** See note to line 2065.
aboughte Incurred, brought upon himself.

2304. **wostow** Thou knowest; a contracted form of 'wost thou'.

2306. **no love ne wyf** No mistress or no wife.

2308. **hunting and venerye** Hunting and the chase.

2310. **noght** Not at all, by no means – a strong negative.

2313. **thre formes** A reference to the threefold divinity of the goddess, namely Luna in heaven, Diana on the earth, and Proserpina in the underworld.

2316. **with-oute more** Without any others, beyond all others.

2317. **as sende** Pray send.

2320. **bisy torment** Uneasy self-torture.

2321. **queynt** Extinguished, quenched.
another place Another direction.

2333–4. The lines 'rhyme' with identical final syllables. See note to line 2172.

2336. **al agon** Gone out entirely.

2338. **thise wete brondes** As we know wet brands always do.

2342. **gan to crye** Began to cry out.

2346. **gan appere** Appeared. 'Gan' without 'to' often forms the past tense.

2357. **thyn aventure of love** Your fortune in love.
as in this cas In this present circumstance.

2365. **the nexte weye** The nearest way.

2367. **the nexte houre of Mars** See note on line 2217.

2374. **honoured art** Art honoured , worshipped.

2376. **of armes al the brydel** The control of arms.

2385. **usedest** Didst enjoy.

2386. **free** Unrestrained.

2388. **thee ... misfille** Things once went wrong for thee.

2389. Vulcan is said to have made, at Jove's request, the first
woman, known as Pandora. Vulcan's own wife was the goddess
Venus, who was untrue to him.

2396. **dooth ... endure** Causes me to suffer this distress.

2398. **er ... hete** Before she becomes well-disposed to me.

2404. **as wel as** Just as much as.

2405. **do that ... victorie** Cause me to have victory.

2409. **craftes stronge** Achievements which demand strength.

2413. **finde** Provide. The word still has this meaning in dialect,
e.g. 'I will *find* the milk if you will bring the tea'.

2423. **ful faste** Very quickly.

2424. At which Arcite was somewhat terrified.

2425. **brighte** Brightly.

2435. **hope wel to fare** Hope to do well.

2436. See line 2172 for identical rhymes.

2438. The scene is now transferred to the Heavens.

2439. **graunting** Promise, favour. Venus, line 2265, had promised
to favour Palamon: now Mars, her spouse, is to support Arcite!

2443. **Saturn** The grandfather of Venus, takes a hand: he was by
nature beneficent.

2446. **every part** Both sides.

2449. 'You may outrun an old man but not out-wit him.'

2451. **agayn his kynde** Against his nature.

2454. **that ... turne** That is the widest of all the orbits to journey through.

2456. 'It is I who cause the drowning in the sea.'

2459. **the cherles rebelling** The Peasants' Revolt of 1381 may be in the poet's mind.

2461. **pleyn correccioun** Open punishment.

2462. **the signe of the Leoun** The Lion and Saturn together would make a formidable combination.

2465. **mynour** One who is preparing a mine during a siege.

2467. **colde** Destructive, hostile

2469. **my loking** A glance from me.

2470. **doon diligence** Do my best to contrive.

2474. **bitwixe yow** Between the two of you.
som tyme At some time.

2482. **the grete effect** The notable ending of the chain of events.

Part 4

2483. **feste** Festivity, rather than feasting.

2495. **stede** Charger.
palfrey Saddle horse.

2496. **maystow seen** You may see, anyone could see.

2497. **uncouth** Strange, unusual, unknown.

2502. **of retenne** Among the retinue of the more important lords.
squyeres Young knights in the service of others.

2503. **nailinge the speres** Nailing the pennons on to the shafts.

2504. **gigginge** Fitting shields with straps. The knights passed their arms through the straps to carry the shield when in the fight.
layneres lacinge Fastening up the straps.

2505. **they weren no-thing** They were not at all, in no way.

2506–7. **brydel gnawinge** Champing the bits.

2508. **priking** Hastening.

2510. **thikke** Packed as tightly as possible, if they were to move at all.

2511. 'Music of various kinds added to the general confusion.'
naker Kettledrum.

2512. **blody sounes** Sounds to urge on the fighting men in battle.

2513. **peples** All kinds of people, in the different retinues.

2514. **holding hir questioun** Arguing about one thing and another.

2515. **divyninge of** Guessing about.

2516. 'Some said it shall be in this way, others in another.'

2517. **helde with** Favoured. The reference is to Lycurgus. See line 2130.

2518. **thikke-herd** Thick-haired.

2522. **gan to springe** Began to rise.

2525. **held yet** Was still within, had not left.

2526–7. **bothe y-liche honoured** Honoured both alike.
fet Brought.

2531. **heigh reverence** Lowly respect.

2533. **made an ho** Shouted 'Ho!', for silence.

2536. **tho showed he** Then he announced.

2539. **in the gyse** After the manner.

2540. **now ... empryse** On this occasion in this tourney.

2542. See line 1860.

2543. **up peyne** Upon pain.

2544–5. 'Shall send or bring into the lists any kind of missile, pole-axe or short knife.'

2548. **un-to his felawe** Up to his opponent.

2549. **but o cours** Not more than one charge.
y-grounde Sharpened.

2550. **if him list** If it pleases him; if he wants to.
to were To protect.

2551. **at meschief** In difficulties.

2552. **stake** Post, where his name shall be recorded as out of further fighting.

2554. **thider he shal** He shall go there.
by force Necessarily, without other option.

2556. **his make** His equal, i.e. the other leader.

2558. **God spede yow** God prosper you.
ley on Strike.

2560. **goth** Go, all of you. (Imperative plural.)

2568. **hanged** Draped.
sarge Serge, an inferior kind of hanging.

2569. **ful lyk a lord** Just like the lord he was.
gan ryde Rode.

2573. **of oon and other** Of one kind and another.

2575. **by tyme** In good time.

2576. **fully prime** Quite 9 a.m. 'Prime' is the division of time from 6 a.m. to 9 a.m.

2579. **in degrees** According to their ranks.

2580. **al the route** All the crowd of citizens.

2581. **under Marte** Refer to lines 2367–2437.

2582. **of his parte** Of his supporting knights.

2585. **under Venus** See lines 2210–70.

2592. **worthiness** Excellence.

2593. **even** Evenly, equally.
for to gesse One might guess.

2597. **cryed was loude** A proclamation was made aloud.

2598. **proude** Valiant, rather than proud.

2599. **lefte hir priking** Discontinued their spurring.

2600. **clarioun** Shrill-sounding trumpet.

2602. **sadly** Firmly.
in arest In position.

2604. **seen men** One could see.

2605. A line noted for its alliterative suggestion of the fighting.

2606. **he** This one, one of them.

2609. **to-hewen and to-shrede** Hack and cut to pieces; *to-* is an intensifying prefix.

2610. **sterne** Violent.

2612. **he** This one; 2614, that one; 2615, another; and so on.

2616. **he him hurtleth** This one throws his foe down with his horse.

2618. **maugree his heed** In spite of anything he could do.
unto the stake See line 2552.

2619. **right ther** The phrase survives in American English.

2620. **another lad is** Another is led to the stake.

2621. **dooth hem ... to reste** Makes them rest.

2623. **ful ofte a-day** Many times that day.

2624. **wroght his felawe wo** Wounded his opponent.

2626. **vale of Galgopheye** It was in this valley in Boeotia that Acteon was turned into a hart. Refer to lines 2065 and 2303.

2629. **jelous herte** Enmity at heart.

2630. **Belmarye** A kingdom in Africa, in which the Knight, as it happens, had seen service. It is now Benmarin, in North Africa.

2635. 'The blood runs out red on both their sides.'

2637. 'Before sunset.' The fight had begun at prime, 9 a.m., but there had been a respite during the day.

2638. **gan hente** Seized.

2641. **by the force of twenty** By the strength of twenty knights.

2656. **it is doon** It's all over.

2657. **no partye** Impartial.

2663. **faire Venus** It was to this goddess that Palamon had prayed and she had apparently acknowledged his prayer in such a way that 'wiste he wel that graunted was his bone' (line 2269).

2666. **fille** Fell.

2667. **'I am ashamed, doutelees'** Venus said this to Saturn her ancestor, who had promised that she would be comforted.
(Line 2478.)

2673. **in hir wele** As happy as could be.

2674. **herkneth me** The Knight has not finished the story yet. A miracle 'bifel anon'.

2675. **which a** What a remarkable.

2676. **hath ... y-don** 'Of y-don' means removed. We still have the word 'doff' or 'do-off' with the same meaning. 'Has doffed his helmet.' Of = off.

2679. **this Emelye** Our heroine Emelye.

2680. **agayn him** Towards him.

2681. **as to speken in comune** Speaking generally, for the most part.

2683. **al his chere** There seems some difficulty in the text here. Clearly Chaucer intended to point out that she was strongly in favour of Arcite: translate by 'in her looks she was all his, as also in her heart'.

2684. **furie** Demon.
infernal From hell.

2685. **Pluto** The God of the Lower World.
requeste of Saturne See line 2670.

2688. **taken keep** Take any precautions.

2689. **pomel** Crown of his head.

2690. **in the place** On the spot.

2691. **to-brosten** Shattered.
with Against.

2692–3. 'The blood had run into his face, so that he lay as black as coal or any crow.'

2695. **with herte soor** With grief at heart.

2696. **corven** Cut out of his armour.

2697. **in a bed** To a bed.

2698. **in memorie** Conscious.

2699. **alway** Continually.

2702. **greet solempnitee** Great ceremony.

2704. **nolde noght** Did not wish at all.

2705. **men seyde eek** They said also.

2706. **maladye** Serious condition. The word had formerly a more serious implication that it has at present.

2710. **that . . . brest-boon** Whose breast bone had been pierced by a spear.

2713. **save** Sage, considered a very potent remedy in the Middle Ages.

2714. **hir limes have** Not lose their limbs.

2719. **holden** Considered.
disconfortinge Defeat.

2720. **but as a justes** Merely a tournament, and not a battle of one army against another.

2722. **falling nis nat but an aventure** Being unhorsed in a tournament is only bad luck.
nis nat Is nothing.

2723–4. 'Nor to be led forcibly to the stake, without surrendering, and be taken with a score of other knights.'

2729–30. 'It was not to be considered shameful at all; nobody would count it cowardice.'

2731. **leet crye** Had it announced.

2733. The sides had done equally well.

2736. **of feste days three** A feast lasting three days.

2738. **largely** With one ceremony.

2740. 'Farewell, and good luck.'

2745. **for any lechecraft** In spite of what any doctor could do.

2747. **veyne-blood** Release of blood by opening a vein.
ventusinge Cupping, whereby blood may be drawn away from a particular part of the body.

2749–51. 'The normal power of the body . . . cannot drive out the poison.'

2755. **him gayneth** There benefit him.
gete his lyf Bring back his life.

2760. 'Good-bye medicine! carry him to the churchyard.'

2761. **this ... som** This is the long and short of the matter.

2766. **o poynt** One detail.

2774. **departing** Separating, severing.

2776. **endere of my lyf** Who hast brought about my death.

2780. **my swete fo** My sweet foe. It was his love for Emelye that was the initial cause of his death.

2785. **jelousye** Jealousy of him.

2786. 'May Jupiter, in his wisdom, so guide my soul to speak as I should of a true lover.'

2788. **circumstaunces** His attributes.

2792. **have of my soule part** Protect my soul.

2793. **as** This word often begins a solemn passage. See lines 2302 and 2325.

2796. **been a wyf** Marry.

2797. **the gentil man** The kindly-hearted man.

2799. **faille gan** Failed.

2809. **chaunged hous** Changed its home, and as I never went there, I cannot tell where it went.

2811. 'Therefore I say no more, I am no theologian.'

2812. 'I find nothing in this narrative about souls.'

2813–14. 'Nor do I wish to tell the opinions of those who write about where they dwell.'

2815. **ther Mars his soule gye** May Mars guide his soul.

2820. **tarien forth** Waste all day. The story teller is hurrying over details.

2823. 'When their husbands have gone from them.'

2832. **Hector** Was slain by Achilles, his body being tied to the chariot and dragged three times round the walls of Troy.

2835. 'Why didst thou have to die?'

2850. **over al this** In addition to this.

2853. **with al his bisy cure** In spite of all his anxious grief.

2858. **ther as** Where.

2862. compleynt Lamenting. See lines 1218–74.

hote fires Ardent passion.

2863–4. office funeral Funeral rites.

2865. leet comaunde anon Had orders given at once.

2873. of the same suyte In the same material.

2877. bare the visage With the face uncovered.

2879. for the peple So that the people.

2881. roreth Resounds.

the crying and the soun The sound of weeping.

2884. y-dropped Bespattered.

2885. passing Surpassing, exceeding.

2887. service Ceremony.

2888. in his degree Because of Arcite's rank.

2889. leet forth three stedes bringe Had three steeds brought.

2895. his bowe Turkeys His Turkish bow. Doubtless this weapon would be more elaborate than that used by the Athenians. Historically Chaucer is incorrect in speaking of the Turks who were not in Europe in the time of Theseus. See **Prussian shield** line 2122.

2901. rede and wete Red with weeping.

2903. wonder hye To a great height.

2911. with fyr in honde Carrying fire.

2913. apparaillinge Preparation.

2915. his grene top The top of the pyre.

2919. At this point begins a long series of lines in which the poet tells us what he cannot or does not purpose to describe. Notice the various references to what the writer does not intend to detail. The first in this section is in line 2924: 'Shal nat be told for me.'

for me As far as I am concerned. The next example begins line 2925. This figure of speech is called 'occupatio'.

2920. highte Were called.

2921–3. asp Aspen; **chasteyn:** chestnut; **lind:** linden; **ew:** yew; **whippeltree:** cornel-tree.

2924. **nat be told for me** Not be told so far as I am concerned.

2928. **nymphes** Minor goddesses who lived in mountains, rivers and trees.

fauns Demi-gods – of which Pan is a good example – represented as men with the legs and tails of goats.

hamadryads Were wood-nymphs who lived in trees but died with the tree they lived in.

2934. **cloven a three** Split into three downwards.

2941. **as was the gyse** As the custom was.

2942. **putte in** Inserted under the pile.

2943. **men made the fyr** The fire was made.

2947. **some caste hir sheeld** Some cast therein their shields.

2948. **whiche that they were** Which they were wearing.

2950. **as it were wood** As if it was mad.

2958. **liche-wake** Vigil. The vigil and the wake-plays were an English funeral custom of Chaucer's own time. It is an historical error to suppose that the Greeks of the time of Theseus, if indeed Theseus is an historical character, celebrated them too.

2960. **ne kepe I nat to seye** I am not troubling to tell you.

wakepleyes Festivals connected with the parish church, not necessarily dramatic.

2962. **in no disjoynt** In any dilemma.

2966. The 'occupatio' ends here.

2970. **than** Then.

semed me It seemed to me.

2976. 'Had this noble Palamon sent for.' He was a Theban.

2984. **ther as was his lest** Where he wished to.

2987. 'The originator of what was created in the heavens.'

2993. **certeyn** Definite.

2995. **wrecched** Miserable.

adoun Below.

3000. 'There is no need for any authority to affirm this.'

3002. 'But I wish to make clear my belief.'

3003. **may . . . discerne** It may be clear from this orderly arrangement.

3005. **but it may be a fool** Unless he is a fool.

3006. 'Every part is derived from its whole.'

3015. **with-out lye** As is obviously true.

3016. **seen at yë** See at a glance.

3020. **is wasted** Comes to nothing, decays completely.

3021. **considereth** Is plural imperative.

3023. **by the weye** Beside the path.

3025. **wane and wende** Dwindle and depart.

3026. **al this thing** The whole creation.

3027. **Of man** With regard to.
seen we wel We see clearly.

3028. **that nedeth** That it is necessary.
termes Periods of life.

3030. **moot be deed** Must die.

3032. **as men may se** As is obvious.

3033. **ther helpeth noght** There is no help for it.

3034. **al this thing** The whole creation.
seyn Declare.

3035. **what maketh this** What is the cause of this.

3037. **his propre welle** Its own source.
converting Turning back.

3041–3. 'Then it is wisdom, as it seems to me, to accept what we cannot avoid and obey willingly what we cannot escape.'

3048. **excellence and flour** Height of his prime.

3055. **as for a worthy fame** With regard to gaining a lasting renoun.

3056. **best of name** At the height of his reputation.

3059. **of chivalrye flour** The flower of chivalry.

3060. **duetee** Reverence, deep respect.

3062. **his wyf** i.e. Arcite's wife, Emelye; though they had not married, she had been won by Arcite's victory in the tourneying.
grucchen ... of his welfare Begrudge his good fortune to his cousin and his wife whom he loved so well.

3064. **he** Arcite.

3065. 'who injure both his soul and himself.'

3066. **lustes** Wishes, desires. There was no sinister suggestion in this word in older English.

3068. **but** Except that.

3072. **o parfyt joye** One perfect happiness.

3073. 'Where there is the greatest sorrow.'

3076. **parlement** Assembly of advisers.

3080. **of your grace** Of your kindly nature.
up-on him rewe Have pity on him.

3083. **let see ... pitee** Show us something of your womanly compassion.

3084. 'The nephew of a king.' See line 1018.
pardee Indeed.

3085. **though he were** Even though he was not yet a knight.

3088. 'It must be taken into consideration, believe me.'

3089. **passen** Take precedence of.
right Mere equity. 'For pitee renneth sone in gentil herte', line 1761.

3090. **ful right** Straight out.

3093. **come neer** Come nearer.

3096. **counseil** Counsellors.

3097. **blisse and melodye** Happiness and music-making.

3100. **that ... a-boght** Who has paid so great a price for it.

3101. **in alle wele** In every happiness.

3104. **gentilly** Honourably, nobly.

3106. **tene** Distress, vexation.

3108. This benediction is spoken by the Knight to the pilgrims to whom he had told his tale.

Words liable to be mistranslated

The words in this list resemble closely words used in modern English, but they must be carefully distinguished from their apparent equivalents. Go over this list frequently, in order not to be caught out in a faulty translation which might easily have been avoided by a thorough knowledge of vocabulary. Against each word is printed the number of the line where it first occurs in this text, and each word should be considered in its context.

accomplice 2864
accuse 1765
adamant 1990
after 1781
ago 1276
al-day 1168
also 3104
amounte 2362
animal 2749
apalle 3053
apparaillinge 2913
areste 1310
ashame 2667
asp 2921
aspect 1087
assh 2922
asshen 1302
astonie 2361
axe 1347

bacheler 3085
baronage 3096
bay 2157
bente 1981
bete 2253
binding 1304
bisinesse 1007

blody 2512
blowen 2241
bole 2139
bone 2269
bore 1658
bouk 2746
bounde 2993
bowe 1642
brede 1970
breste 1980
burne 1983
by and by 1011

cage 1294
care 1321
careful 1565
cas 1074
cas 2080
caste 2468
caste 2081
char 2138
charge 1284
charitee 1433
chasteyn 2922
chere 913
cherl 2459
chivalrye 865

clench 1991
clerk 1163
commune 1251
compas 1889
compassing 1996
compleynt 2012
complexion 2475
composicioun 2651
conclusion 1845
condicioun 1431
contenaunce 1916
contrarie 1667
converting 3037
corps 2819
correccioun 2461
cote 2457
couch 2161
couch 2933
counseil 1141
craft 2409
crafty 1897
croppe 1532
cure 1007

dampne 1175
daunger 1849
debat 1754

liven 916
lust 1250
lyves 2395

make 2556
manye 1374
mat 955
meschief 2551
mete 1900
meynee 1258
ministre 1663
mister 1710
mone 1366
mone 2077

naught 2068
neer 968
nere 875
nothing 1703

offence 1083
office 1418
oratorie 1905
ought 3045
out of 1141

pan 1165
parlement 1306
partie 2657
payen 2370
pilour 1007
plat 1845
pleyn 1464
pleyne 1251
pose 1162
pryme 2189
pure 1279
pyne 1324

pyne 1746

quike 1015
quike 2335
quyte 1032

rather 1153
rede 3068
regne 1624
rehersing 1650
remedye 1216
rente 1443
rente 990
right 1534
rood 966
route 889

sad 2985
sadly 2602
sangwyn 2168
save 2713
save 1561
sawe 1163
scaffold 2533
scriptures 2044
see 1956
serie 3067
servaunt 1421
shine 1279
shortly 1485
siker 3049
sin 1240
singe 2210
sleighte 1948
slepy 1387
slider 1264
slough 980
slow 2466

slyly 1444
smoking 2281
solempnitee 870
sone 1022
sone 1963
soor 1454
sooth 1521
sore 1755
sore 1115
sore 2743
sory 2004
sotil 1054
sowe 2019
spare 1396
spede 2558
spore 1704
sterve 1249
stevene 1524
stiken 1565
stinten 1334
stoke 2546
straunge 2718
streit 1984
streme 1495
stubbe 1978
studie 1530
successioun 3014
sum 1088
suyte 2873
swich 862
sythe 1877

table 1305
tare 1570
tarien 2820
tester 2499
than 1479
theatre 1885

thing 885
thinke 2207
thought 954
to 2726
tonne-greet 1994
toret 2152
trapped 2157
travaille 2406
trays 2139
trespas 1764
tronchoun 2615
trouthe 1610
twyn 2030

uncouth 2497
unset 1524

up-riste 1051
up-sterte 1080

vasselage 3054
venerye 2308
vertu 2249
vileinye 2729

wake-pleyes 2960
wan 2456
wanting 2665
war 896
wayke 887
wedde 1218
wede 1006
were 2550

were 1929
what 865
whether 1856
whyle 1437
wisly 1863
with-oute 1888
wol 1662
wonder 2073
wonder 1654
wont 1195
wood 1329
wreke 961
wyse 1338

yet 1156
yore 1813
yvele 1127

General questions

1 From what source did Chaucer derive *The Knight's Tale*, and how did he make use of that source?

2 What descriptions does Chaucer give of Hippolyta and Emelye? Why is this information so scanty?

3 As you read through *The Knight's Tale* collect references to the fact that it is being told by a knight to a number of other pilgrims travelling to Canterbury.

4 Write an account of Duke Theseus, as depicted in this tale, pointing out how he is influenced by those with whom he comes into contact.

5 Indicate whether Theseus impresses you favourably or not, referring to text in support of your opinion.

6 Why was Arcite released from prison, what conditions did Theseus lay down for his release, and how far did Arcite observe them?

7 What were Arcite's feelings on the matter of his release from prison?

8 How did Palamon view Arcite's release?

9 How was it that Arcite was able to spend so many years in Athens after his return without being recognized? (Answer this question in some detail, with direct reference to the text.)

10 By what means was Palamon able to escape from prison and how soon was he recognized?

11 From information derived from the third part, make a plan of the lists constructed by the command of Theseus.

12 What details which cannot be shown in a diagram does Chaucer give of the lists?

13 What do you gather from the poem about the way in which the month of May was welcomed in Chaucer's time? Was he right in assuming that it was similarly celebrated in Athens?

14 What indications are there in the poem that Chaucer himself had seen service as a soldier?

15 Why did Palamon offer his prayer to Venus, Arcite to Mars, and Emelye to Diana? Make a summary of each of the prayers.

16 Summarize, paragraph by paragraph, the final speech of Theseus, beginning at line 2987. At what point in his address does he begin to apply his reasoning to the actual matter in hand?

17 Quote a few examples of Chaucer's humour as found in this poem.

Glossary

The character of the Knight from the Prologue to *The Canterbury Tales*

aboven *above*
agayn *against*
al-so *in addition*
armee *armed expedition*
array *dress equipment*
ay *always*
bataille *battle*
be *been*
bigan *began*
bismotered *soiled*
bord *table for meals*
chivalrie *knightly conduct*
comen *come back, return*
Cristen *Christian*
curtesye *courtly behaviour*
degree *rank, station in life*
evermore *always*
feith *religion, faith*
ferre *farther*
fiftene *fifteen*
fighten *fight*
fo *foe, enemy*
foughten *fought*
fredom *liberality, generosity*
fro *from*
fustian *coarse cloth*
gay *finely dressed*
gentil *of noble birth*
gipoun *tunic, short vest*
habergeoun *coat of mail, hauberk*

hethen *heathen, infidel*
hethenesse *heathendom*
honour *honourable conduct*
hors *horse, horses*
ilke *same*
late *lately, recently*
listes *lists at a tournament*
lord *lord, master*
lyf *life*
maner *sort, kind*
mayde *maid, girl*
meeke *modest*
mortal *deadly*
nacion *nation*
nat *not*
never *never*
noble *noble, notable, distinguished*
oftetyme *often*
out *out, away from home*
parfit *perfect*
port *bearing, manner, demeanour*
prys *reputation, renown, praise, esteem*
reyse *go on a military expedition*
see *sea*
seege *siege*
sayde *said*
slayn *slain*
somtyne *at one time, formerly*
sovereyn *supreme, very high*
ther *there*

therto *moreover*
though *although*
thryes *thrice, three times*
trouthe *truth*
verray *true*
viage *journey, expedition, voyage*
vileynye *anything unbecoming a knight*
wente *was on his way*

wered *wore*
werre *war, quarrel*
wight *person*
worthy *distinguished*
worthinesse *distinction, prowess*
wys *discreet, prudent*
y-come *returned*

'Who shal telle the Firste Tale?' – lines 822–58

a *in on*
accord *contract, decision*
ale *ale*
alle *all*
aller gen. pl., *of all*
amorwe adv., *on the next day*
anon *at once*
areste *stop*
assent *assent, agreement*
aventure *luck, chance, accident*
blithe *glad, happy*
cas *chance, accident, luck*
chere *manner, fashion*
clerk *scholar, student for holy orders*
cometh *come*
composition *agreement*
cut *lot, choice, decision*
draweth *draw*
even-song *what is sung in the evening*
ferrer *farther*
fil *fell*
flok *flock, group*
foreward *promise*

forth *forward*
free *voluntary*
ful *very*
gadrede *gathered*
game *jest, fun, entertainment*
gan *began*
han *have*
herd *heard*
herkneth *listen to*
hond *hand*
juggement *opinion, decision, verdict*
kepe *keep, hold to*
lat *let*
leste *it pleases*
ley *place*
litel *little*
lordinges *sirs, my masters*
maister *master*
manere *way, fashion*
mo *more*
morwesong *what is sung in the morning*
moste *must*
mote *may*

myre *merry, happy*
nedeth *are needed*
neer *nearer*
noght *at all, by any means*
paas *foot rate, walking pace*
paye *pay*
rebel *rebellious*
recorde *recall*
resoun *reasonable, fair, in order*
riden *rode*
right *indeed*
rise *rise*
roos *rose*
saugh *saw*
seye *say*
seyde *said*
shamefastnesse *modesty, shyness*
shortest *shortest*

shortly *in a few words, briefly*
sin *since*
sire *sir*
sort *accident, luck, chance*
sothe *truth*
springe *arise, dawn*
studieth *meditate*
tellen *tell*
togidre *together*
twinne *proceed on our way*
waterynge *place for watering horses*
weye *way, route*
what *well then*
wight *person*
word *word*
woot *know, remember*
wyn *wine*
wys *wise*

The Knight's Tale – Lines 859–3108

a *in, into*
able *capable*
abood *delay*
abought *bought*
about *in turn*
above *on high*
aboven *above*
abregge *shorten, abridge*
abyden *abide, wait*
abye *pay for, buy*
accepte *accept, receive*
accomplice *carry out, perform*

accuse *reveal, betray*
acord *agreement, bargain*
acorde *agree*
adamant *steel*
a-day *in the day*
adoun *downwards*
adversitee *adversity, hardship*
afered *frightened*
aferen *frighten*
affeccioun *love, desire*
afferme *decree*
after *afterwards*
after *according to*

agast *terrified, frightened*

agayn *again, once more*

ageyn *again, once more*

ago *gone, departed*

agon *go away, depart*

agoon *gone, departed*

al *all*

al *entirely*

al *although*

alaunts *mastiffs, wolf-hounds*

al-day *continually, constantly, always*

alder *alder tree*

alight *alight from horse-back*

allas *alas*

alle *all, one and all*

allegge *affirm in evidence*

alliaunce *alliance*

allone *alone*

almost *almost*

al-so *so much, to such a degree*

al-though *notwithstanding that*

alway *always, for ever*

alyve *alive, living*

Amadrides *hamadryads*

Amazones *Amazons*

amen *the end*

amende *make good, amend, put right, improve, change*

amiddes *in the midst of*

amorous *full of love*

amorwe *on the next day, in the morning*

amounte *mean, come to, signify*

ancle *ankle*

and *if, and*

angwish *grief of body or mind, anguish*

a-night *in the night time*

animal *physical*

anoon *at once, immediately*

answer *answer, reply*

apalle *become weaker, lose renown*

apaye *content, satisfy*

apparaillinge *preparation*

appere *appear*

appetyt *desire, inclination, appetite*

approche *draw near, approach*

areste *durance, confinement, duress*

arette *consider, ascribe, impute*

arise *get up, bestir oneself*

arm *armour, arms*

arm-greet *as thick as one's arm*

armipotente *powerful in arms*

armurer *armourer*

array *condition, dress*

ars-metrik *arithmetic*

art *skill, occupation*

artow contr. for **art thou**

arwe *arrow*

as (this word introduces a prayer), *pray*

ashame *put to shame*

aske *beg, pray for*

aslake *assuage, soften, diminish*

asp *aspen tree*

aspect *planetary positioned, usually evil*

aspye *see, detect*

assaut *assault*

assaye *test, try, sum up the qualities of*

assege *besiege*

assemblen *summon, call together*

assent *agreement, consent*

assente *agree, consent*

assh *ash tree*

asshen *ashes from a fire, cinders*

asshy *as if sprinkled with ashes*

assure *be certain, be sure*

asterte *escape*

astonie *be astounded*

asyde *aside*

athamaunt *adamant*

Athenes *Athens*

at-rede *surpass in counsel, outwit*

at-renne *outrun*

atte *at the*

atteyne *reach, attain to*

auctoritee *person in authority*

aught *anything*

aungel *angel*

auter *altar*

availle *be sufficient*

avauntage *advantage, prestige*

aventure *adventure, fortune, good or bad*

avow *vow, promise*

avys *opinion, advice*

awake *wake up, awaken*

ax *axe*

axe *ask, ask for, beg*

axing *request*

ay *always*

ayeins *opposite*

ayel *grandfather*

bacheler *one aspiring to knighthood*

bad *prayed, begged*

bak *back*

bal *ball*

balled *bald*

bane *destruction, cause of death, death*

baner *banner*

banishe *banish*

bar *carried, pierced*

bare *uncovered*

bareyne *devoid of, barren*

baronage *assembly of barons*

barre *bar*

bataille *battle*

batayle *battle*

bathe *bathe*

bauderie *mirth, gaiety, wantonness*

bay *bay-coloured*

beat *kindle*

beautee *beauty*

bedde *bed*

beddynge *couch, sleeping place*

beech *beech tree*

ben *be*

be(e)ste *animal, beast, creature*

beginning *beginning, origin*

ben(edi)cite *bless*

benigne *kindly, gracious*

bente *slope, hillside*

ber *carry, pierce*

berd *beard*

bere *bear*

bere *bier*

bere *carry, pierce, give birth to*

beste *best*

bete *beat, hammer*

bete *kindle*

bibledde *covered with blood*

bidde *pray, beg, command*

bifalle *happen, occur, take place*
bifel *happened, occurred*
bifore *before*
biforn *in front, previously*
biginne *begin*
bihinde *behind*
biholde *behold*
biknowe *confess, acknowledge*
biloved *beloved*
binde *bind, pledge*
binding *bond, pledge*
biquethe *bequeath*
biraft *deprived of*
bireve *deprive of, take from*
biseke *beseech, ask*
bisette *employ, occupy*
bisily *industriously*
bisinesse *occupation, activity*
bisy *busy*
bisyde *beside, by the side of*
bittre *bitter*
bitwene *between*
bitwixen *between*
biwreye *reveal, expose*
blake *black*
blede *bleed*
blenche *start back*
bleynte *started back*
blind *blind*
blis *happiness, blessedness*
blisful *happy, blessed*
blisfully *joyfully, happily*
blisse *happiness*
blody *inciting to bloodshed*
blood *blood, lineage*
blowen *proclaim*
blythe *happy, joyful*
blyve *quickly*

bocher *butcher*
boghte *bought*
boke *book*
bokelinge *buckling*
boket *bucket, pail*
bokle *buckle*
bole *bull*
bond *agreement, covenant*
bond *pledged*
bone *bone*
bone *boon, requests*
boon *bone*
boor *boar*
bore *born*
born *born*
borwe *surety, pledge*
bothe *both*
bothe *more than two*
bough *bough, branch of a tree*
bouk *belly, body*
bounde *boundary, limit*
bounden *bound*
bowe *bough*
bowe *bow*
boxtree *box-tree*
brak *broke*
braun *muscle*
braunch *branch of a tree*
brede *breadth, width*
breeth *breath*
breke *break*
breme *fiercely*
brend *burnished*
brenne *burn, cremate*
brenne *burn*
brenninge *cremation, burning*
brenningly *fiercely, fervently, hotly*

brent *burnt*

brere *briar, thorn*

brest *breast*

brest-boon *breast-bone*

breste *shatter, burst*

brest-plat *breast-plate*

bret-ful *completely covered*

brid *bird*

bright *bright*

bringen *bring*

brode *broad*

broghte *brought*

broke *broke*

broken *broken*

brondes *burning pieces of wood, logs*

brook *brook*

brother *brother, comrade-in-arms*

browding *embroidery*

brow *brow, eye-brow*

broyded *plaited*

brydel *bridle*

bulde *build*

bulte *built*

burgen *bury*

burne *burnish*

burned *burnished*

bush *bush*

busk *thicket*

but *except, unless*

by *by, beside*

by and by *side by side*

byde *remain, wait*

bye *buy*

by-japed *deceived*

byte *penetrate, get through*

bytinge *keen, bitter, biting*

cacche *seize, catch*

cage *prison*

caitif *wretched, miserable*

caitif *prisoner*

calle *cry out, call out*

cam *came*

can *be able, understand, know how*

cantel *piece, portion*

care *trouble, anxiety*

careful *sorrowful, troubled*

careyne *corpse, dead body*

carie *carry*

caried *carried*

carieden *carried*

carole *dance with vocal accompaniment*

carpenter *carpenter*

carte *chariot, cart*

cas *accident, chance*

cas *quiver*

caste *plot, plan, contrivance*

caste *glance, consider, reckon*

castel *castle*

caught *caught*

cause *cause, origin, reason, beginning*

cause *bring about, cause, originate*

caytif *wretched*

cerial *holm oak*

certes *indeed, certainly, truly*

certeyne *definite, fixed, certain*

chamberleyn *attendant in the bedchamber*

champartye *partnership, equality*

char *chariot*

charge *account, burden, responsibility*

charitee *act of kindness or benevolence*

charme *spell, charm*

chaste *pure, chaste*

chasteyn *chestnut tree*

chastitee *chastity, purity of conduct*

chaunce *chance, accident*

chaunge *change, vary, alter*

chaungeable *inconstant, changeable*

chaunging *altering, changing*

cheke *cheek*

chere *appearance, countenance*

cherl *peasant*

chese *choose*

cheyne *chain*

chief *chief, principal*

chieftayn *chieftain, leader*

child *child*

children *children*

chirche *church*

chirking *grating sound, screaming*

chivalrye *knighthood, company of knights*

circuit *circumference, distance round*

circumstance *circumstance*

citee *city*

citole *a stringed instrument*

citryn *lemon-coloured*

cladde *dressed*

clamour *noise, outcry*

clarioun *trumpet*

clarree *clarified wine*

clateren *clatter, rattle*

clateringe *clattering, clanking, rattling*

clause *sentence, a few words*

clench *rivet*

clene *pure*

clepen *call, name*

clere *brightly, clearly*

clerk *scholar*

cleve *split asunder*

clothe *dress*

clothered *clotted*

clothes *clothes, coverings*

cloven *split*

cokkow *cuckoo*

col-blak *coal-black, black as coal*

colde *cold, destructive, gloomy*

cole *coal*

colpon *billet*

comaunde *command*

comaundement *commandment, instruction*

come *come*

commune *association*

communes *common people, commoners*

companye *company, number*

compas *circle*

compassing *contrivance, planning*

compleint *lamentation*

complexioun *temperament, disposition*

compleyne *make moan, lament, crave pity*

composicioun *agreement*

concluden *decide, sum up*

conclusioun *decision, judgement*

condicioun *disposition*

confort *comfort*

confort *comfort, encourage, strengthen*

confus *bewildered, confused*

confusioun *discomfiture, bewilderment*

conquerour *conqueror, victor*

conquest *victory, conquest*

conserve *preserve, protect*

considere *think over, consider, ponder*

constellacioun *position of stars*

contek *quarrel, contest*

contrarie *opposite*

contree *kingdom, nation*

converten *change, turn*

converting *changing*

converten *convert*

convey *escort, conduct*

corage *courage, spirit*

coral *coral*

corde *rope, cord*

coroune *crown, garland*

corps *corpse, dead body*

correccioun *reproof, punishment*

corrumpable *corruptable*

corrupt *become corrupt*

corven *carved*

cosin *cousin*

cote *cottage, house, dungeon*

cote-armure *coat-of-arms*

couch *cover, lay*

coude *could*

counseil *opinion, secret*

countenaunce *appearance, demeanour*

cours *orbit, pursuit, charge*

courser *war horse*

court *court*

couthe *could*

covenant *vow, promise*

cover *cover*

cowardye *cowardice*

cracching *scratching, tearing*

cradel *cradle, child's bed*

craft *skill, achievement*

crafty *skilled, clever, skilful*

creature *human being, creature*

croppe *top of a tree*

croune *crown*

croune *crown*

crowe *crow*

crowned *crowned*

cruel *cruel, merciless*

cruelly *cruelly*

crueltee *cruelty*

cry *cry, exclamation*

crye *cry, weep*

cr333inge *crying, lamentation*

cure *care, diligence*

curse *curse*

dampne *condemn*

dar *to dare*

darreyne *decide a claim to, decide*

dart *arrow, dart*

daun *sir, lord*

daunce *dance, game*

daunce *dance*

daunger *power, liability*

daunsinge *dancing*

dawe *dawn*

day *day*

debat *strife, quarrel, conflict*

debonaire *gracious, kindly*

declaren *declare, announce, reveal*

decree *enactment, declaration*
dede *dead*
dede *deed, action*
deduyt *delight, pleasure*
deed *dead*
deedly *deadly, death-like*
deer *deer*
deere *at a high price, dearly*
deeth *death, corpse*
defye *mistrust, defy, deny*
degree *rank, step, position*
delay *delay*
delivere *free, set free, deliver*
delyt *delight, pleasure*
deme *consider, judge*
departe *separate, part*
depe *deep*
depe *deeply*
depeynted *painted, depicted, pictured*
dere *dear*
dere *injure, harm*
derke *dark, evil, wicked*
derre *dearer*
deryve *derive, have a beginning*
descend *deteriorate*
deserve *deserve*
desiring *eager desire*
desirous *desiring eagerly*
despeir *despair*
despitous *scornful, spiteful*
desplay *unfurl, exhibit, display*
despyt *scorn, spite*
destinee *destiny, fate*
destreyne *distress, harass*
destroy *destroy*
destruccioun *destruction*
desyr *desire, longing*

desyre *wish for*
devocioun *devotion, piety*
devoir *knightly duty*
devyse *describe, tell, instruct*
devysing *description, design*
deye *die*
deys *dais*
diapred *variegated, sprinkled with figures*
diched *moated*
diden *did*
dight *prepared, ready*
dighte *prepare*
digne *worthy*
diligence *care, devoted service*
dim *indistinct, faint, low*
disconfitinge *defeat, uneasiness*
disconfiture *defeat, confusion*
disconfort *unhappiness, sorrow*
disconforten *discourage, distress*
discrecioun *discrimination, discretion*
disfigure *alter, change*
disjoynt *perplexity, difficulty*
dispence *expenditure, expense*
dispitously *scornfully*
disposicioun *disposition, arrangement, guidance*
distresse *misery*
distreyne *lay hold upon, oppress*
divinistre *one who can foretell the future*
divisioun *distinction*
divyninge *forecasting the future*
divyn *theologian, divine*
dominacioun *power, control*
dongeoun *keep, 'donjon' tower*

doon *do, make, cause, carry out*
doth *do*
double adj., *twofold, double*
double v., *double*
doughter *daughter*
doun *down, downward*
doute *doubt*
doutelees *without doubt,*
certainly
downward *downwards*
dowve *dove*
drawen *draw, recall*
drede *fear, terror, dread*
drede *fear, dread*
dredful *cautious, timid*
drenching *drowning*
dresse *dress, array, put in order*
dreye *dry*
dronke *drunken*
droppe *drop*
drope *tear, drop*
drugge *act as a drudge*
drye *dry*
drye *dry*
dryve *drive*
duetee *duty, homage, reverence*
duk *leader, duke*
duracioun *length of life,*
duration
dure *remain, last*
durre *dare*
duske *grow dim*
dwelle *remain, dwell, stop*
dwelling *abode*
dyamaunt *diamond*
dye *die*
dys *dice*
ech *each*

echoon *each one*
eek *also*
eet *ate*
effect *result, purpose, conclusion*
eft *again*
egle *eagle*
eir *air*
either *either*
elde *old age*
eldest *oldest*
elles *otherwise, else*
elles-where *elsewhere*
elm *elm tree*
emforth *to the extent of*
empoysoning *poisoning*
empryse *enterprise, undertaking*
encens *incense*
enchauntment *enchantment*
encombre *hamper, encumber*
encrees *increase*
encrese *increase*
ende *end, agreement*
ende *come to an end*
endelong *lengthways, from end*
to end
endere *finisher, cause of the end*
endure *endure, put up with,*
suffer
endyte *write, tell*
enemy *enemy*
engendre *produce, bring forth,*
give birth to
enhauncen *improve, raise*
enhorte *exhort*
enoynt p.p., *anointed*
ensample *example*
entente *purpose, intention*
enter *enter, come into*

entree *entrance*

envye *envy, jealousy*

ere *ear*

ere *plough*

erle *earl, nobleman*

ernest *seriousness, earnest*

erst *formerly, earlier, sooner*

erthe *earth*

earthly *earthly, mortal*

escapen *escape*

eschue *escape, avoid*

ese *ease, comfort, pleasure*

esen *set at ease, comfort*

espye *notice, observe*

estat *condition*

estres *interior of a building*

est-ward *towards the east*

ete *eat, devour*

eternally *eternally, forever*

eterne *unchangeable*

eve *evening*

evene *exactly, steadily*

ever *always, ever*

everemo *always*

evermore *continually*

everich *each*

everichoon *each one, every one*

ew *yew tree*

excellence *highest reputation*

excuse *excuse, pardon*

execute *carry out*

exercyse *practise, exercise*

expelle *drive out, expel*

experience *experience*

expulsif *expellent*

exyle *banish, drive into exile*

eye *eye*

eyle *ail, trouble, disturb*

fader *father*

fadme *fathom*

faire *fair, lovely, beautiful*

faire *properly, without mishap*

fairer *fairer*

fairnesse *beauty, loveliness*

falle *befall, happen, occur, fell*

falling *falling, collapse*

fals *false*

falsly *falsely, traitorously*

falwe *yellowish, pallid*

fame *reputation*

fantastyk *fantastic*

fare *behaviour, conduct*

fare *behave, act*

farwel *farewell, goodbye*

faste *close, near*

faste *keenly, eagerly, quickly*

faunes *fauns*

favour *caprice, vagaries, favour*

fayn *happy, glad*

fayn *happily, gladly*

feble *weak, feeble*

fecchen *fetch*

fee *payment*

feeld *field, area*

feele *feel*

feith *promise, word*

fel *cruel, savage*

fel *befell, happened*

felawe *companion, comrade, fellow*

felawshipe *comradeship, fellowship*

feld *fell (a tree)*

felicitee *happiness*

felle *cruel*

felle *cause to fall*

felonye *crime*
felingly *with real feeling*
fer *farther*
ferden *behaved, acted*
fere *fear, dread*
ferforthly *thoroughly*
fermacies *remedies, medicines*
ferre *farther, additionally*
feste *feast*
feste *entertain*
fet *fetched*
feterien *fetter*
fether *plumage*
fettres *fetters*
fewe *few*
fey *faith, honour*
fiers *fierce*
fifty *fifty*
fight *fight, combat*
fighte *fight*
fighting *fighting*
figure *statue, arrangement*
fille *satisfaction, desire*
fillen *happened*
finde *provide, find*
firre *fir tree*
first *first of all*
flaterye *flattery*
fledden *fled*
fleen *flee from, escape*
fleeth *flee*
flesh *flesh*
flete *float*
fleting *floating*
flight *flight*
fliker *flutter*
flikeringe *fluttering*
florin *florin, a coin*

flotery *rugged, dishevelled*
flour *prime example*
fo *foe, enemy*
folde *sheepfold*
folk *people*
folwe *follow*
folye *foolishness*
fomy *foaming*
fond *found*
fool *fool*
foolhardinesse *foolhardiness*
foom *foam*
foot *foot*
footman *servant on foot*
for *for, in spite of, against*
forbere *desist from, leave alone*
for-blak *very black*
force *strength, power*
fordo *destroy, defeat, overthrow*
foreste *forest, wood*
forge *forge, hammer on an anvil*
forme *form, appearance*
for-old *very old*
forpyned *wasted away*
forth *at once, straightway*
forther-moor *further on, beyond*
forthren *aid, promote one's interests*
for-thy *for this reason*
fortune *fortune, fate*
fortunen *prosper*
fortunest *prosper*
forward *agreement, bargain*
foryete *forget*
foryeve *forgive*
fother *cartload, a great quantity*
foule *foul, disgusting, filthy*
foundre *stumble violently*

foure *four*
fowel *bird*
foyne *thrust (as in fencing)*
frakin *freckle*
fredom *freedom*
free *unfettered, free*
freend *friend*
freendlich *friendly*
freendly *in a friendly fashion*
fresh *brightly*
fresshe *bright, fresh*
fressher *fresher*
freten *eat, devour*
fro *backwards*
frosty *frosty*
frothen *foam at the mouth*
fruyt *benefit, fruit*
ful *very*
fulfille *satisfy*
fully *in full, fully*
funeral *associated with a funeral*
furie *fiend, monster*
fy *fie!, for shame!*
fyle *file, rasp*
fyle *smooth with a file*
fynally *in the end, lastly*
fyr *fire*
fyr-makinge *kindling, making a fire*
fyry *fiery, as if in flames*
gadere *gather*
gaf *gave*
game *fun, amusement, pleasure*
gan *began*
gape *gape, stare*
gappe *gap*
gardin *garden*
gardin-wal *garden-wall*

gastly *terrible*
gat *got, obtained*
gate *gate*
gaude *yellowish green*
gayler *gaoler, jailer*
gayne *avail, profit*
gelpen *boast*
general *general*
gentil *noble, tender-hearted, kindly*
gentilesse *courtesy*
gentilly *courteously*
geometrie *geometry*
gere *armour, equipment*
gere *moods, changeful ways*
gerful *changeable*
gerland *garland*
gesse *think, suppose*
gete *get, obtain, acquire*
gigginge *clatter of fitting with straps*
gilt *guilt, wrongdoing*
giltelees *innocent, guiltless*
ginne *begin*
gipoun *doublet*
girden *pierce*
girt *wearing a girdle, girt*
glad *cheerful, happy*
gladen *make happy*
glader *one who makes another happy*
gladnesse *gladness, happiness*
glass *glass*
glede *glowing coal*
gliteren *shine, glitter*
glorie *glory*
glorious *glorious*
glove *glove*

glowe *glow*

glyde *glide, pass*

gnawen *gnaw, champ the bit*

gnawinge *gnawing*

god *heathen god*

goddes *gods*

goddesse *goddess*

goldes *marigolds*

godhede *godhead*

goldhewen *made of gold*

gon *gone*

gonne *began*

goode *good*

goon *go*

gost *ghost*

goth *began*

governaunce *order, method, plan*

governe *rule, govern*

governour *governor, ruler*

grace *favour, boon, grace*

graunt *promise*

graunte *promise*

graunting *promise, favour*

grave *tomb, grave*

gray *gray, grey*

gree *advantage*

grete *great*

grene *green*

gretter *greater*

greve *bough, twig, branch*

greve *grieve, vex*

grevous *dangerous, grievous*

griffon *griffin*

grim *grim*

grinden *grind*

grisly *fearful, terrible, grim*

ground *ground, earth*

grounde *ground*

grove *grove, boughs*

groyning *groaning*

grucche *murmur, grumble*

gruf *prostrate, grovelling*

gye *guide, control*

gyle *deceit*

gyse *manner, fashion, custom*

habergeoun *coat of mail*

habit *habit, attitude to life*

habitacioun *dwelling, home*

hadden *had*

haf *lifted*

hakke *cut down, hack*

halle *hall, castle*

half *half*

halp *helped*

han *have*

hange *hang*

harde *strong, firm, hard*

hardinesse *boldness, bravery*

hardy *bold, brave*

hare *hare*

harie *drag, harry, push*

harm *suffering, injury*

harnays *suit of armour*

harneys *ornaments on armour*

hasel *hazel tree*

haste *hasten, hurry*

hastily *quickly, hurriedly*

hat *hat*

haten *to be named*

hauberk *coat of mail*

hauke *hawk*

have *have*

hawethorn-leve *hawthorn leaf*

he *he*

hedd *head*

hede *head*

heed *head*

heeld *held*

heep *heap*

heer *here*

heer *hair*

heer-biforn *before this, already*

heigh *high*

heighte *height*

helden *supported*

hele *health, happiness*

helle *Hell, Hades, the infernal regions*

helm *helmet*

help *help, aid*

helpe *help, assist*

helping *assistance, remedy*

hem *them*

hem-self *himself*

henne *hence*

hent *seized, caught*

hente *seize, embrace, catch*

heraud *herald*

herbe *herb*

herd *heard*

herde *heard*

here *her*

here *hear, listen to*

heres *hair*

here-agayns *against this, to the contrary*

herknen *listen to, hearken*

herneis *armour*

hert *hart*

herte *heart*

herte-blood *heart's blood*

herte-spoon *pit of the stomach*

hest *command, behest*

hete *promise*

heve *lift*

hevene *heaven, the heavens*

hevenly *in a heavenly manner*

hevinesse *sorrow, grief*

hewe *colour, tint*

hewen *cut, cut down*

hider *hither, here*

hidous *dreadful, hideous*

hidously *fiercely, terribly*

highte *height*

hight(e) *is called, was called*

hille *hill*

him *him, to him*

hindren *thwart, hinder, cross*

hir *their, of them*

hir *her*

hire *her*

his *his, its*

hitte *strike, hit*

ho! interj., *demanding silence*

holde *continue, observe, show, hold, consider*

holm *evergreen oak*

holpe *help*

holwe *hollow*

holy *holy*

holinesse *holiness*

homward *homeward*

hond *hand*

honestly *in honourable fashion*

honge *hang*

honour *honour*

honouren *honour*

honten *hunt*

honurable *honourable*

hony *honey*

hool *whole*

hoolly *wholely*

hoom *homewards*

hoom-cominge *home-coming, return*

hoost *host, army*

hoot *hot*

hope *hope*

hoppesteres *dancers*

horn *horn*

horrible *loathsome*

hors *horse*

hostelrye *hostel, inn*

hote *fervently*

hote *command, promise, be called*

hound *hound, dog*

houre *hour*

housbond *husband*

how *how, however much*

howle *howl*

huge *huge, great*

humble *humble*

humblesse *humility*

humour *humour, disposition*

hundred *hundred*

hunte *huntsman*

hunte *hunt, hunting*

hunter *hunter*

hunteresse *huntress*

hunting *hunting*

hurt *hurt, injure*

hurtlen *attack, push*

hust *hushed, quiet*

hyde *hide*

hye *high*

hye *on high*

hye *haste, speed*

hye *hasten, hurry*

ilke *same*

image *image, idol*

imaginacioun *delusion, fantastic notion*

imagining *plotting, scheming*

in *in, into*

Inde *India, the East*

inequal *unequal*

infernal *belonging to Hell, or Hades*

infortune *ill-luck, malevolence*

iniquitee *wickedness*

inn *lodge, put up*

inne *in, within*

inne *lodging*

innocence *innocence, innocent people*

instrument *musical instrument*

intellect *intelligence*

ire *anger*

iren *iron*

ivy-leef *ivy leaf*

jalous *jealous*

jape *trick, deceive*

jelous *jealous*

jelousye *jealousy*

jewele *jewel*

jolitee *fun, amusement*

journee *day's journey*

joye *joy, happiness*

joynant *adjoining, adjacent to*

juge *judge*

juste *tourney, joust*

juwyse *judicial sentence*

kan *be able*

keep *notice, heed, care*

kemb *comb, trim*

kempe *coarse, shaggy*

kene *sharp*

kepe *take care of, tend, guard*
keper *keeper, guardian*
kerve *carve*
kerver *carver*
kerving *carving*
kinde *kind, sort, nature*
king *king*
kinrede *kindred, family*
kisse *kiss*
kist *kissed*
knarry *gnarled, knotty*
knave *lad, servant*
knee *knee*
knewe *knew*
knight *knight*
knighthede *knightly rank*
knitte *knit*
knotty *gnarled*
know *know, recognise*
knowe *known*
knyf *knife*
koude *could*
kynde *sort, kind*
kyte *kite, bird of prey*
laborer *labourer*
labour *labour, toil*
labouren *labour, toil*
lacerte *muscle*
lacing *fastening*
lad *led*
ladde *accompanied*
ladel *ladle*
lady *lady*
laft *left standing*
lakke *lack, fail, be in need of*
lamentacioun *weeping, lament*
langage *words, language*
large *liberty*

large *spacious, open, wide*
largely *for the most part, almost*
larke *lark, a wild bird*
las *snare*
lasse *less*
laste *endure, continue*
lat *let, allow, permit*
laughe *rejoice, laugh*
launde *field*
laurer *laurel*
lawe *law*
laxatif *laxative, relaxing*
lay *stayed*
layneres *strap*
lechecraft *medical skill, art of healing*
lede *lead, conduct*
leef *dear, pleasing, pleasant*
leen *lend*
leep *leap, spring*
leeste *least*
leet *allowed*
leeve *dear, beloved*
lefte *left*
legge *leg*
lene *lean, thin*
lene *lend*
lenger *longer*
lengthe *length*
leoun *lion*
lepart *leopard*
lese *lose*
lesinge *lie, untruth*
lest *pleasure, desire*
leste *it pleased*
lete *leave, allow*
letten *desist from, hinder*
leve *dear*

leve *leave, departure*
leve *leaf of a tree*
leve *leave alone, forsake*
leve *trust, believe*
leye *lay, place*
leyser *leisure*
lichewake *funeral wake*
liggen *lie down*
lighte *light, bright*
lighte *light*
lighte *light up*
lightly *rapidly, quickly, cheerfully*
ligne *lineage, line of descent*
lilie *lily*
lime *limb*
linage *lineage, descent*
lind *lime tree*
lippes *lips*
list *it pleases*
liste *pleased*
listes *lists, a place for tournaments*
litel *little*
liven *live, spend one's life*
livinge *alive*
lode-sterre *pole-star*
loke *look*
loking *look, glance*
lond *land*
long *long, tedious, tiresome*
longen *belong*
looth *unwilling*
lord *lord*
lordshipe *authority, lordship, protection*
los *loss*
lost *lost*
love *lover, mistress*
love *love*

lowe *low*
lust *desire, longing, delight*
lustily *joyfully, merrily*
lustinesse *delight, joy, exuberance*
lusty *gay, merry*
lye *untruth, falsehood*
lye *stay, encamp*
lyfly *to the life*
lyk *like*
lyketh *it pleases*
lyknesse *likeness, resemblance*
lyte *small, little*
lyte *short period*
lyth *remain*
lyven *live*
lyves *living, alive*
mace *club*
mad *mad, out of one's mind*
made *made*
maister-strete *main street*
maistow *mayest thou*
make *mate, friend*
make *make*
maladye *ailment, illness*
malencolyk *characterized by melancholy*
manace *menace, threatening*
manasinge *threatening*
manere *kind, sort*
manhede *manliness*
mankinde *mankind*
manly *bold*
manly *courageously, in fair fight*
mansioun *mansion*
mantelet *cloak*
many *many*
manye *mania*

mapul *maple tree*
marbel *marble*
mariage *marriage*
martirdom *martyrdom*
martyren *torture*
mat *down-hearted*
matere *concern, business*
matrimoine *matrimony*
maugree *in spite of*
may *can*
mayde *young girl*
mayden *unmarried woman*
maydenhede *purity,*
  maidenliness
maystow *mayest thou*
melodye *melody, song music*
memorie *memory*
men *one, you*
mencioun *mention*
mene *mean, intend*
mengen *mingle, mix*
mercy *mercy*
mery *merry, happy*
meschaunce *misadventure,*
  mischance
mescheef *misfortune, trouble*
meschief *misfortune, trouble*
messager *herald, messenger*
met *met*
mete *food, meat*
mete *meet, encounter, come upon*
meth *mead, drink made of honey*
meynee *household, retainers,*
  servants
midnight *the middle of the night,*
  midnight
might *power*

mighty *powerful, strong*
milk *milk*
minde *mind, thought, memory*
ministre *servant, overseer,*
  administrator
minstralcye *minstrelsy*
miracle *miracle*
mirour *mirror*
mirre *myrrh*
misbede *offend, insult*
misboden *offended*
misfille *go amiss*
mishappe *befall*
mister *business, occupation, trade*
mo *compar., more*
modifye *modify*
moevere *mover, originator*
moment *moment, instant*
mone *moan*
mone *moon*
mood *anger, mood*
moorninge *mourning,*
  lamentation
moot *must, is compelled to*
mordre *murder*
mortal *to the death*
morwe *morrow, morning*
morwening *morning*
mosel *muzzle*
moste *greatest*
mot *must, have to*
mote *must, have to*
mount *mountain*
mountaunce *amount, value*
mous *mouse*
mouth *mouth*
mowen *be able*

muche *much*

muchel *much*

murmure *murmur of discontent*

murmuringe *murmur*

murye *merry*

myle *mile*

myn *my*

mynour *miner*

myrie *delightful*

myte *mite, farthing*

nailinge *nailing*

naked *naked*

naker *kettledrum*

nam *am not, am nothing*

name *name, reputation, fame*

namely *especially, particularly*

namo *no more, no one else*

namore *no more*

nas *was not*

nath *hath not, has not*

natheless *nevertheless*

natural *natural*

naught *not at all*

navele *navel*

nayl *nail, claw*

ne *nor*

necessitee *necessity*

necligence *neglect, negligence*

nede *be necessary*

nedes *necessarily*

nedes-cost *necessarily*

nedeth *need*

neede *necessity*

neer *nearer*

neither *neither*

nekke *neck*

nercotikes *narcotics*

nere *were not*

never *never*

never-mo *no more, nevermore*

nexte *nearest, next*

newe *new*

newe *newly, recently*

night *night*

nis *is not*

nobleste *noblest*

noght *not, not at all, certainly not*

nolde *would not, did not wish* (for **ne wolde**)

nombre *number, company*

nones *for the occasion*

noon *no, none, no one*

noot *know not* (for **ne woot**)

norisshinge *nourishment, food*

northren *northern*

north-ward *to the north, northwards*

nose *nose*

no-thing *in no way, not at all*

now *now, at present*

noyse *noise*

ny *near*

nymphe *nymph*

o *one*

obeisaunce *obedience, homage*

obsequies *funeral rites*

observaunce *rites, customary ceremonies*

obstacles *hindrances, obstacles*

odour *odour, scent, perfume*

of *about, concerning, of*

offence *injury*

offende *harm, injure*

offensioun *hurt, harm*

office *position, appointment, service, rite*

officere *official*

of-spring *descendant*

ofte *often, frequently*

oille *oil*

oke *oak, oak tree*

olde *old, ancient, of long ago*

ones *once*

onward *adv., further on*

ook *oak, oak tree*

oon *one, a one*

oonly *only, merely*

ooth *oath*

open *open, not secret*

opie *opium*

opinioun *opinion, judgement*

opposit *opposite, contrary*

oratorie *shrine, oratory, temple*

ordeyne *provide, place, fix*

ordinaunce *decree, arrangement*

ordre *ordering, provision*

orient *the eastern sky*

orisoun *prayer*

oth *oath*

ought *anything*

out-hees *alarm, hue and cry*

outher *either*

out of *without*

outrage *cruelty, injustice, outrage*

outrely *completely, entirely*

out-run *run out*

over *over, in addition to*

over-al *everywhere, anywhere*

overcaste *make gloomy, become gloomy, darken*

overcome *overcome, conquer*

over-ride *ride over, run over*

over-sprede *cover, spread over*

over-thwart *across*

oxen *oxen, cattle*

owne *own*

paas *walking pace, step*

pace *go, pass*

pacience *patience*

page *foot page*

paleys *palace*

palfrey *palfrey, saddle-horse*

pan *brain-pan, head*

paradys *paradise*

paraments *rich robes, mantles*

par amour *passionately, devotedly*

paramours *as* **par amour**

pardee! *by heaven! by God!*

parfyt *perfect*

parlement *assembly*

parlement *decision*

part *share, lot, portion, side in a contest*

partie *part, portion*

partie *partisan, unfair judge*

party *partly*

passant *notable, surpassing*

passe *surpass, pass away*

payen *pagan, heathen*

pees *peace*

penaunce *sorrow, penance*

pencel *small brush, pencil*

penoun *pennon*

peple *people, crowd*

perche *perch*

perfit *perfect*

perles *pearls*

perpetuelly *perpetually*

perrye *precious stones*

person *individual, person*

perturben *thoroughly disturb*

pestilence *epidemic, plague*

peyne *torture, torment*

peynten *paint*

peyre *pair, couple*

picchen *pitch, throw*

pighte *pitched*

piler *pillar*

pilgrime *pilgrim*

pilgrymage *pilgrimage*

pilour *robber*

pitee *pity, matter for regret*

pitous *compassionate, full of pity, pitiable, pious*

pitously *sadly, solemnly*

place *place, field of combat, spot*

plane *plane tree*

plat *certain, sure*

plate *plate of mail*

plesaunce *pleasure*

plesen *please, give satisfaction*

pley *fun, sports, games*

pleye *amuse oneself*

pleyinge *amusement*

pleyn *open*

pleyn *plainly*

pleyne *complain*

pleynly *plainly, openly, frankly*

pollax *pole-axe*

pomel *top of the head*

popler *poplar tree*

porter *doorkeeper, porter*

portreitures *paintings*

portreying *picture*

pose *put a case, suggest, suppose*

positif *positive, definite, fixed*

possessioun *possession*

possible *possible*

possibilitee *what is possible, opportunity*

pound *pound in weight*

povre *poor*

povrely *meanly, shabbily, poorly*

power *power, authority*

poynt *aim, purpose, object*

preesse *throng, press forward*

prescience *foreknowledge*

presence *presence*

present *in her presence*

preve *prove*

prey *booty*

preye *ask, beg*

preyere *prayer, petition*

prike *spur*

prikke *prick, stab*

prince *prince*

princesse *princess*

principal *chief*

pris *fame, renown*

prisoner *prisoner*

prisoun *prison*

prively *secretly*

privetee *secrets, private business*

processe *course, passage*

profre *offer*

progressioun *development*

propre *own, personal, correct*

proprely *duly, fittingly*

proud *haughty, proud*

proudly *haughtily*

pryde *pride*

pryme *dawn, first light*

pryvee *secret*

pure *very*

purgatorie *purgatory*

purpos *intention, purpose*

purtreyour *draughtsman, painter, artist*

purveyaunce *providence*

putten *place, put*

pykepurs *pickpocket*

pyne *punishment, torture*
pyne *punish*
pype *pipe, fife*
pypen *pipe, whistle*
quake *tremble, shiver*
qualm *plague, pestilence, disease*
quenche *extinguish, quench*
quene *queen*
questioun *argument, debate, discussion*
queynt *quenched*
queynte *strange, odd*
quethe *speak*
quike *alive, living*
quike *revive, burst into flame*
quitly *entirely, completely*
quod *spoke*
quook *trembled*
quyte *ransom, set free*
rad *read, advised*
rafter *rafter, beam*
rage *passion, raging, fury*
ran *ran*
rancour *ill-feeling, malice, hatred*
ransake *ransack, search*
rasour *razor*
rather *sooner, rather*
raughte *reached*
raunsoun *ransom*
recche *heed, care*
reche *reach, touch*
reconforte *take courage*
recorde *remember, keep in mind*
rede *red*
rede *advise, recommend, read, interpret*
redily *in readiness, at hand*

redoutinge *reverence, worship*
redy *ready, prepared*
refuge *shelter, place of safety*
regioun *district, part of the body*
registre *book of recordings*
regne *region, dominion, kingdom*
rehersing *repeating*
rekke *heed, care*
rekne *reckon, count up*
remedye *remedy, cure, help*
remembraunce *reminder*
remenant *rest, remainder*
rende *tear*
rendingen *tearing*
renges *ranks*
renne *run*
renoun *reputation, fame*
rente *income, revenue*
rente *tore*
repentaunce *repentance*
replicacioun *reply, contradiction*
requeste *request, petition*
rescous *rescue*
rese *tremble, shake*
reson *reason, justice*
resoune *resound, re-echo*
respyt *delay, postponement*
reste *rest*
restore *restore, give back*
retenue *train of servants*
retourninge *return*
reule *govern, rule*
revel *revelry*
reve *seize, plunder*
reverence *respect, honour*
rewe *row, line*
rewe *show pity on*

rewefulleste *saddest, most sorrowful*

reyne *rain*

reyne *rein*

richely *richly, handsomely*

richesse *wealth, riches*

richest *richest*

ride *ride*

right *just, exactly*

right *point, detail*

righte *direct, straight*

rightful *just, lawful*

ringe *resound, ring out*

rinnen *run*

risen *risen*

rit *ride*

river *river*

rolle *roll, revolve*

rome *wander, stroll, roam*

ronnen *ran*

rood *rode*

roos *rose*

rore *roar*

rouke *crouch, huddle, cower*

route *company*

routhe *pity, compassion*

royally *in royal splendour*

ruby *ruby*

ruggy *rugged, rough*

ruine *ruin*

rumbel *rumbling noise*

ryde *ride*

rydeth *ride*

rydinge *riding*

ryme *put into verse, tell in verse*

ryse *rise, rise from bed*

ryte *rite, religious observance*

sacred *pious*

sacrifyse *sacrifice*

sad *grave, sober, heavy*

sadel *saddle*

sadel-bowe *saddle bow*

sadly *firmly*

sake *sake*

salte *salt*

salue *greet, welcome*

saluing *greeting*

salve *ointment, balm*

same *same*

sangwyn *blood-red, red as blood*

sarge *serge*

sauf *except*

saugh *saw*

save *sage, a herb*

save *except*

savinge *except*

sawe *proverb, saying*

sayde *said*

scaffold *platform*

scalded *scalded*

scalden *scald*

scapen *escape*

Scithia *Scithia*

scriptures *manuscripts, writings*

see *sea*

seen *see*

seest *see*

seet *sat*

seete *seat*

sege *siege*

seigh *see*

seith *say*

seke *seek, search*

seken *seek*

selde *seldom*

selve *exact, very same, identical*

seme *seem, appear*
semely *pleasing, becoming*
send *send*
sene *visible, seen*
sene *see*
sentence *sentence, decision, verdict*
sepulture *burial, tomb*
serie *speech, argument, series*
sermoning *preaching*
serpent *serpent*
servage *servitude, slavery*
servaunt *lover*
serve *serve as a lover, or devotee*
servyse *service, devotion, rites*
seten *sat*
sette *set, place, fix*
seurtee *promise, pledge*
seven *seven*
seventhe *seventh*
seyden *say*
seye *say, declare*
seyn *saw*
shaft *arrow, shaft, stick*
shake *shake*
shal *shall, must*
shame *disgrace, shame*
shamfast *modest*
shap *shape, form*
shape *shape, prepare, arrange*
sharpe *severe*
sheld *shield*
shende *injure, disgrace, corrupt*
shene *bright, shining*
shent *injured*
shepne *stable, shed, shippon*
shere *shears, scissors*
sherte *shirt*

shet *shut*
shette *shut*
shew *show*
shine *shin*
ship *ship*
shiver *shiver to pieces*
shode *parting of the hair, the temple*
sholde *should*
shoon *shone*
shortly *in a few words, in brief*
shot *missile*
showe *show*
shrighte *shrieked*
shriken *shriek*
shuldre *shoulder*
shul *shall*
shyne *shine*
sight *sight*
signe *sign of the Zodiac*
signifye *mean*
sik *sick, ill*
siker *sure, certain*
sikerly *certainly, surely, indeed*
silver n., *silver*
silver adj., *silver*
sin *since*
singe *sing*
sinke *sink*
sit *sit*
sith *since*
sithen *afterwards*
sitte *sit, dwell, assemble*
sixty *sixty*
skin *skin*
slakke *slow*
slaughtre *slaughter, slaying*
slawe *slew*

slayn *slain*
slee(n) *slay, kill*
sleep *sleep*
sleep *sleep, slept*
sleere *slayer, killer*
sleighte *skill, dexterity*
slepy *inducing sleep*
slider *slippery*
slogardye *laziness, slothfulness*
slough *slain*
slow *slew*
slyly *carefully, wisely, discreetly*
smale *small*
smellinge *scented*
smerte *stinging, smarting, painful*
smerte *sting, hurt, cause pain*
smith *blacksmith*
smoke *smoke*
smoking *filling with incense*
smoot *smote*
smyler *one who smiles, flatterer*
smyte *smite, strike, pierce*
snare *trap, snare*
socour *help, aid*
sodeinly *suddenly*
sodeynliche *suddenly*
sodeynly *suddenly*
softe *softly*
soghte *sought*
solempnitee *due ceremony*
solitarie *solitary, lonely*
som *some*
somdel *somewhat, a little*
somer *summer*
som-tyme *sometime or other*
som-what *to some degree, a little*
sone *soon*

sone *son*
song *song, singing*
song *sang*
songen *sung*
sonne *sun*
soor *sorrow*
sooth *truth*
soothly *truly*
soper *supper*
sore *sorrowful, sore, grievous*
sore *sorely, grievously*
sore *pain, distress*
sorwe *sorrow, grief, distress*
sorwe *mourn, grieve*
sorweful *sorrowful, sad*
sorwefully *sadly*
sory *dreary, sad*
sothe *truth*
sotil *skilful, cunning, dainty, thin*
soule *soul*
soun *sound, noise*
sovereyn *excellent, supreme*
sowe *sow, pig*
space *period of time*
spak *spake*
sparcle *sparkle*
spare *refrain from, refuse*
sparklynge *sparkling*
sparre *beam, spar*
sparth *battle axe*
speces *species, kind*
speche *way of speaking, voice*
special *special, particular*
spedde *hurried*
spede *prosper, hurry*
speke *speak*
spende *spend*
spente *spent*

spere *spear*
spirit *spirit, soul*
spore *spur*
spouse *wife, consort*
sprad *spread*
sprede *spread*
sprenge *sprinkle*
springe *grow*
spronge *sprung*
spycerye *spices, spicery*
square *square*
squyer *squire, servant*
stable *firm, unmoveable*
stablisse *fix firmly, stabilize*
staf *stick, staff*
stake *post, staff*
stalk *stalk of a plant*
stalke *stride stealthily*
starf *died*
statue *statue, figure*
staves *sticks, staffs*
stede *steed, war-horse*
steel *steel*
steer *steer, bullock*
stelen *steal*
stente *stop, cause to stop*
sterne *bold, strong, mighty*
sterre *star*
stert *start, moment*
sterte *leap, spring*
sterve *die*
stevene *voice, sound, time*
stiken *pierce*
stille *quietly, still*
stinge *sting, pierce*
stinten *desist from, leave off*
stith *anvil*
stok *descent, line, family*
stok *stump of wood*

stoke *stab*
stole *stole*
stomble *stumble*
stonden *stand*
stongen *stung*
stoon *stone*
storm *storm*
story *story*
stounde *any time*
stout *strong*
strangle *strangle*
strangling *strangling*
straughte *stretched*
straunge *foreign*
strecche *stretch*
stree *straw*
streighte *straight, direct*
streit *narrow*
streme *ray of sunshine*
strengthe *strength*
strepe *strip*
strete *road*
stronge *strong*
stroof *strove*
strook *blow, stroke*
stryve *strive, struggle, compete*
stryf *strife, struggle*
stubbe *stump, root of a tree*
studie *fit of abstraction, brown study*
successioun *generation*
suffisaunt *sufficient*
suffise *suffice*
suffyce *prove sufficient*
sum *some*
sustene *support, sustain*
suster *sister*
suyte *dress, uniform*
swelle *swell*

swelte *swoon, despair*

swerd *sword*

swere *take an oath, swear*

swete *kindly, dear, sweet*

swich *such, so great*

swifte *swift*

swoor *swore*

swore *swore*

swote *sweet*

swough *sighing of a breeze, murmur*

swowne *swoon, faint*

swowninge *swooning*

syde *side, party*

syke *sigh*

sythe *time, occasion*

table *tablet, slab*

tak *take*

take *seize, capture, take, value*

taken *taken*

tale *tale, story*

tame *tame*

tare *weed, tare*

targe *shield*

tarien *drag out, spend, prolong*

tas *heap, pile*

tellen *tell, inform*

tempest *storm*

temple *temple, place for worship*

tendre *young, tender*

tendrely *tenderly, gently*

t'endyte contraction for **to endyte**

tene *grief, sorrow, vexation*

tente *tent*

tere *tear, weeping*

terme *period*

tester *headpiece, helmet*

than *then*

than *than*

thank *gratitude, thanks, consent, free will*

thank *return thanks, thank*

that *so that*

that *that, who*

th'avys contraction for **the avys**

theatre *arena*

theef *thief*

th'effect contraction for **the effect**

th'encens contraction for **the encens**

th'enchauntement contraction for **the enchauntment**

thenke *think, imagine*

thentree contraction for **the entree**

ther *there*

ther-aboute *about that place*

ther-as *where, in what place*

ther-biforn *beforehand*

ther-for *for that reason*

ther-out *from thence*

ther-to *in addition*

ther-with *by this means*

ther-with-al *therupon*

thider *thither, in that direction*

thider-ward *in that direction*

thikke *thick*

thikke-herd *thick-haired*

thilke *that same*

thing *affair, business, episode, subject*

thinke *seem, appear*

thinketh *think*

thirle *pierce*

this *this*
thise *these*
tho *then*
tho *those*
thorn *thorn tree*
though *although*
thought *thought*
thought *it seemed*
thousand *thousand*
thral *enslaved*
threed *thread*
threste *thrust, push one's way*
thridde *third*
throng *throng, crowd*
thryes *thrice, three times*
thunderinge *noise of thunder*
thurgh *through, by means of*
thurghfare *thoroughfare*
thurgh-girt *pierced through*
thurgh-out *right through*
thus *in this manner*
thy-selven *thyself*
til conj., *until*
til prep., *until*
tirannye *tyranny*
tiraunt *tyrant*
to *too*
to *toe*
to *to, towards*
to-breste *burst through*
to-brosten *burst through*
togidre *together*
to-hewen *hack into pieces*
tolde *told*
to-morwe *tomorrow*
tonne-greet *as big as a barrel*
top *top, head*
toret *small ring in a dog's collar*

torment *torment, torture*
tormente *torture*
to-shredde *tear to pieces*
touch *reach, touch*
touched *touched*
tough *unyielding*
toun *town*
tour *tower*
touret *turret*
toward *towards*
Trace *Thrace, part of Greece*
traitour *traitor*
transfigure *transfigure*
transmutacioun *inconstancy*
trapped *having trappings*
trappure *trappings*
traunce *trance*
travaillinge *labouring in childbirth*
travaille *labour, toil*
trays *traces, harness*
traytour *traitor*
trede *tread*
tree *tree*
treson *treason*
trespas *wrong doing, crime*
tresse *plait of hair*
tretee *treaty, agreement*
trewe *true, honest, faithful*
trewely *faithfully*
trompe *trumpet*
tronchoun *broken shaft of a spear*
trone *throne*
trouthe *promise, fealty, pledge, word of honour*
trowe *believe, trust*
truste *take one's word*

turne *turn away, turn towards, transform*
turneyinge *tournament*
twenty *twenty*
tweye *two*
tweyne *twain, two*
twyn *twine*
tygre *tiger*
tyme *time*
tyraunt *tyrant*
unborn *unborn*
uncouth *unusual*
under *under*
undernethe *beneath, underneath*
understonde *understand*
unhorsed *unseated*
unknowe *unknown*
unkonning *ignorant*
unset *not fixed, not arranged*
untressed *unplaited*
unwist *unknown*
unyolden *not surrendered*
up-haf *lifted up*
up-heve *lift up*
upright *upright*
up-riste *rising of the sun*
up-so-doun *upside down*
up-sterte *sprang up*
upward *upwards*
up-yaf *gave up, surrendered*
up-yolden *yielded up*
usage *custom, usage*
utterly *utterly, completely*
vale *valley*
vanisshinge *disappearance*
variacioun *variation*
vasselage *knightly exploits, service*

venerye *hunting*
vengeaunce *vengeance, punishment*
venim *poison*
ventusinge *cupping*
verraily *in truth, truly*
verray *true, undoubted*
vertu *power, qualities*
vese *rush of wind, blast, hurry*
vestiments *clothing*
veyne-blood *blood in the veins*
victorie *victory*
vileinye *boorishness, disrespect, spite*
visage *face, countenance*
visyte *visit*
vital *vital*
vois *voice*
vomyt *vomit*
voyden *empty, drive out*
voys *voice*
wages *wages*
wailling *wailing*
wake *awaken, be awake*
wake-pleyes *funeral games*
wal *wall*
walk *walk*
walke *walk*
walled *walled-in*
wan *gloomy*
wan *won*
wane *wane, diminish*
wanhope *despair, hopelessness*
wanie *wane, diminish*
wanting *desire for, lack*
war *aware, wary*
wasshe *wash*
waste *ruined, laid waste*

waste *destroy*

water *water*

wayke *weak, feeble*

wayle *wail, lament*

wawe *wave*

wayten *watch, await*

wedde *pledge*

wedde *wed, marry*

weddinge *marriage, wedding*

wede *garment, clothing*

weep *weep*

wel *well, much*

wel-come *welcome*

wele *prosperity, success, happiness*

welfare *welfare, prosperity*

welle *source, spring*

wende *depart, go away*

wende *supposed*

wenen *suppose, think*

wente *go, go away*

wepe *weep*

weping *weeping, lamenting*

wepne *weapon*

werche *work, make, create*

were *defend*

were *wear*

werede *wear*

weren *were*

werre *war, contest*

werreyen *make war upon*

wessh *washed*

west-ward *westward, towards the west*

wete *wet*

wex *grew*

wexen *grow, increase, become*

wey(e) *way, road*

weyen *weigh*

weymentinge *lamentation*

weylaway *alas*

weyeth *weigh*

whan *when*

what *partly, how much*

wheel *wheel*

whelpe *puppy*

wher adv., *where*

wher conj., *where*

wheras *where*

whereby *by means of which*

wherfor *for which reason, wherefore*

whether *which of two*

whether *whether*

which *which*

whippeltre *cornel tree*

whistelinge *whistling*

whyl *while*

whyle *space of time*

whylom *once upon a time*

whyte *white*

widwe *widow*

wif *wife, woman*

wight *person, man*

wighte *weight*

wikke *wicked, baleful, malicious*

wikkedly *wickedly*

wilfulnesse *self-will, perversity*

wille *self-will*

willen *wish, desire*

wilnen *wish, desire*

wilow *willow tree*

wilt *wish*

wiltow contraction for **wilt thou**

window *window*

wing *wing*

winged *winged*
winnen *win*
wirche *work, act, do*
wisdom *wisdom*
wisly *surely*
wiste *know*
wistest *know*
wit *wits, intelligence*
witen *know*
with *with, by*
with-outen *round about*
withseye *contradict, deny*
witing *knowledge*
wo *sorrow, distress, harm,*
lamentation
wode *wood, forest*
wodebinde *woodbine,*
honeysuckle
woful *woeful, sorrowful*
wofullere *more distressing*
wol *will, intend, desire*
wolf *wolf*
woltow *contraction for* **wolt**
thou
wolt *wish*
womman *woman*
wommanhede *womanliness*
wonder *wonderful*
wonder *wondrously, remarkably*
wone *habit, custom*
wone *dwell, live, be accustomed,*
remain
woneden *live*
wonne(n) *win*
wont *accustomed*
wood *mad*
woodly *madly, without restraint*
woodnesse *madness*

wook *waken*
woost *know*
woot *know*
world *world, everyone*
worse *worse*
worse *worse fate*
worshipe *honour, reverence*
worshipful *worthy, honourable*
worthy *notable, distinguished*
wost *know*
wostow *contraction for* **wost**
thou
wot *know*
wounde *wound*
wounded *wounded*
wrastle *wrestle*
wrecche *wretched person*
wrecche *wretched, miserable*
wrecched *wretched*
wreke *avenge*
wrethe *wreath*
wrihen *hide, cover*
write *write*
wroght *wrought*
wrong *astray, wrong*
wrothe *angry quarrelsome, at*
variance
wrye *hide, cover*
wryten *written*
wyde *wide, spacious*
wyke *week*
wynnen *win, gain by effort*
wys *far-seeing, prudent*
wyse *way, fashion, manner*
wysly *wisely, prudently*
wyve *wife*

Words beginning **y-** are past participles

yaf *gave*
y-bete *beaten*
y-born *born*
y-bounden *pledged*
y-brent *burnt*
y-brought *brought*
y-buried *buried*
y-clenched *riveted*
y-cleped *called*
y-clothed *clothed*
y-corve *carved*
ydel *useless, idle*
ydelnesse *idleness*
y-don *done*
y-drawe *drawn*
y-droppe *dropped*
y-dryve *driven*
ye *ye, you*
yë *eye*
yeer *year*
yere *year*
yelow *yellow*
yelpe *boast*
yelwe *yellow*
yeman *yeoman, servant*
yerde *yard in length*
yet *just, quite*
yeve *give*
y-fetered *fettered*
y-founde *found*
y-grounde *ground*
y-holde *held*
y-hurt *hurt*
y-laft *left*
yliche *in the same way, alike*
yif *give*

yift *gift*
yiven *given*
y-lyke *alike*
y-maked *made*
y-met *met*
y-meynd *mingled*
y-nough *enough*
yolle *shout, yell*
yond *yonder, over there*
yonder *that over there*
yonge *young*
yore *once, formerly*
y-payed *paid*
youling *loud weeping*
your *your*
youthe *youthfulness, youth*
yow *you*
y-raft *seized*
y-ronnen *run*
y-sayd *said*
y-scalded *scalded*
y-sent *sent*
y-served *served*
y-set *sat*
y-slayn *slain*
y-spoken *spoken*
y-spreynd *grown*
y-stiked *pierced*
y-storve *died*
y-sworn *sworn*
y-take *taken*
y-turned *turned*
yvele *with difficulty, evilly*
y-wedded *wedded*
y-wonnen *won*
y-wrye *covered*